Globalism

GLOBALISM
The New Market Ideology

MANFRED B. STEGER

ROWMAN & LITTLEFIELD PUBLISHERS, INC.
Lanham • Boulder • New York • Oxford

ROWMAN & LITTLEFIELD PUBLISHERS, INC.

Published in the United States of America
by Rowman & Littlefield Publishers, Inc.
4720 Boston Way, Lanham, Maryland 20706
www.rowmanlittlefield.com

12 Hid's Copse Road, Cumnor Hill, Oxford OX2 9JJ, England

British Library Cataloguing in Publication Information Available

Library of Congress Cataloging-in-Publication Data
Steger, Manfred B., 1961–
    Globalism : the new market ideology / Manfred B. Steger.
        p. cm.
    Includes bibliographical references and index.
    ISBN 0-7425-0072-1 (alk. paper) — ISBN 0-7425-0073-X (pbk. : alk. paper)
        1. International trade. 2. International economic integration. 3. Free
    enterprise. 4. Globalization—Economic aspects. 5. Globalization—Social
    aspects. I. Title.
    HF1379 .S738 2001
    337—dc21

                                                                2001041702

Printed in the United States of America

♾️™ The paper used in this publication meets the minimum requirements of
American National Standard for Information Sciences—Permanence of Paper
for Printed Library Materials, ANSI/NISO Z39.48-1992.

TO MY DEAR FRIEND STEVE BRONNER

whose cosmopolitan vision continues to inspire me

CONTENTS

Preface, ix

Acknowledgments, xiii

ONE

The Roots of Globalism, *1*

TWO

The Academic Debate over Globalization, *17*

THREE

Five Central Claims of Globalism, *43*

FOUR

Antiglobalist Challengers from the Political Left and Right, *81*

FIVE

The "Battle of Seattle" and Its Aftermath, *117*

SIX

Future Prospects, *135*

Notes, 151

Selected Bibliography, 175

Index, 187

About the Author, 195

PREFACE

At the outset of the new century, it has already become a cliché to observe that we live in an age of globalization. Although it may not constitute an entirely new phenomenon, globalization in its current phase has been described as an unprecedented compression of time and space reflected in the tremendous intensification of social, political, economic, and cultural interconnections and interdependencies on a global scale. But not everybody experiences globalization in the same way. In fact, people living in various parts of the world are affected very differently by this gigantic transformation of social structures and cultural zones. Globalization seems to generate enormous wealth and opportunity for the privileged few, while relegating the many to conditions of abject poverty and hopelessness.

And yet, we must remember that globalization is an incipient process, slowly giving rise to a new condition of globality whose eventual qualities and properties are far from being determined. What we *do* know from past experience, however, is that periods of rapid social transformation threaten the familiar, destabilize old boundaries, and upset established traditions. Like the mighty Hindu god Shiva, globalization is not only a great destroyer, but also a powerful creator of new ideas, values, identities, practices, and movements.

The public interpretation of the origin, direction, and meaning of these profound social changes that go by the name of "globalization" has fallen disproportionately to a powerful phalanx of social forces that has arrayed itself around the ideology of globalism. Putting before the public a particular agenda of topics for discussion, questions to ask, and claims to make, globalists simultaneously distort social reality, legitimate and advance their power interests, and shape collective and personal identities. To a large extent being creatures of the very material and ideal conditions whose meanings they expound, globalists supply people with simplified images of a free-market world far more coherent and desirable than it really is. Thus market ideologists not only endow social processes with their own meanings, but also attempt to soothe the heightened sense of existential insecurity that accompanies all epochal shifts.

But what exactly is *globalism*? What are its central claims? How does it function? Has it been challenged by other systems of ideas? These are the central questions I seek to answer in this book. I submit that globalism is the dominant ideology of our time. It is an Anglo-American free-market doctrine that endows the relatively new concept of globalization with neoliberal norms, values, and meanings—all of which are produced and reproduced within the media and popular culture for public consumption. But I wrote this study out of a firm conviction that globalization does not necessarily have to mean or be what globalists say it means or is. Indeed, my skepticism toward the central claims of globalism has fueled my desire to explore the workings of an ideology that strike me as diminishing the capacity of human beings to participate in shaping their destinies and live in dignity and relative material security. However, my skeptical posture toward globalism should not be interpreted as a blanket rejection of globalization. I take comfort in the fact that the world is becoming a more interdependent place in which people have a better chance of discovering their common humanity. Hence, I welcome the progressive transformation of social structures, provided that modernity and the development of science and technology go hand in hand with greater forms of freedom and equality for all people, as well as with a more effective protection of our global environment.

The overarching intent of this study, then, is not to denounce globalization, but to offer a thoughtful analysis and critique of globalism. Such a critical project encourages the reader to recognize the internal contradictions and the many biases of the globalist discourse. Guided by the regulative ideal of a more egalitarian global order, a critical theory of globalization must, therefore, transcend narrow disciplinary boundaries in its attempt to understand the ways in which global forces threaten to create a totalitarian market order in the twenty-first century.

Derived from the Greek verb *krinein*—to discern, to reflect, to judge—and the Greek noun *theoria*—contemplation—the concept of "critical theory" signifies the noble human impulse to reflect upon the validity and desirability of social institutions and their normative foundations. In its best moments, social criticism weakens the authoritarian tendency inherent in all political ideologies to silence the irksome Socratic gadfly. Embraced and cultivated by a global civil society, the critical impulse thus represents the lifeblood of all democratic politics—past, present, and future.

ACKNOWLEDGMENTS

It is a pleasant duty to record my debts of gratitude. The research and writing of this book were generously funded by a 2000–2001 research grant from the Globalization Research Center at the University of Hawai'i at Mānoa. I am very grateful to the Center's director, Deane Neubauer, and his dedicated staff for their generous support and encouragement. In addition, I am grateful to Illinois State University for supporting my work on this book with two summer research grants. I am also thankful for the opportunity to hone the ideas presented in this book at various professional lectures, colloquia, and seminars in North America, Europe, Japan, and the Middle East.

Many people contributed their efforts to this book. My good friends and colleagues Lane Crothers and Franz Broswimmer offered important suggestions. Lane spent much time combing through the manuscript, and Franz provided me with a steady stream of pertinent information. Their criticisms and insights surely made this a better book. I would also like to thank Ibrahim Aoudé, Uschi Baatz, Stephen Eric Bronner, Terrell Carver, Susan Craig, Thomas Eimermann, Dale Fitzgibbons, Michael Forman, Manfred Henningsen, Fumio Iida, Micheline Ishay, Timothy Kaufman-Osborn, John Kautsky, Elizabeth Kelly, Douglas Kellner, Bradley Macdonald, Peter Manicas, Khalil Marrar, Valentine Moghadam, Issam Nassar, Carlos Parodi, Richard Payne, James Reid, Mohamad Tavakoli-Targhi, and James White for their perceptive comments on my work.

Special thanks are due to Jamal Nassar, my department chair and loyal friend, for his untiring support. My two graduate research assistants, Sherri Replogle and Amentahru Wahlrab, did a fantastic job. Without their outstanding investigative abilities, many important sources would never have been unearthed. They also read the entire manuscript and provided me with their valuable feedback. Jennifer Knerr, my editor at Rowman & Littlefield Publishers, has been a genuine beacon of support, understanding, and encouragement. Robert Kowkabany, too, did a great job as copyeditor. Finally, as always, my deepest expressions of gratitude go to my soul mate Perle Besserman—thanks for everything.

THE ROOTS OF GLOBALISM

"The End of Ideology Debate"

More than forty years ago, a major intellectual controversy erupted in the United States over whether ideological politics had ended in Western industrialized countries. Prominent European commentators quickly joined the discussion, and the political pundits on both sides of the Atlantic soon found themselves embroiled in what came to be known as "The End of Ideology Debate."[1] The book that set the terms of this controversy bore the suggestive title, *The End of Ideology: On the Exhaustion of Political Ideas in the Fifties*. Widely hailed as a landmark in American social thought, the study was authored by Daniel Bell, a rising intellectual star who would eventually establish himself as one of the most influential American sociologists of the twentieth century.

Bell's book postulated the utter exhaustion of both Marxist socialism and classical liberalism, the two great nineteenth-century Western ideologies. According to the author, old ideas such as the "inevitability of history" or the "self-regulating market" had lost their power to rally modern constituencies who had witnessed the economic desperation of the Great Depression, the hypocrisy of the Moscow Trials and the Hitler–Stalin Pact, the horrors of the Nazi concentration camps, and the unleashing of nuclear weapons against defenseless civilians. Most Westerners had abandoned their simplistic beliefs in nineteenth-century utopias that projected visions of perfect social harmony—be it the classless society of Marxist socialists or the commercial paradise of laissez-faire liberals. Although new ideologies had emerged in the newly independent states of Africa and Asia, Bell conceded, their nationalist message was too parochial and limited to appeal to post–World War II audiences in Europe and the United States.

In spite of its nostalgic tone, Bell's book showed much appreciation for the virtues of a world without ideological battles. He noted that people in the West had become less prone to pledge their allegiance to dangerous forms of political extremism, and more accepting of a pragmatic middle way embodied in the modern welfare state of the 1950s. On one hand, this middle way offered the political stability and economic security most people were craving after the traumatic events of the first half of the century. On the other hand, however, its technocratic framework seemed to provide hardly any outlets for political passions and heroic ideals.

Ideology—being for Bell largely an emotional "all-or-none affair"— had become intellectually devitalized and increasingly displaced by an instrumental reformism built on the virtues of compromise, utility, and scientific objectivity. The preoccupation with administrative solutions for largely technical problems related to the state and national economies had rendered ideology obsolete. Bell cautiously applauded the alleged demise of nineteenth-century ideologies, implying that a deideologized politics of the 1950s was facilitating Western progress toward a more rational and less divisive society.[2]

However, as his critics were quick to point out, Bell's analysis contained a number of uncritical assumptions. For one, in implying a necessary link between the "ideological" and "extremism," he painted the pragmatic mode of empirical problem-solving in overly rosy colors. He made the demise of ideology appear as an attempt to refashion a new age of rational moderation—a natural state lost in nearly a century's worth of irrational attempts to put utopian ideas into practice. In particular, some commentators interpreted Bell's assertion of a deideologized climate in the United States as a deeply ideological attempt to reclaim objectivity and prudence as the essential attributes of a superior Anglo-American culture. They considered *The End of Ideology* a sophisticated defense of the West that was itself thoroughly pervaded by the ideological imperatives of the cold war.

Secondly, several reviewers argued that Bell was trying to substitute technocratic guidance by experts for genuine political debate in society. They charged him with evoking a myth of a popular consensus around basic norms and values in order to forestall a potentially divisive discussion on the remaining inequalities in America. Thirdly, the international tensions produced by the cold war, together with the sudden upsurge of ideological politics in the 1960s and 1970s, seemed to disprove Bell's thesis entirely. The Civil Rights movement, the numerous protest movements against the Vietnam War, the feminist movement, and the meteoric rise of environmentalism all pointed to the distinct possibility that at least some of the central norms and values contained in radical Western nineteenth-century ideologies were still alive and well a century later.

However, the sudden collapse of communist regimes in Eastern Europe and the Soviet Union from 1989 to 1991 unexpectedly resurrected the end-of-ideology debate. In a seminal article he later expanded into a full-length study, Francis Fukuyama, then a deputy director of the U.S. State Department's policy-planning staff, argued that the passing of Marxism-Leninism as a viable political ideology marked nothing less than the "end point of mankind's ideological evolution." This end state was "evident first of all in the total exhaustion of viable systematic alternatives to Western liberalism." Fukuyama also postulated the emergence of a "deideologized world," but he insisted that this new era would not be characterized by the convergence between liberalism and socialism as predicted earlier by Daniel Bell. Rather, it represented the "unabashed victory of economic and political liberalism." Downplaying the significance of rising religious fundamentalism and ethnic nationalism in the "New World Order" of the 1990s, Fukuyama predicted that the global triumph of the "Western idea" and the spread of its consumerist culture to all corners of the earth would prove to be unstoppable. Driven by the logical development of market forces and the unleashing of powerful new technologies, Western capitalist democracy had emerged as the "final form of human government."[3]

Hence, Fukuyama's vision of a deideologized world only partially overlapped with Bell's similar analysis. While Fukuyama agreed with his colleague on the irrevocable demise of socialism, he disagreed with Bell's bleak assessment of free-market liberalism. Indeed, Fukuyama expected a hi-tech realization of the old nineteenth-century free-market utopia. Expressing some discomfort at the coming ideological vacuum at the "end of history," he predicted the rapid marketization of most social relations in a globalized world dedicated to self-interested economic calculation, the endless solving of technological problems, and the satisfaction of ceaseless consumer demands.[4]

In two recent articles on the subject, Fukuyama defends and expands his central idea that the end of ideology would be connected to free-market globalization. He not only reiterates that these developments constitute an "irreversible process," but also adds that Anglo-American norms and values would largely underwrite the cultural makeup of the new deideologized world. Indeed, Fukuyama concludes that the current position of the United States as the sole remaining superpower has made it "inevitable that Americanization will accompany globalization."[5]

In my view, any pronouncement of an end of ideology ought to be considered from a more sober historical perspective. Bell's thesis makes sense insofar as it coincided with a major postwar shift away from unregulated capitalism toward the welfare state. Fukuyama's triumphalism constituted a sensible response in the late 1980s because it echoed the central ideas of rising free-market forces. As Fred Dallmayr notes, "Western liberalism and liberalization have emerged as the triumphant ideological panacea, spreading its effects around the globe."[6] Hence, twentieth-century end-of-ideology visions should be seen as historically contingent attempts to universalize the dominant ideological imperatives of their time by presenting them as a natural finality to which history no longer poses an alternative. But in so doing, they imitate nineteenth-century ideologies. This suggests that some of the old conceptual building blocks have been discarded prematurely.

Hence, this study rejects the thesis of the coming of a deideologized world. Instead, I will advance the argument that ideology is still very much with us today. As I see it, far from condemning people to ideological boredom in a world without history, the opening decade of the twenty-first century is quickly becoming a teeming battlefield of clashing ideologies. The chief protagonist—the currently dominant market ideology I call "globalism"—has encountered serious resistance. Ideological challengers on both the political left and right have already begun to flex their conceptual muscles. Defining the meaning and predicting the direction of globalization, globalist forces will continue to struggle with their antiglobalist opponents as each side tries to impress its agenda on the public mind. This ideological contest over the meaning and direction of globalization will deeply impact the political and ethical issues of the new century. However, before I elaborate on my arguments in more detail, let me turn to a brief discussion of the main elements of ideology and clarify their relationship to globalism.

Ideology: Elements and Functions

Most political and social theorists define *ideology* as a system of widely shared ideas, patterned beliefs, guiding norms and values, and regulative ideals accepted as fact or truth by some group. Ideologies offer individuals a more or less coherent picture of the world not only as it is, but also as it should be. In doing so, they organize the tremendous complexity of human experience into fairly simple and understandable images that, in turn, provide people with a normative orientation in time and space, and in means and ends.[7] In an excellent essay on the historical development of the concept of ideology from the early nineteenth century to the present, political theorist Terrell Carver rightly emphasizes the connection between ideology and politics. He argues that ideology is neither a template against which something is or is not an ideology, nor is it a recipe stating how to make an ideology correctly. "Rather," Carver writes, "it is an agenda of things to discuss, questions to ask, hypotheses to make. We should be able to use it when considering the interaction between ideas and politics, especially systems of ideas that make claims, whether justificatory or hortatory."[8]

Following Carver's argument, one could say that there exists a specific place for ideology in politics. After all, politics is the public arena where various "agendas of things to discuss" are linked to the power interests of particular groups and classes. Thus ideology always contains a political dimension, for it is ultimately about the many ways in which power is exercised, justified, and altered in society. Ideologists speak to their audiences in stories and narratives that persuade, praise, condemn, distinguish "truths" from "falsehoods," and separate the "good" from the "bad." Ideology enables people to act, while at the same time constraining their actions by binding them to a particular set of norms and values. Hence, ideology connects theory and practice by orienting and organizing human action in accordance with generalized codes of conduct.

In this book, I contend that globalism is the dominant political ideology of our time—that is, the dominant system of ideas that make claims about social processes. Globalists put before the public an "agenda of things to discuss" that supports their neoliberal political agenda. The following example provides a first glimpse into the workings of globalist ideology. The headlines of a *Newsweek* cover story on economic globalization contained the following phrases: "Like It or Not, You're Married to the Market"; and "The Market 'R Us."9 Equating globalization with marketization, these statements seek to entice their readership to accept a particular representation of social reality as a general truth. A closer analysis of these headlines reveals the following ideological elements and functions.

First, the postulated link between the reader's identity and the impersonal market offers an *explanation* of economic globalization. It is couched in objective terms that emphasize the "factuality" of the market. Market principles are portrayed as pervading even the most intimate dimensions of our social existence. And there is nothing consumers can do about it. In other words, socially created relations are depicted as exterior, natural forces that are more powerful than human will.

Second, the headlines suggest *standards of normative evaluation*. Although marketization is portrayed as an objective process, there is the implication that its effects are nonetheless beneficial. After all, the concept of "marriage" resonates on a deeply positive note with most *Newsweek* readers. Who would want to be married to a "bad" person? Who would want to assume the identity of a "bad" person? Thus the market must be a benign force, after all, worthy of becoming our most intimate partner.

Third, the statements serve as a *guide* and *compass for action*. As the stories below the headlines make abundantly clear, markets reflect a natural and superior way of ordering the world. Hence, they ought to command the reader's approval and support. The implication is that good citizens should demand from their political regimes that they facilitate globalization as understood in market terms.

Fourth, the headlines offer a *simplification* of complex social reality. Most importantly, market interests are presented as general interests. Moreover, the clever permutation of a well-known brand name—Toys 'R Us—serves as a marker of positive identity. Lack of choice ("like it or not")—a seemingly undesirable condition—is resolved in a marriage of convenience that appears to harbor great financial opportunity for those who know how to treat their (market) spouse. Finally, the gender dynamics at work in these headlines are far from subtle. There is little doubt as to who is the commanding husband in this patriarchal marriage.

In his *Lectures on Ideology and Utopia*, the French philosopher Paul Ricoeur integrates these ideological elements and functions into a comprehensive conceptual framework.[10] Drawing on the insights of Marxist thought, Ricoeur characterizes the first functional level of ideology as *distortion*—that is, the production of contorted images of social reality. Most importantly, the process of distortion hides the contrast between things as they may be envisioned in theory and things as they play themselves out on the plane of material reality. Indeed, all ideologies assemble a picture of the world based on a peculiar mixture that both represents and distorts social processes. Yet, Ricoeur disagrees with Karl Marx's notion that distortion explains all there is to ideology. For the French philosopher, distortion is merely one of the three main functions of ideology, representing the surface level of a phenomenon that contains two more functions at progressively deeper levels.

Inspired by the writings of the German sociologist Max Weber, Ricoeur identifies *legitimation* as the second functional level of ideology. Two main factors are involved here: the claim to legitimacy made by the ruling authority, and the belief in the authority's legitimacy granted by its subjects. Accepting large parts of Weber's explanation of social action, Ricoeur highlights ideology's function of mediating the gap between belief and claim. In other words, Ricoeur argues that there will always remain some discrepancy between the popular belief in the authority's right to rule and the authority's claim to the right to rule. It is one of ideology's functions to supply the people with additional justification in order to narrow this gap.

Ricoeur's model is completed in his description of *integration*, the third functional level of ideology. Drawing on the writings of anthropologist Clifford Geertz, who emphasizes the symbolic structure of social action, Ricoeur claims that, on the deepest level, ideology plays a mediating or integrative role. It provides society with stability as it creates, preserves, and protects the social identity of persons and groups. In its constructive function, ideology supplies the symbols, norms, and images that go into the process of assembling and holding together individual and collective identity. Thus ideology assumes a conservative function in both senses of that word. It preserves identity, "but it also wants to conserve what exists and is therefore already a resistance."[11] Such rigid forms of resistance to change contribute to turning beliefs and ideas into a dogmatic defense of dominant power structures.

Ricoeur's model inspires my own view that the study of ideology yields a better understanding of human action as mediated, structured, and integrated by symbolic systems such as language. Ideologies permeate all societies, with different segments of the population holding particular ideas about power and social order. However, in no case will a given society be so completely dominated by a single ideology as to have no alternatives available within the system. At the same time, there are periods in modern history when a particular ideology becomes predominant or "hegemonic."

Made famous by Antonio Gramsci, a leading socialist thinker who died in the late 1930s in an Italian fascist prison, *hegemony* can be defined as a power relationship between social groups and classes in which one class exercises leadership by gaining the active consent of subordinate groups. According to Gramsci, this process involves the internalization on the part of the subordinate classes of the moral and cultural values, the codes of practical conduct, and the worldview of the dominant classes. As a result, the subordinate groups give their spontaneous consent to the social logic of domination that is embedded in hegemonic ideology. This allows dominant groups to maintain a social order favorable to their own interests by only rarely having to resort to open coercion.

In his discussion of hegemony, Gramsci also comments on the power of ideology to shape personal and collective identities. Indeed, the two *Newsweek* headlines discussed above represent a good example of how ideological integration contributes to hegemony. As Gramsci scholar William I. Robinson notes, "Under a hegemonic social order, embedded in ideology are definitions of key political, economic, and philosophical concepts and the ideological framework establishes the legitimacy or illegitimacy of the demands placed on the social order."[12]

As I interpret the claims of hegemonic globalism and evaluate the responses of its antiglobalist challengers in chapters 3 and 4, I draw heavily on the insights provided by Gramsci and Ricoeur. Their respective explanations of the elements and functions of ideology provide a helpful framework for my own discussion of globalism.

Neoliberalism and Globalism: Pouring Old Philosophical Wine into New Ideological Bottles

In the last two decades, Anglo-American proponents of the nineteenth-century market utopia have found in the concept of "globalization" a new guiding metaphor for their neoliberal message. The central tenets of neoliberalism include the primacy of economic growth; the importance of free trade to stimulate growth; the unrestricted free market; individual choice; the reduction of government regulation; and the advocacy of an evolutionary model of social development anchored in the Western experience and applicable to the entire world.

Neoliberalism is rooted in the classical liberal ideals of British philosophers such as Adam Smith (1723–1790), David Ricardo (1772–1823), and Herbert Spencer (1820–1903). Smith is often credited with creating the Scottish Enlightenment image of *homo economicus*—the view that people are isolated individuals whose actions reflect mostly their economic self-interest. In Smith's view, economic and political matters are largely separable, with economics claiming a superior status because it supposedly operates best without government interference under a harmonious system of natural laws. The market is seen as a self-regulating mechanism tending toward equilibrium of supply and demand, thus securing the most efficient allocation of resources. Any constraint on free competition is said to interfere with the natural efficiency of market mechanisms. Composed of small buyers and sellers, the market's "invisible hand" translates individual pursuit of self-interest into optimal public benefit. Attacking the seventeenth-century economic doctrine of mercantilism—absolute control of the economy by a powerful state with the objective of building up large gold reserves—Smith argued vigorously in favor of "liberating" markets from intrusive state regulation. His classical understanding of liberalism defends freedom as a person's right to be "left alone" by social demands so that the individual may act in the market as *homo economicus* unencumbered by social regulations. This early vision of economic liberty still forms the backbone of contemporary neoliberal doctrine.

Smith complemented his laissez-faire market ideal with a defense of free trade and its principles of laissez-passer, most importantly the elimination of tariffs on imports and other barriers to trade and capital flows between nations. But it was David Ricardo's "theory of comparative advantage" that became the gospel of modern free traders. Ricardo argued that free trade amounted to a win-win situation for all trading partners involved, because it allowed each country to specialize in the production of those commodities for which it had a comparative advantage. For example, if Italy could produce wine more cheaply than England, and England could produce cloth more cheaply than Italy, then both countries would benefit from specialization and trade. In fact, Ricardo even went so far as to suggest that benefits from specialization and trade would accrue even if one country had an absolute advantage in producing all of the products traded. Politically, Ricardo's theory amounted to a powerful argument against government interference with trade.[13]

Perhaps the most influential formulation of classical liberalism appears in Herbert Spencer's justification of the dominance of Western laissez-faire capitalism over the rest of the world by drawing on Charles Darwin's theory of evolution by natural selection. For Spencer, free-market economies constitute the most civilized form of human competition in which the "fittest" would naturally rise to the top. Establishing himself as the leading proponent of early industrial capitalism, Spencer limited the required tasks of the state to protecting individuals against internal and external forms of aggression. Any interference with the workings of private enterprise would inevitably lead to cultural and social stagnation, political corruption, and the creation of large, inefficient state bureaucracies.

Spencer denounced socialism, trade unions, and even rudimentary forms of social regulation such as factory safety laws as examples of "over-regulation" inimical to rational progress and individual freedom. In his early study *Social Statics*, he enshrined laissez-faire capitalism as the final system toward which all societies were evolving under the leadership of Anglo-American countries. Spencer's elevation of free-market competition as the natural source of humankind's freedom and prosperity proved to be extremely influential with the commercial interests of Victorian England. Late in his life, he reported total sales of his books at close to 400,000 copies. No doubt, Spencer's theories greatly contributed to the hegemony of free-market economic doctrine in nineteenth-century Britain.[14]

The collapse of world trade during World War I and the economic crises and conflicts during the interwar years caused free-market ideas to lose much of their appeal. Virulent forms of nationalism and trade protectionism emerged as extreme reactions to laissez-faire capitalism, and it was not until the end of World War II that modified versions of liberalism reappeared on the political agenda of Western countries. Until the 1970s, even the most conservative political parties in Europe and the United States embraced rather extensive forms of state interventionism propagated by British economist John Maynard Keynes. Culminating in the creation of the modern welfare state, Keynes's advocacy of a "social market" represented the impressive attempt to combine some redeemable values of socialism with the virtues of liberalism in a system of mixed economy and political pluralism that balanced capitalist markets with demands for greater social equality.

However, the rise of neoliberal ideas in the late 1970s found a favorable economic context as inflation, high unemployment, and other structural problems plagued Western industrial countries. Making a strong case for the return to free-market policies of the past, neoliberal politicians drew on the neoclassical laissez-faire economic theories of Anglo-American economists such as Friedrich Hayek and Milton Friedman. In the early 1980s, British conservatives under the intellectual leadership of Keith Joseph and Margaret Thatcher created the ideological foundations of what some commentators have called "Second-Coming Capitalism" or "Turbo-Capitalism."[15] Their social conservatism combined with neoliberal economic policies, ultimately weakening the power of labor unions and initiating drastic market-oriented reforms. By the late 1980s, British Prime Minister Margaret Thatcher and U.S. President Ronald Reagan were both revered and reviled as the founding figures of a new market paradigm. Since then, their ideological heirs have marshaled their considerable resources to expand the neoliberal project into a full-blown globalist ideology.

Neoliberal globalists seek to cultivate in the popular mind the uncritical association of "globalization" with what they claim to be the universal benefits of market liberalization: Rising global living standards, economic efficiency, individual freedom and democracy, and unprecedented technological progress. Ideally, the state should only provide the legal framework for contracts, defense, and law and order. Public-policy initiatives should be confined to those measures that liberate the economy from social constraints: privatization of public enterprises, deregulation instead of state control, liberalization of trade and industry, massive tax cuts, strict control of organized labor, and the reduction of public expenditures.

Hence, globalists support a model of economic organization based on classical liberal ideals that is adjusted to the increasingly global framework of our times. In what amounts to an updated version of Adam Smith's self-regulating market, they seek to enshrine laissez-faire capitalism as the self-evident and natural order of our era. In that sense, neoliberal globalists are "market fundamentalists" who believe in the creation of a single, global market in goods, services, and capital.[16] They suggest that all peoples and states are equally subject to the logic of globalization, which is in the long run beneficial and inevitable, and that societies have no choice but to adapt to this world-shaping force.[17] This interpretation of globalization as driven by the irresistible forces of the market and technology is frequently expressed in quasi-religious language that bestows almost divine wisdom upon the market.[18]

Since globalists draw on ideas and prescriptions that have been formulated over the last two centuries by classical liberal thinkers, their ideology offers few new political or economic insights. Largely, it constitutes a gigantic repackaging enterprise—the pouring of old philosophical wine into new ideological bottles. Still, globalism deserves the label "new market ideology," for its proponents have been able to make an innovative connection between quaint free-market ideas and cutting-edge global talk. Indeed, by calling the ideological-economic framework of our time "the *new* economy," globalists want to signal the novelty of their paradigm.

Conceptual Framework of the Book

Globalism constitutes a coherent discursive regime that shapes the social understandings of authority, but it is not a monolithic ideology. A complex phenomenon, it comes in many variations on the main theme of market liberalization. Lately, some globalists even seek to incorporate parts of their opponents' arguments in order to forestall more serious objections. In the last decade, globalism has spread to most parts of the world. Still, the expansion of this market narrative has encountered considerable resistance, forcing globalists to respond with their powerful arsenal of ideological representation, the co-option of local elites, political coercion, and market power.

Yet globalism's preferred method is to employ its dominant codes and hegemonic meanings as battering rams to crush the remaining obstacles in the path of global capital. Developing countries are "persuaded" to follow the economic dictates of international economic institutions by donning what *New York Times* correspondent Thomas Friedman calls the "golden straitjacket" of neoliberalism. Thus, globalism's claims and political maneuvers remain conceptually tied to a Spencerian nineteenth-century narrative of "modernization" and "civilization" that presents Western countries—particularly the United States and the United Kingdom—as the privileged vanguard of an evolutionary process that applies to all nations.

But what distinguishes globalism from previous market ideologies is the innovative attempt of its believers to fill the concept of "globalization" with neoliberal meanings. Hence, this book distinguishes between *globalism*—a neoliberal market ideology endowing globalization with certain norms, values, and meanings—and *globalization*—a social process defined and described by various commentators in different, often contradictory ways.

However, I do not mean to suggest that globalism (the rhetorical package) exists in isolation from globalization (the material process). Ideologies are never imaginary constructs without foundations in material phenomena. Social institutions, concrete political and economic processes, and the selective ideological interpretation of these processes form an interconnected whole.[19] I employ the distinction between globalization and globalism because I do not want to lose sight of the considerable role played by ideas, beliefs, language, and symbols in shaping the conditions of the social world. In following Weber's suggestion to broaden Marx's materialist account of social formation, I refuse to bestow upon economic "materiality" the unquestioned causal primacy it has received from the pens of orthodox Marxists. Rather, I suggest that a society and an epoch must be understood as being as much the product of ideas as the outcome of material forces.

This study's focus on the ideational and normative dimensions of globalization is important for a variety of reasons. For one, most existing books on globalization tend to concentrate on the economic aspects of it. Undoubtedly, such accounts are important, but it is equally necessary to explore the role of ideas in these processes. Conventional books on globalization often take one aspect of global dissemination, such as trade or investment, and talk about the ways in which the phenomenon is causing changes elsewhere. That globalization is a material process is taken for granted. This book, however, suggests that globalization is also a linguistic and ideological practice. It is also a persuasive story, embedded in a neoliberal political project that most of us are being asked to go along with. Hence, my analysis of globalism adopts a less conventional approach, one that critically examines the neoliberal narrative of globalization. Seeking to contribute to the development of a critical theory of globalization, my study follows the suggestion of several prominent researchers who have called for a more extensive analysis of the production and global circulation of neoliberal market ideology.[20]

Second, my focus on the ideological dynamics of globalism as it unfolds in the public arena permits me to explore in more detail the discursive strategies of neoliberal forces as they attempt to harness the concept of globalization to their material interests. Such a "critical discourse analysis" contributes to a better understanding of the complex ideological dynamics behind the spread of globalism—a process that itself represents an important dimension of globalization. Given globalism's deep roots in Anglo-American neoliberal ideas, most of the evidence assembled in this book is drawn from statements made in the public arena by both the North American and European framers of the new market ideology. It is my intention to spell out clearly, and with as many instructive examples as possible, how various claims and assumptions of globalism legitimize, reinforce, and defend a particular political agenda with global implications, and how these claims clash with antiglobalist arguments.

Situating itself squarely within the tradition of critical theory, this study seeks to provide readers with an understanding of how dominant beliefs about globalization fashion their realities, and to show them that these ideas can be changed to bring about a more egalitarian and cosmopolitan order.[21] Pointing to concrete instances of human suffering and environmental degradation and showing how particular social forces justify these developments, critical theorists of globalization have challenged the claims of the new market ideology.[22] As a result of such critical interventions, alternative stories of globalization have emerged. Rather than heralding the end of ideology, these narratives remind people that history contains no predetermined outcomes.

THE ACADEMIC DEBATE
OVER GLOBALIZATION

The Blind Scholars and the Elephant

The ancient Buddhist parable of six blind scholars and their encounter with the elephant illustrates the nature of the current academic debate on globalization. Since the blind scholars did not know what the elephant looked like and had never even heard its name, they resolved to obtain a mental picture, and thus the knowledge they desired, by touching the animal. Feeling its trunk, one blind man argued that the elephant was like a lively snake. Another man, rubbing along its enormous leg, likened the animal to a rough column of massive proportions. The third person took hold of its tail and insisted that the elephant resembled a large, flexible brush. The fourth man felt its sharp tusks and declared it to be like a great spear. The fifth man examined its waving ear and was convinced that the animal was some sort of fan. Occupying the space between the elephant's front and hind legs, the sixth blind scholar groped in vain for a part of the elephant. Con-

17

sequently, he accused his colleagues of making up fantastic stories about nonexisting things, asserting that there were no such beasts as "elephants" at all. Each of the six blind scholars held firmly to his story of what he knew an elephant to be. Since their scholarly reputation was riding on the veracity of their respective findings, the blind men eventually ended up arguing and fighting about which story contained the correct definition of the elephant. As a result, their entire community was riven asunder. Suspicion and general distrust became the order of the day.[1]

The parable of the blind scholars and the elephant contains many valuable lessons. First, one might conclude that reality is too complex to be fully grasped by imperfect human beings. Second, although each observer correctly identified one aspect of reality, the collective mistake of the blind men lay in their attempts to reduce the entire phenomenon to their own partial experience. Third, the maintenance of communal peace and harmony might be worth much more than the individual sense of superiority that comes with stubbornly clinging to one's— often one-sided—understanding of the world. Fourth, it might be wise for the blind scholars to return to the elephant and exchange their positions. As a result, they might be able to appreciate better the whole of the elephant as well as the previous insight of each man.

Representing a contemporary version of this ancient parable, the debate over globalization takes place in two separate, but related arenas. One battle is mostly fought within the narrow walls of academia, while the other unfolds in the popular arena of public discourse. Although there are some common themes and overlapping observations, the academic debate differs from the more general discussion in that its participants tend to focus on the analytical rather than the normative/ideological dimension of globalization.

The principal participants in the academic debate reside and teach in the wealthy countries of the Northern Hemisphere, particularly the United States and the United Kingdom. Their disproportionate intellectual influence reflects not only existing power relations in the world, but also the global dominance of Anglo-American ideas. Although they share a common intellectual framework, these scholars hold radically different views regarding the definition of globalization, its scale, chronology, impact, and policy outcomes.

As the parable of the blind scholars and the elephant suggests, academics often respond to the analytical challenge by trying to take conceptual possession of globalization—as though it were something "out there" to be captured by the "correct" analytical framework. Indeed, as Stephen J. Rosow points out, many researchers approach globalization as though they were dealing with a process or an object without a meaning of its own prior to its constitution as a conceptual "territory."[2] Moreover, since it falls outside the boundaries of established academic disciplines, the study of globalization has invited armies of social scientists, scholars in the humanities, and even natural scientists to leave their mark on an intellectual *terra incognita*.

As a result, various scholars have invoked the concept of globalization to describe a variety of changing economic, political, and cultural processes that are alleged to have accelerated since the 1970s. No generally accepted definition of globalization has emerged, except for such broad descriptions as "increasing global interconnectedness," "the rapid intensification of worldwide social relations," "the compression of time and space," "a complex range of processes, driven by a mixture of political and economic influences," and "the swift and relatively unimpeded flow of capital, people, and ideas across national borders."[3] A number of researchers even object to those characterizations; a few go so far as to deny the existence of globalization altogether.

It is the purpose of this chapter to introduce the reader to the principal academic approaches to the subject. These range from the suggestion that globalization is little more than "globaloney," to interpretations of globalization as an economic, political, or cultural process. Although such analytical perspectives are necessary for gaining a better understanding of globalization, I will make a case at the end of the chapter that scientific approaches to the subject need to be complemented by explorations of the ideational and normative dimensions of globalization.

Globalization Is "Globaloney"

Scholars who champion this perspective contend that existing accounts of globalization are incorrect, imprecise, or exaggerated. They note that just about everything that can be linked to some transnational process is cited as evidence for globalization and its growing influence. Hence, they suspect that such general observations often amount to little more than "globaloney."[4] The arguments of these globalization skeptics fall into three broad categories. Representatives of the first group dispute the usefulness of globalization as a sufficiently precise analytical concept. Members of the second group point to the limited nature of globalizing processes, emphasizing that the world is not nearly as integrated as many globalization proponents believe. In their view, the term "globalization" does not constitute an accurate label for the actual state of affairs. The third group of critics disputes the novelty of the process while acknowledging the existence of moderate globalizing tendencies. They argue that those who refer to globalization as a recent process miss the bigger picture and fall prey to their narrow historical framework. Let us examine the respective arguments of these three groups in more detail.

First Group

Scholars who dismiss the utility of globalization as an analytical concept typically advance their arguments from within a larger criticism of such vague words employed in academic discourse. Besides globalization, another often-cited example for such analytically impoverished concepts is the complex and ambiguous phenomenon of nationalism. Craig Calhoun, for example, argues that nationalism and its corollary terms "have proved notoriously hard concepts to define," because "nationalisms are extremely varied phenomena," and "any definition will legitimate some claims and delegitimate others."[5] Writing in the same critical vein, Susan Strange considers globalization a prime example of such a vacuous term, suggesting that it has been used in academic discourse to refer to "anything from the Internet to a hamburger."[6] Similarly, Linda Weiss objects to the term as "a big idea resting on slim foundations."[7]

Scholarly suggestions for improvement point in two different directions. The first is to challenge the academic community to provide additional examples of how the term "globalization" obscures more than it enlightens. Such empirically based accounts would serve as a warning to extreme globalization proponents. Ultimately, the task of more careful researchers should be to break the concept of globalization into smaller, more manageable parts that contain a higher analytical value because they can be more easily associated with empirical processes. This rationale underlies Robert Holton's suggestion to abandon all general theoretical analyses in favor of middle-range approaches that seek to provide specific explanations of particulars.[8]

The second avenue for improvement involves my own suggestion offered at the end of this chapter to complement the social-scientific enterprise of exploring globalization as an objective process with more interpretive studies of the ideological project of globalism. Following this argument, the central task for scholars working in the new field of globalization studies would be to identify the many ways in which various ideologists have filled the term with values and meanings that bolster their respective political agendas.

Second Group

The second group of skeptics emphasizes the limited nature of current globalizing processes. This perspective is perhaps best reflected in the writings of Paul Hirst and Graham Thompson.[9] In their detailed historical analysis of economic globalization, Hirst and Thompson claim that the world economy is not a truly global phenomenon, but one centered on Europe, East Asia, and North America. The authors emphasize that the majority of economic activity around the world still remains primarily national in origin and scope. Presenting recent data on trade, foreign direct investment, and financial flows, the authors warn against drawing global conclusions from increased levels of economic interaction in advanced industrial countries. Hirst and Thompson advance an argument against the existence of economic globalization based on empirical data in order to attack the general misuse of the concept. Without a truly global economic system, they insist, there can be no such thing as globalization: "[A]s we proceeded [with our economic research] our skepticism deepened until we became convinced that globalization, as conceived by the more extreme globalizers, is largely a myth."[10]

Buried under an avalanche of relevant data, one can nonetheless detect a critical-normative message in the Hirst-Thompson thesis: It is to show that exaggerated accounts of an "iron logic of economic globalization" tend to produce disempowering political effects. For example, the authors convincingly demonstrate that certain political forces have used the thesis of economic globalization to propose national economic deregulation and the reduction of welfare programs. The implementation of such policies stands to benefit neoliberal interests.

But there also remain a number of problems with the Hirst-Thompson thesis. For example, as several critics have pointed out, the authors set overly high standards for the economy in order to be counted as "fully globalized."[11] Moreover, their efforts to construct an abstract model of a perfectly globalized economy unnecessarily polarizes the topic by pressuring the reader to either completely embrace or entirely reject the concept of globalization. Perhaps the most serious shortcoming of the Hirst-Thompson thesis lies in its attempt to counteract neoliberal economic determinism with a good dose of Marxist economic determinism. Their argument implicitly assumes that globalization is primarily an economic phenomenon. As a result, they portray all other dimensions of globalization—culture, politics, and ideology—as reflections of deeper economic processes. While paying lip service to the multidimensional character of globalization, their own analysis ignores the logical implications of this assertion. After all, if globalization is truly a complex, multilevel phenomenon, then economic relations constitute only *one* among *many* globalizing tendencies. It would therefore be entirely possible to argue for the significance of globalization even if it can be shown that increased transnational economic activity appears to be limited to advanced industrial countries.

Third Group

The third and final group of globalization skeptics disputes the novelty of the process, implying that the label "globalization" has often been applied in a historically imprecise manner. In his most recent study, Robert Gilpin confirms the existence of globalizing tendencies, but he also insists that many important aspects of globalization are not novel developments. Citing relevant data collected by the prominent American economist Paul Krugman, Gilpin notes that the world economy in the late 1990s appears to be even less integrated in a number of important respects than it was prior to the outbreak of World War I. Even if one were to accept the most optimistic assessment of the actual volume of transnational economic activity, the most one could say is that the postwar international economy has simply restored globalization to approximately the same level that existed in 1913. Gilpin also points to two additional factors that seem to support his position: the globalization of labor was actually much greater prior to World War I, and international migration declined considerably after 1918. Hence,

Gilpin warns his readers against accepting the arguments of "hyper-globalizers."[12]

Similar criticisms come from the proponents of world-system theory. Pioneered by neo-Marxist scholars such as Immanuel Wallerstein and Andre Gunder Frank, world-system theorists argue that the modern capitalist economy in which we live today has been global since its inception five centuries ago.[13] Driven by the exploitative logic of capital accumulation, the capitalist world system has created global inequalities based on the domination of modernizing Western "core" countries over non-Western "peripheral" areas. These forms of exploitation were inscribed in nineteenth-century systems of colonialism and imperialism and have persisted in the twentieth century in different forms. World-system theorists reject, therefore, the use of the term "globalization" as referring exclusively to relatively recent phenomena. Instead, they emphasize that globalizing tendencies have been proceeding along the continuum of modernization for a long time.

The greatest virtue of the world-system critique of globalization lies in its historical sensitivity. Any general discussion of globalization should include the caution that cross-regional transfers of resources, technology, and culture did not start only in the last few decades. Indeed, the origins of globalizing tendencies can be traced back to the political and cultural interactions that sustained the ancient empires of Persia, China, and Rome. On the downside, however, a world-system approach to globalization suffers from the same weaknesses as the Marxist economic-determinist view pointed out above in my discussion of the Hirst-Thompson thesis. Wallerstein leaves little doubt that he considers global integration to be a process driven largely by economic forces whose essence can be captured by economistic analytical models. Accordingly, he assigns to culture and ideology merely a subordinate role as "idea systems" dependent on the "real" movements of the capitalist world economy.[14]

However, more recent studies produced by world-system scholars acknowledge that the pace of globalization has significantly quickened in the last few decades of the twentieth-century.[15] Ash Amin, for example, has suggested that much of the criticism of globalization as a new phenomenon has been based on quantitative analyses of trade and output that neglect the qualitative shift in social and political relations. This qualitative difference in the globalizing process, he argues, has resulted in the world-capitalist system's new configuration as a complex network of international corporations, banks, and financial flows. Hence, these global developments may indeed warrant a new label.[16] In their efforts to gauge the nature of this qualitative difference, world-system theorists have begun to focus more closely on the interaction between dominant-class interests and "cultural-ideological transnational practices." In so doing, they have begun to raise important normative questions, suggesting that the elements of the "ideological superstructure"—politics, ideas, values, and beliefs—may, at times, neutralize or supersede economic forces.[17]

Overall, then, all three groups of globalization skeptics make an important contribution to the academic debate on the subject. Their insistence on a more careful and precise usage of the term forces the participants in the debate to hone their analytical skills. Moreover, their intervention serves as an important reminder that some aspects of globalization may neither constitute new developments nor reach to all corners of the earth. However, by focusing too narrowly on abstract issues of terminology, the globalization skeptics tend to dismiss too easily the significance and extent of today's globalizing tendencies. Finally, the representatives of these three groups show a clear inclination to conceptualize globalization mostly along economic lines, thereby often losing sight of its multidimensional character.

Globalization Is an Economic Process

The widespread scholarly emphasis on the economic dimension of globalization derives partly from its historical development as a subject of academic study.[18] Some of the earliest writings on the topic explore in much detail how the evolution of international markets and corporations led to an intensified form of global interdependence. These studies point to the growth of international institutions such as the European Union (EU), the North American Free Trade Association (NAFTA), and other regional trading blocs.[19] Economic accounts of globalization convey the notion that the essence of the phenomenon involves "the increasing linkage of national economies through trade, financial flows, and foreign direct investment (FDI) by multinational firms."[20] Thus expanding economic activity is identified as both the primary aspect of globalization and the engine behind its rapid development.

Many scholars who share this economic perspective consider globalization a real phenomenon that signals an epochal transformation in world affairs. Their strong affirmation of globalization culminates in the suggestion that a quantum change in human affairs has taken place as the flow of large quantities of trade, investment, and technologies across national borders has expanded from a trickle to a flood.[21] They propose that the study of globalization be moved to the center of social-scientific research. According to their view, the central task of this research agenda should be the close examination of the evolving structure of global economic markets and their principal institutions.

Studies of economic globalization are usually embedded in thick historical narratives that trace the gradual emergence of the new postwar world economy to the 1944 Bretton Woods Conference.[22] Under the leadership of the United States and Great Britain, the major economic powers of the West decided to reverse the protectionist policies of the interwar period (1918–1939) by committing themselves to the expansion of international trade. The major achievements of the Bretton Woods Conference include the limited liberalization of trade and the establishment of binding rules on international economic activities. In addition, the Bretton Woods participants agreed on the creation of a stable currency exchange system in which the value of each country's currency was pegged to a fixed gold value of the U.S. dollar. Within these prescribed limits, individual nations were free to control the permeability of their borders, which allowed them to set their own economic agendas, including the implementation of extensive socialwelfare polices. Bretton Woods also set the institutional foundations for the establishment of three new international economic organizations. The International Monetary Fund (IMF) was created to administer the international monetary system. The International Bank for Reconstruction and Development, or World Bank, was initially designed to provide loans for Europe's postwar reconstruction. Beginning in the 1950s, its purpose was expanded to fund various industrial projects in developing countries around the world. In 1947, the General Agreement on Tariffs and Trade (GATT) became the global trade organization charged with fashioning and enforcing multilateral trade agreements. Founded in 1995, the World Trade Organization (WTO) emerged as the successor organization to GATT. As will be shown in later chapters of this study, both the philosophical purpose and the neoliberal policies of this new international body became the focal points of intense ideological controversies over the effects of economic globalization in the late 1990s.

During its operation for almost three decades, the Bretton Woods system contributed greatly to the establishment of what some observers have called the "golden age of controlled capitalism."[23] According to this interpretation, existing mechanisms of state control over international capital movements made possible full employment and the expansion of the welfare state. Rising wages and increased social services secured in the wealthy countries of the global North a temporary class compromise.

Most scholars of economic globalization trace the accelerating integrationist tendencies of the global economy to the collapse of the Bretton Woods system in the early 1970s. In response to profound changes in the world economy that undermined the economic competitiveness of U.S.-based industries, President Richard Nixon decided in 1971 to abandon the gold-based fixed-rate system. The combination of new political ideas and economic developments—high inflation, low economic growth, high unemployment, public-sector deficits, two major oil crises within a decade—led to the spectacular election victories of conservative parties in the United States and United Kingdom. These parties spearheaded the neoliberal movement toward the expansion of international markets, a dynamic supported by the deregulation of domestic financial systems, the gradual removal of capital controls, and an enormous increase in global financial transactions.[24]

During the 1980s and 1990s, Anglo-American efforts to establish a single global market were further strengthened through comprehensive trade-liberalization agreements that increased the flow of economic resources across national borders. The rising neoliberal paradigm received further legitimation with the 1989–1991 collapse of command-type economies in Eastern Europe. Shattering the postwar economic consensus on Keynesian principles, free-market theories pioneered by Friedrich Hayek and Milton Friedman established themselves as the new economic orthodoxy, advocating the reduction of the welfare state, the downsizing of government, and the deregulation of the economy. A strong emphasis on "monetarist" measures to combat inflation led to the abandonment of the Keynesian goal of full employment in favor of establishing more "flexible" labor markets. In addition, the dramatic shift from a state-dominated to a market-dominated world was accompanied by technological innovations that lowered the costs of transportation and communication. The value of world trade increased from $57 billion in 1947 to an astonishing $6 trillion in the 1990s.[25]

Perhaps the two most important aspects of economic globalization relate to the changing nature of the production process and the internationalization of financial transactions. Indeed, many analysts consider the emergence of a transnational financial system the most fundamental feature of our time. As sociologist Manuel Castells points out, the process of financial globalization accelerated dramatically in the late 1980s as capital and securities markets in Europe and the United States were deregulated. The liberalization of financial trading allowed for the increased mobility among different segments of the financial industry, with fewer restrictions and a global view of investment opportunities.[26] In addition, advances in data processing and information technology contributed to the explosive growth of tradeable financial value. However, a large part of the money involved in expanding markets had little to do with supplying capital for productive investment—putting together machines, raw materials, and employees to produce saleable commodities and the like. Most of the growth occurred in the purely money-dealing currency and securities markets that trade claims to draw profits from future production. Aided by new communication technologies, global rentiers and speculators earned spectacular incomes by taking advantage of weak financial and banking regulations in the emerging markets of developing countries. By the late 1990s, the equivalent of nearly two trillion U.S. dollars was exchanged daily in global currency markets alone.[27]

While the creation of international financial markets represents a crucial aspect of economic globalization, another important economic development of the last three decades also involves the changing nature of global production. Transnational corporations (TNCs) consolidated their global operations in an increasingly deregulated global labor market. The availability of cheap labor, resources, and favorable production conditions in the Third World enhanced both the mobility and the profitability of TNCs. Accounting for over 70 percent of world trade, these gigantic enterprises expanded their global reach as their direct foreign investments rose approximately 15 percent annually during the 1990s.[28] Their ability to disperse manufacturing processes into

27

many discrete phases carried out in many different locations around the world is often cited as one of the hallmarks of economic globalization. Indeed, the formation of such "global commodity chains" allows huge corporations such as Nike and General Motors to produce, distribute, and market their products on a global scale. Nike, for example, subcontracts 100 percent of its goods production to 75,000 workers in China, South Korea, Malaysia, Taiwan, and Thailand.[29]

Transnational production systems augment the power of global capitalism by enhancing the ability of TNCs to bypass the nationally-based political influence of trade unions and other workers' organizations in collective wage-bargaining processes. While rejecting extreme accounts of economic globalization, the political economist Robert Gilpin nonetheless concedes that the growing power of TNCs has profoundly altered the structure and functioning of the global economy:

> These giant firms and their global strategies have become major determinants of trade flows and of the location of industries and other economic activities around the world. Most investment is in capital-intensive and technology-intensive sectors. These firms have become central in the expansion of technology flows to both industrialized and industrializing economies. As a consequence, multinational firms have become extremely important in determining the economic, political, and social welfare of many nations. Controlling much of the world's investment capital, technology, and access to global markets, such firms have become major players not only in international economic, but political affairs as well.[30]

Globalization Is a Political Process

As the above example of TNCs shows, economic perspectives on globalization can hardly be discussed apart from an analysis of political processes and institutions. Most of the debate on political globalization involves the weighing of conflicting evidence with regard to the fate of the modern nation-state. In particular, two questions have moved to the top of the research agenda. First, what are the political causes for the massive flows of capital, money, and technology across territorial boundaries? Second, do these flows constitute a serious challenge to the power of the nation-state? These questions imply that economic globalization might be leading to the reduced control of national governments over economic policy. The latter question, in particular, involves an important subset of issues pertaining to the principle of state sovereignty, the growing impact of intergovernmental organizations, and the prospects for global governance.

An influential group of scholars considers political globalization as a process intrinsically connected to the expansion of markets. In particular, steady advances in computer technology and communication systems such as the World Wide Web are seen as the primary forces responsible for the creation of a single global market.[31] According to this view, politics is rendered almost powerless in the face of an unstoppable and irreversible technoeconomic juggernaut that will crush all governmental attempts to reintroduce restrictive policies and regulations. Economics is portrayed as possessing an inner logic apart from and superior to politics. According to this view, it is this combination of economic self-interest and technological innovation that is responsible for ushering in a new phase in world history in which the role of government will be reduced to that of a handmaiden to free-market forces. As Lowell Bryan and Diana Farrell assert, the role of government will ultimately be reduced to serving as "a superconductor for global capitalism."[32]

Perhaps the most influential representative of this view is Kenichi Ohmae. Projecting the rise of a "borderless world" brought on by the irresistable forces of capitalism, the Japanese business strategist argues that the nation-state is becoming irrelevant in the global economy. Seen from the perspective of real flows of economic activity, Ohmae asserts that nation-states have already lost their role as meaningful units of participation in the global economy. As territorial divisions are becoming increasingly irrelevant to human society, states are less able to determine the direction of social life within their borders. Since the workings of genuinely global capital markets dwarf their ability to control exchange rates or protect their currency, nation-states have become vulnerable to the discipline imposed by economic choices made elsewhere over which states have no practical control. In the long run, the process of political globalization will lead to the decline of territory as a meaningful framework for understanding political and social change. No longer functioning along the lines of discrete territorial units, the political order of the future will be one of regional economies linked together in an almost seamless global web that operates according to free-market principles.[33]

It is important to note that many neo-Marxist scholars also share such an economistic interpretation of political globalization. Caroline Thomas, for example, portrays politics merely as a consequence of global processes driven by a reinvigorated capitalism that has entered the stage wherein accumulation is taking place on a global rather than a national level. Consequently, she insists that the concept of globalization "refers broadly to the process whereby power is located in global social formations and expressed through global networks rather than through territorially-based states."[34]

A second group of scholars disputes the view that large-scale economic changes simply happen to societies in the manner of natural phenomena such as earthquakes and hurricanes. Instead, they highlight the central role of politics—especially the successful mobilization of political power—in unleashing the forces of globalization.[35] This view rests on a philosophical model of active human agency. If the shape of economic globalization is politically determined, then shifting political preferences are capable of creating different social conditions. Daniel Singer, for example, argues that at the root of the rapid expansion of global economic activity there lies neither a "natural law of the market" nor the development of computer technology, but political decisions made by governments to lift the international restrictions on capital: "Once the decisions were implemented in the 1980s, the technology came into its own. The speed of communication and calculation helped the movement of money to reach astronomical proportions."[36] The clear implication of Singer's view is that nation and territory still do matter—even in a globalized context.

Hence, this group of scholars argues for the continued relevance of conventional political units, operating either in the form of modern nation-states or "global cities."[37] At the same time, most proponents of this view understand that the development of the last few decades has significantly constrained the set of political options open to states, particularly in developing countries. Jan Aart Scholte, for example, points out that globalization refers to gradual processes of "relative deterritorialization" that facilitate the growth of "supraterritorial" relations between people.[38] Scholte emphasizes, however, that his concession to deterritorialization does not necessarily mean that nation-states are no longer the main organizing forces in the world. Equipped with the power to regulate economic activities within their sphere of influence, states are far from being impotent bystanders to the workings of global forces. If concrete political decisions were responsible for changing the international context in the direction of deregulation, privatization, and the globalization of the world economy, then different political decisions could reverse the trend in the opposite direction.[39] To be sure, it might take a crisis of international proportions brought on by various globalization processes to provide states with the incentive to make their boundaries less permeable to transnational flows. Still, even this scenario shows that it is possible to reverse seemingly irresistible globalizing tendencies. The core message of this group of academics is loud and clear: Politics is the crucial category upon which rests a proper understanding of globalization.

A third group of scholars suggests that globalization is fueled by a mixture of political and technological factors. John Gray, for example, presents globalization as a long-term, technology-driven process whose contemporary shape has been politically determined by the world's most powerful nations. According to Gray, it is the ultimate objective of the neoliberal Anglo-American initiative to engineer a global free market. Regardless of the ultimate success or failure of this political project, however, the British political theorist predicts that the "swift and inexorable spawning of new technologies throughout the world" will continue, making the technology-driven modernization of the world's societies "a historical fate."[40] Still, Gray asserts that no nation has the hegemonic power to realize a universal free market. In fact, he predicts that the world economy will fragment as its imbalances become insupportable. Thus the political theorist foresees a gloomy ending to the current political efforts to establish a single global market: "Trade wars will make international cooperation more difficult. . . . As global *laissez-faire* breaks up, a deepening international anarchy is the likely human prospect."[41]

A far less pessimistic version of a perspective that combines technology and politics to explain globalization can be found in Manuel Castells's seminal three-volume study on the rise of the "network society." The Spanish sociologist separates the powerful forces fueling globalization into three independent processes: "The information technology revolution; the economic crisis of both capitalism and statism, and their subsequent restructuring; and the blooming of cultural social movements."[42] As a result of these developments, elaborate networks of capital, labor, information, and markets have linked up to create conditions favorable to the further expansion of the global economy. Castells points to the rise of a new "informational capitalism" based on information technology as the indispensable tool for the effective implementation of processes of socioeconomic restructuring. In this context, he acknowledges both the crisis of the nation-state as a sovereign entity and the devolution of power to regional and local governments as well as to various supranational institutions.

On the other hand, Castells also emphasizes the continued relevance of nation-states as crucial bargaining agencies that influence the changing world of power relationships. As new political actors emerge and new public policies are implemented, the role of culture increases: "Culture as the source of power, and power as the source of capital, underlie the new social hierarchy of the Information Age."[43] While pointing to the potential for global economic and ecological disasters brought on by globalization, Castells ends on a far more positive note than Gray: "The dream of the Enlightenment, that reason and science would solve the problems of humankind, is within reach."[44]

A fourth group of scholars approaches political globalization primarily from the perspective of global governance. Representatives of this group analyze the role of various national and multilateral responses to the fragmentation of economic and political systems and the transnational flows permeating through national borders.[45] Political scientists such as David Held and Richard Falk articulate in their respective writings the need for effective global governance as a consequence of various forces of globalization. Both authors portray globalization as diminishing the sovereignty of national governance, thereby reducing the relevance of the nation-state.

Much to their credit, Held and Falk are two of the most vociferous advocates for moving the academic debate on globalization in a more ideational and normative direction. Falk in particular calls for a closer analysis of the ways in which neoliberal ideology has played a major role in associating globalization with a particular set of ideas and assumptions.[46] In this regard, his writings have served as an inspiration for the present study.

In Held's view, neither the old Westphalian system of sovereign nation-states nor the postwar global system centered on the United Nations (UN) offers a satisfactory solution to the enormous challenges posed by political globalization. Instead, he predicts the emergence of a multilayered form of democratic governance based on Western cosmopolitan ideals, international legal arrangements, and a web of expanding linkages between various governmental and nongovernmental institutions. Rejecting the charge of utopianism often leveled against his vision, Held provides empirical evidence for the existence of a tendency inherent in the globalization process that seems to favor the strengthening of supranational bodies and the rise of an international civil society. He predicts that democratic rights will ultimately become detached from their narrow relationship to discrete territorial units.

If Held's perspective on political globalization is correct, then its final outcome might well be the emergence of a "cosmopolitan democracy" that would constitute the "constructive basis for a plurality of identities to flourish within a structure of mutual toleration and accountability." His vision of a cosmopolitan democracy includes the following political elements: a global parliament connected to regions, states, and localities; a new charter of rights and duties locked into different domains of political, social, and economic power; the formal separation of political and economic interests; and an interconnected global legal system with mechanisms of enforcement from the local to the global.[47]

In a similarly hopeful vein, Richard Falk argues that political globalization might facilitate the emergence of democratic transnational social forces anchored in a thriving civil society. Distinguishing his vision of a popular-democratic "globalization-from-below" from the market-driven, corporate "globalization-from-above," Falk analyzes the capacities of political actors to challenge the prevailing dominance of neoliberal globalization in a series of key arenas. These include the role of international institutions and regimes, the influence of the media, the changing nature of citizenship, and the reorientation of state activities. Falk retains a strong thematic focus on the capacities of nation-states to implement a cosmopolitan agenda. His writings consistently raise the important question of "whether the state will function in the future mainly as an instrument useful for the promotion and protection of global trade and investment or whether, by contrast, the state can recover its sense of balance in this globalizing setting so that the success of markets will not be achieved at the expense of the well-being of peoples."[48]

A number of academic critics have challenged the idea that political globalization is fueling a development toward cosmopolitan democracy. Most of their criticism boils down to the charge that Held and Falk indulge in an abstract idealism that fails to engage with current political developments on the level of policy. Moreover, skeptics raise the suspicion that the authors do not explore in sufficient detail the cultural feasibility of global democracy. As cultural patterns become increasingly interlinked through globalization, critics argue, the possibility of resistance and opposition becomes just as real as their vision of mutual accommodation and tolerance of differences.[49]

Globalization Is a Cultural Process

Held and Falk might respond to these criticisms that one major strength of their approach lies in approaching globalization not as a one-dimensional phenomenon, but as a multidimensional process involving diverse domains of activity and interaction, including the cultural sphere. Indeed, any analytical account of globalization would be woefully inadequate without an examination of its cultural dimension. A number of prominent scholars have emphasized the centrality of culture to contemporary debates on globalization. As sociologist John Tomlinson puts it: "Globalization lies at the heart of modern culture; cultural practices lie at the heart of globalization."[50] The thematic landscape traversed by scholars of cultural globalization is vast and the questions they raise are too numerous to be completely fleshed out in this short survey. Rather than presenting a long laundry list of relevant topics, this section focuses on one of the central questions raised by scholars of cultural globalization: Does globalization increase cultural homogeneity, or does it lead to greater diversity and heterogeneity? Or, to put the matter into less academic terms, does globalization make people more alike or more different?

Most commentators preface their response to this question with a general analysis of the relationship between the globalization process and contemporary cultural change. Tomlinson, for example, defines cultural globalization as a "densely growing network of complex cultural interconnections and interdependencies that characterize modern social life." He emphasizes that global cultural flows are directed by powerful international media corporations that utilize new communication technologies to shape societies and identities. As images and ideas can be more easily and rapidly transmitted from one place to another, they profoundly impact the way people experience their everyday lives. Culture remains no longer tied to fixed localities such as town and nation, but acquires new meanings that reflect dominant themes emerging in a global context. This interconnectivity caused by cultural globalization challenges parochial values and identities, because they undermine the linkages that connect culture to fixity of location.[51]

A number of scholars argue that these processes have facilitated the rise of an increasingly homogenized global culture underwritten by an Anglo-American value system. Referring to the global diffusion of American values, consumer goods, and lifestyles as "Americanization," these authors analyze the ways in which such forms of "cultural imperialism" are overwhelming more vulnerable cultures. The American sociologist George Ritzer, for example, coined the term "McDonaldization" to describe the wide-ranging process by which the principles of the fast-food restaurant are coming to dominate more and more sectors of American society as well as the rest of the world. On the surface, these principles appear to be rational in their attempts to offer efficient and predictable ways of serving people's needs. Only toward the end of his study does the author allow himself to address the normative ramifications of this process: When rational systems serve to deny the expression of human creativity and cultural difference, they contribute to the rise of irrationality in the world. In the long run, McDonaldization leads to the eclipse of cultural diversity and the dehumanization of social relations.[52]

The prominent American political theorist Benjamin R. Barber also enters the normative realm when he warns his readers against the cultural imperialism of what he calls "McWorld"—a soulless consumer capitalism that is rapidly transforming the world's diverse population into a blandly uniform market. For Barber, McWorld is a product of a superficial American popular culture assembled in the 1950s and 1960s and driven by expansionist commercial interests: "Its template is American, its form style. . . . Music, video, theater, books, and theme parks . . . are all constructed as image exports creating a common taste around common logos, advertising slogans, stars, songs, brand names, jingles, and trademarks."[53]

Much to its credit, Barber's analysis moves beyond offering a "value-free" account of the forces of McWorld. His insightful account of cultural globalization contains the important recognition that the colonizing tendencies of McWorld provoke cultural and political resistance in the form of "Jihad"—the parochial impulse to reject and repel Western homogenization forces wherever they can be found. Fueled by the furies of ethnonationalism and/or religious fundamentalism, Jihad represents the dark side of cultural particularism. In the words of the author, Jihad is the "rabid response to colonialism and imperialism and their economic children, capitalism and modernity." Guided by opposing visions of homogeneity, Jihad and McWorld are dialectically interlocked in a bitter cultural struggle for popular allegiance. Barber insists that both forces ultimately work against a participatory form of democracy, for they are equally prone to undermine civil liberties and thus thwart the possibility of a global democratic future.[54]

Proponents of the cultural homogenization thesis offer ample empirical evidence for their interpretation. They point to Amazonian Indians wearing Nike sneakers, denizens of the Southern Sahara purchasing Texaco baseball caps, and Palestinian youths proudly displaying their Chicago Bulls sweatshirts in downtown Ramallah. Documenting the spread of Anglo-American culture facilitated by the deregulation and convergence of global media and electronic communication systems, some commentators even go so far as to insist that there no longer exist any viable alternatives to the "Americanization" of the world. For example, French political economist Serge Latouche argues that the media-driven, consumerist push toward "planetary uniformity" according to Anglo-American norms and values will inevitably result in a worldwide "standardization of lifestyles."[55]

It is one thing to acknowledge the powerful cultural logic of global capitalism, but it is quite another to assert that the cultural diversity existing on our planet is destined to vanish. In fact, several influential academics offer contrary assessments that link globalization to new forms of cultural diversity.[56] Roland Robertson, for example, contends that global cultural flows often reinvigorate local cultural niches. Arguing that cultural globalization always takes place in local contexts, Robertson predicts a pluralization of the world as localities produce a variety of unique cultural responses to global forces. The result is not increasing cultural homogenization, but "glocalization"—a complex interaction of the global and local characterized by cultural borrowing.[57] These interactions lead to a complex mixture of both homogenizing and heterogenizing impulses. Often referred to as "hybridization" or "creolization," the processes of cultural mixing are reflected in music, film, fashion, language, and other forms of symbolic expression. Ulf Hannerz, for example, emphasizes the complexity of an emerging "global culture" comprised of new zones of hybridization. In these regions, meanings derive from different historical sources that were originally separated from one another in space, but have come to mingle extensively. Hence, rather than being obliterated by Western consumerist forces of homogenization, local difference and particularity evolve into new cultural constellations and discourses.[58]

In addition to addressing the question of whether globalization leads to cultural homogeneity or heterogeneity, scholars such as Hannerz and Robertson seek to expand the concept of globalization by portraying it as a multidimensional "field." In their view, globalization is both a material and a mental condition, constituted by complex, often contradictory interactions of global, local, and individual aspects of social life. Cultural theorists such as Ulrich Beck and Arjun Appadurai have refined this argument by contrasting common interpretations of globalization as a "process" with the less mechanical concept of "globality," referring to "the experience of living and acting across borders."[59]

Appadurai identifies five conceptual dimensions or "landscapes" that are constituted by global cultural flows: ethnoscapes (shifting populations made up of tourists, immigrants, refugees, and exiles); technoscapes (development of technologies that facilitate the rise of TNCs); finanscapes (flows of global capital); mediascapes (electronic capabilities to produce and disseminate information); and ideoscapes (ideologies of states and social movements). Each of these "scapes" contains the building blocks of the new "imagined worlds" that are assembled by the historically situated imaginations of persons and groups spread around the globe."[60] Suspended in a global web of cultural multiplicity, more and more people become aware of the density of human relations. Their enhanced ability to explore and absorb new cultural symbols and meanings coexists in uneasy tension with their growing sense of "placelessness." Focusing on the changing forms of human perception and consciousness brought on by global cultural flows, Beck and Appadurai discuss subjective forms of cultural globalization that are often neglected in more common analyses of "objective" relations of interdependence.

Sociologist Martin Albrow also uses the concept of globality to describe a new condition where people and groups of all kinds refer to the globe as the framework for their beliefs and actions. Analyzing the complex web of interactions underlying this epochal shift in people's consciousness, he concludes that a dawning "Global Age" is slowly supplanting the old conceptual framework of modernity. A proper understanding of this new era demands that researchers revise dogmatic Enlightenment ideas of progress and science and instead embrace a more cautious and pragmatic universalism that explicitly recognizes the uncertainties and contingencies of the Global Age. Albrow speaks of a new condition of "globality" that is profoundly different from modernity in that there is no presumption of centrality of control. In short, the project of modernity has ended.[61]

On this issue, then, the debate on cultural globalization has linked up with the longstanding controversy in political and social theory over whether our present age should be understood as an extension of modernity, or whether it constitutes a new condition of "postmodernity" characterized by the loss of a stable sense of identity and knowledge.[62] Indeed, scholars of cultural globalization have shown more willingness to engage in sustained investigations of the normative dimension of globalization than their colleagues in political science or economics.

Globalization and Ideology:
Toward a Critical Examination of Globalism

This chapter has introduced some of the main analytical perspectives in the academic debate on globalization. Still, this overview does not encompass all topics of the ever-expanding discourse on the subject. In addition to exploring the economic, political, and cultural dimensions of globalization, many scholars have raised a number of additional topics, such as the collective impact of globalization on the ecological health of the planet's natural systems, the structure and direction of transnational migration flows, the emergence of transnational social movements such as the women's movement, the spread of global diseases, and the globalization of military technology linked to a transnationalization of defense production.[63]

But rather than providing a full account of every conceivable aspect of the debate, the purpose of this chapter is to show that there exists no scholarly agreement on a single conceptual framework for the study of globalization. Academics remain divided on the validity of available empirical evidence for the existence and extent of globalization, not to mention its normative and ideological implications. Fredric Jameson, for example, questions the utility of forcing such a complex social phenomenon as globalization into a single analytical framework.[64] He argues that such attempts result frequently in either further disagreements or the elevation of a partial view to the unassailable truth and last word on the subject.

To be sure, there is much value in the intellectual advances brought about by analytical research programs for the study of globalization. No serious scholar would wish to disavow the importance of conceptual clarity and precise formulations. But the impulse to separate the social-scientific study of globalization from ideological and normative matters often serves to further perpetuate stale disputes over definitions and methodological differences. As Ian Clark puts it: "While there can be no objection to a precise definition of globalization, definitions should not be permitted to resolve the underlying issues of substance and historical interpretation."[65]

Any overly objectivist approach to globalization is bound to overlook the insight that all social-scientific concepts are simultaneously analytical and normative. This dual status of concepts means that they never merely describe that to which they refer, but are also necessarily engaged in a normative process of meaning construction.[66] Yet, many scholars believe that the normative/ideological nature of the globalization debate that takes place mostly in the public arena actually interferes with and obstructs the formulation of more "objective" or "value-free" accounts of globalization. This instinctive scholarly fear of ideological "contamination" derives partly from the historic mission of academic institutions. Like their nineteenth-century predecessor, today's universities subscribe to the belief that the world is, in principle, knowable and controllable through a balanced operation of human rationality. This means that scholars are encouraged to conduct their research within established parameters of objectivity and neutrality in order to reach a clear understanding of the phenomenon in question. Matters of ideology—particularly one's own political and moral preferences—are seen as compromising the scientific integrity of the research project. Therefore the normative dimension of ideology is often excluded from academic attempts to understand globalization.

In fact, a discussion of the normative/ideological dimension of the phenomenon is often seen as unscientific "journalism." However, this argument misses the dynamics of globalization as a public discourse. The public debate over globalization that occurs largely outside the walls of academia represents an important aspect of the phenomenon itself. If the researcher wants to understand the material and ideal stakes raised in the debate, then public judgments regarding the meanings and likely consequences of globalization represent an important subject of study. Thus the researcher must enter the value-laden arena of ideology. The task can no longer be limited to an objective classification of the constitutive parts of the elephant called "globalization," but a critical assessment of the *language about globalization* that is constitutive of the phenomenon itself. Rather than being rejected as a confusing cacophony of subjective assertions, the exhibited normative preferences and the rhetorical and polemical maneuvers performed by the main participants in the public debate on globalization become the focus of the researcher's critical task.

In my view, it is virtually impossible for globalization scholars to interpret the public discourse on the subject apart from their own ideological and political framework. In spite of the obvious dangers inherent in this move, the inclusion of one's own beliefs and values does not necessarily invalidate one's research project. As the German philosopher Hans-Georg Gadamer has pointed out, the motivations and prejudices of the interpreter condition every act of understanding.[67] Hence, it would be a mistake to consider the researcher's values and preconceptions solely as a hindrance to a proper understanding of social processes. In fact, the interpreter's inescapable normative involvement enables the very act of understanding. Thus the study of globalization as a real-life phenomenon must include an investigation of the ideological project that I have called "globalism."

Fortunately, the tendency of the academic discourse to separate ideological and normative matters from analytical concerns has been increasingly subjected to criticism from a variety of scholars who reject a narrow scientist approach to the study of globalization. For example, the writings of Stephen Gill and Robert W. Cox probe the extent to which neoliberal conceptions of the market have been shaping the public debate on globalization.[68] This book also is anchored in a more interpretive approach to understanding social phenomena that does not shy away from normative and ideological matters. I seek to avoid a general discussion of *globalization* (the material process) without a proper recognition that the former is inextricably intertwined with *globalism* (the dominant ideological package). Academic efforts to capture the nature of globalization apart from the ongoing ideological claims made in the public arena reinforce, intentionally or not, the dominant globalist project that alternately masks and transmits a neoliberal worldview, thus making it easier for existing power interests to escape critical scrutiny. As Alan Scott notes, the separation of analytical concerns from ideological and normative matters harbors the danger that the ethos of scientific detachment might unintentionally serve politically motivated attempts to provide "people with persuasive arguments to the effect that little can be done in the face of these enormous economic, political and social developments."[69]

Seeking to avoid this danger, the next chapter of this book introduces the major claims of globalism. Ironically, both globalist forces and their antiglobalist challengers often situate their respective views within a powerful narrative of science and objectivity. Both sides offer statistical data, display elaborate tables and elegant flip charts, and quote authoritative sources in order to legitimize their claims as "factual knowledge." However, their collections of "facts" mostly serve a particular political agenda. Various political groups sell globalization to their audiences in order to advance their preferred policies and political projects.[70] An analysis of their arguments, offered in the next chapter, brings to light underlying power interests and subjects them to critical reflection. I identify and examine five central claims of globalism in order to gain a better understanding of how neoliberal forces associate the concept of globalization with codes and meanings that bolster their political vision of a world functioning according to the principles of the free market.

FIVE CENTRAL CLAIMS
OF GLOBALISM

Selling Globalization

Recently, the neoliberal American magazine *BusinessWeek* featured a cover story on globalization that contained the following statement: "For nearly a decade, political and business leaders have struggled to persuade the American public of the virtues of globalization." Citing the results of a national poll on globalization conducted in April 2000, the article goes on to report that most Americans seem to be of two minds on the subject. On one hand, about 65 percent of the respondents think that globalization is a "good thing" for consumers and businesses in both the United States and the rest of the world. On the other, they are afraid that globalization might lead to a significant loss of American jobs. In addition, nearly 70 percent of those polled believe that free-trade agreements with low-wage countries are responsible for driving down wages in the United States. Ending his article on a rather combative note, the author issues a stern warning to American politicians and business leaders not to be "caught off guard" by the arguments of antiglobalist forces. In order to assuage people's increasing anxiety on the subject, American "decision makers" ought to be more effective in highlighting the benefits of globalization. After all, the journalist concludes, the persistence of public fears over globalization might result in a significant backlash, jeopardizing the health of the international economy and "the cause of free trade."[1]

The cover story contains two important pieces of information with regard to the ideological dimensions of globalization. First, there is the author's open admission that political and business leaders are actively engaged in selling their preferred version of globalization to the public. In fact, he sees the construction of arguments and images that portray globalization in a positive light as an indispensable tool for the realization of a global order based on free-market principles. No doubt, such favorable visions of globalization pervade public opinion and political choices. Language and ideas *do* matter in the ongoing "struggle to persuade the American public of the virtues of globalization." This means that neoliberal decision makers have had to become expert designers of an attractive ideological container for their market-friendly political agenda. Given that the exchange of commodities constitutes the core activity of all market societies, the discourse on globalization itself has turned into an extremely important commodity destined for public consumption.

Second, the polling data presented in the *BusinessWeek* cover story reveal the existence of a remarkable cognitive dissonance between the American people's normative orientation toward globalization and their personal experiences in the globalizing world. How can one explain that a sizeable majority of respondents are afraid of the negative economic impact of globalization on their lives while at the same time deeming globalization to be a "good thing"? One obvious answer is ideology. Neoliberal visions of globalization have shaped a large part of American public opinion, even if people's daily experiences reflect a less favorable picture. For example, the magazine article tells the harrowing story of a factory worker employed by the Goodyear Tire & Rubber Company in Gadsden, Alabama. Having lost his job after Goodyear shifted most of its tire production to low-wage jobs in Mexico and Brazil, the worker was only recently rehired by the same company for less money. Still, the article concludes this disturbing story by reaffirming the overall positive impact of economic globalization: "Polls have shown for years that a solid majority of Americans believe that open borders and free trade are good for the economy."[2]

BusinessWeek is only one among dozens of magazines, journals, newspapers, and electronic media published in the wealthy countries of the Northern Hemisphere that feeds their readers a steady diet of globalist claims. Their neoliberal market ideology serves a concrete political purpose. It presents globalization in such a way as to advance the material and ideal interests of those groups in society who benefit the most from the liberalization of the economy, the privatization of ownership, a minimal regulatory role for government, efficient returns on capital, and the devolution of power to the private sector. Like all ideologists, globalists engage continuously in acts of simplification, distortion, legitimation, and integration in order to cultivate in the public mind the uncritical attitude that globalization is a "good thing." When people accept the claims of globalism, they simultaneously accept as authority large parts of the comprehensive political, economic, and intellectual framework of neoliberalism. Thus the ideological reach of globalism goes far beyond the task of providing the public with a narrow explanation of the meaning of globalization. Most importantly, globalism is a compelling story that sells an overarching neoliberal worldview, thereby creating collective meanings and shaping personal and collective identities.

Protected by this powerful discursive regime, the marketization tendencies in the world have grown stronger than at any point in history. Globalism has become what some social and political thinkers call a "strong discourse." Such a hegemonic discourse is notoriously difficult to resist and repel because it has on its side powerful social forces that have already preselected what counts as "real" and, therefore, shape the world accordingly. As American social philosopher Judith Butler notes, the constant repetition, public recitation, and "performance" of an ideology's central claims and slogans frequently have the capacity to produce what they name.[4] As more neoliberal policies are enacted, the claims of globalism become even more firmly planted in the public mind. They solidify into what French social philosopher Michel Foucault calls a solid "ground of thinking."[5] The political realization of the neoliberal agenda, in turn, leads to the further weakening of those political and social institutions that subject market forces to public control. Neoliberal policies are made to appear as the most rational response to inevitable, but efficient, market forces. Growing global disparities in wealth and well-being are shrugged off as mere temporary dislocations on the sure path to a brighter future.

This chapter analyzes significant passages in the utterances, speeches, and writings of influential advocates of globalism. These persons usually reside in wealthy Northern countries and include corporate managers, executives of large transnational corporations, corporate lobbyists, journalists and public-relations specialists, intellectuals writing to a large public audience, state bureaucrats, and politicians. Putting before the public a globalist agenda of things to discuss, questions to ask, and claims to make, this powerful phalanx of neoliberal forces seeks to imbue the concept of globalization with values, beliefs, and meanings that support the global realization of societies based on free-market principles. This perspective is being promoted on a daily basis to the U.S. public and lawmakers alike by the spokespersons of major corporations and corporate associations. As Sandra Masur, of Eastman Kodak and the U.S. Business Roundtable, emphasizes: "The Companies of the [Business] Roundtable are seeking across-the-board liberalization of trade in goods, services, and investment."[6]

After introducing the reader to what I consider to be five central globalist claims, I subject these assertions to critical examination. In so doing, I employ a methodological approach usually referred to as "critical discourse analysis." Recognizing the importance of communication through the media, this method focuses on the interpretation of coherent units of spoken and written language. At the same time, it places ideas in their historical context. As Andrew Chadwick points out, by scrutinizing texts in the public domain, critical discourse analysis is particularly suited to help the researcher comprehend the role played by language use in producing and reinforcing asymmetrical power relations that sustain certain forms of social and political identity.

Rejecting a sharp distinction between the realm of "real politics" and "ideas," Chadwick suggests that any analysis of political practice is incomplete if it does not refer to the discourses that surround and construct it.[7] The French democratic theorist Claude Lefort also has argued that social reality constitutes a symbolic order, or a "discourse." Such articulatory practices contribute to the formation of social institution and the organization of social relations. Consequently, the study of globalization should be extended beyond its predominantly econo-mistic grounding.[8]

My critical examination of the five central claims of globalism sug-gests that the neoliberal language about globalization is ideological in the sense that it is politically motivated and contributes toward the construction of popular beliefs and values. Exposed to a shifting con-text of political competition, rivalry, and conflict, the claims of global-ism seek to fix a particular meaning of globalization in order to pre-serve and stabilize existing asymmetrical power relations. Although these meanings undergo ceaseless contestation and redefinition in the public arena, the dominant party of this struggle enjoys the advantage of turning its ideological claims into the foundation of a widely shared framework of understanding. Thus the claims of globalism become an important source of collective and individual identity.[9]

I wish to conclude my introductory remarks with a note of caution. Some readers might view my discussion of the five globalist claims as an attempt to present my audience with a greatly exaggerated account of globalism. Critics might object to my exposition as a project of building up a straw person that can be easily dismantled. In his critical study of economic globalization, Michael Veseth responds to the same objection by pointing out that this artificial straw person is actually the product of the globalists' own making.[10] In other words, globalists themselves construct these claims to sell their political agenda. It may be true that no single globalist speech or piece of writing contains all of the five assertions discussed below. But all of them contain some of these claims.

Claim No. 1: Globalization Is about the Liberalization and Global Integration of Markets

The first claim of globalism is anchored in the neoliberal ideal of the self-regulating market as the normative basis for a future global order. According to this perspective, the vital functions of the free market—its rationality and efficiency, as well as its alleged ability to bring about greater social integration and material progress—can only be realized in a democratic society that values and protects individual freedom. For Friedrich Hayek and his neoliberal followers, the free market rep-resents a state of liberty, because it is "a state in which each can use his knowledge for his own purpose."[11] Thus the preservation of individual freedom depends on the state's willingness to refrain from interfering with the private sphere of the market. Liberals refer to this limitation on governmental interference as "negative liberty." This term refers to the protection of a private area of life within which one "is or should be left to do or be what he is able to do or be, without interference by other persons."[12] Since neoliberals allege that the free market relies on a set of rules applying equally to all members of society, they consider it both just and meritocratic. While the existence of the market depends on human action, its resulting benefits and burdens are not products of human design.[13] In other words, the concrete outcomes of market interactions are neither intended nor foreseen, but are the result of the workings of the "invisible hand."

Opposing the expansion of governmental intervention in the economy that occurred in Western industrialized nations during the first three-quarters of the twentieth century, globalists call for the "liberalization of markets"; that is, the deregulation of the national economies. In their view, such neoliberal measures would not only lead to the emergence of an integrated global market, but they would also result in greater political freedom for all citizens of the world. As Milton Friedman notes: "The kind of economic organization that provides economic freedom directly, namely competitive capitalism, also promotes political freedom because it separates economic power from political power and in this way enables the one to offset the other."[14] This citation highlights the crucial neoliberal assumption that politics and economics are separate realms. The latter constitutes a fundamentally unpolitical, private sphere that must remain sheltered from the imposition of political power. Governments ought to be limited to providing an appropriate legal and institutional framework for the fulfillment of voluntary agreements reflected in contractual arrangements.

A passage in a recent *BusinessWeek* article implicitly conveys this neoliberal suspicion of political power in defining globalization in market terms: "Globalization is about the triumph of markets over governments. Both proponents and opponents of globalization agree that the driving force today is markets, which are suborning the role of government. The truth is that the size of government has been shrinking relative to the economy almost everywhere."[15] Joan Spiro, former U.S. Undersecretary of State for Economic, Business, and Agricultural Affairs in the Clinton administration, echoes this assessment: "One role [of government] is to get out of the way—to remove barriers to the free flow of goods, services, and capital."[16] Claiming that it is the liberalization of markets that "makes globalization happen," the British *Financial Times* reporter Martin Wolf conveys a similar perspective to his mass readership. He argues that globalization "marks the worldwide spread of the economic liberalization that began nearly fifty years ago in Western Europe with the Marshall Plan." Celebrating the most "precious right of democracy, the right to be left alone," the British journalist Peter Martin takes Wolf's argument a step further: "The liberal market economy is by its very nature global. It is the summit of human endeavor. We should be proud that by our work and by our votes we have—collectively and individually—contributed to building it."[17] In short, the globalist voices cited above present globalization as a natural economic phenomenon reflected in the liberalization and integration of global markets and the reduction of governmental interference in the economy. Privatization, free trade, and unfettered capital movements are portrayed as the best and most natural way for realizing individual liberty and material progress in the world.

Globalists usually convey their assertion that globalization is about the liberalization and global integration of markets in the form of moral demands and rational imperatives. For example, former U.S. trade representative Charlene Barshefsky admonished her audiences in both the United States and developing countries to realize that globalization requires a rational commitment "to restructure public enterprises and accelerate privatization of key sectors—including energy, transportation, utilities, and communication—which will enhance market-driven competition and deregulation. . . ."[18] Asserting that the realization of "open, dynamic economies" constitutes "the very essence of globalization," IMF managing director Michael Camdessus argues that in order "to optimize the opportunities and reduce the risks of globalization, we must head towards a world with open and integrated capital markets."[19] Fred Theobald, president of The Esus Group, a global business-consulting firm, refers to globalization as a rational-moral process of "transitioning to where the quest for growth supersedes a domestic or regional mind-set, where the entire world and its people are seen as its [the company's] market, and where boundaries do not exist—only opportunities."[20] Tom Weidemeyer, president of UPS Airlines, conveys a similar moralistic message: "I'm confident that those of us who favor open markets will be victorious because our message is one of inclusion, empowerment, and opportunity."[21]

Perhaps the most eloquent exposition of the neoliberal claim that globalization is about the liberalization and global integration of markets can be found in Thomas Friedman's recent bestseller, *The Lexus and the Olive Tree: Understanding Globalization.* Indeed, many commentators have emphasized that Friedman's book provides the "official narrative of globalization" in the United States today.[22] Although the award-winning *New York Times* correspondent claims that he does not want to be considered as "a salesman of globalization," he eagerly admonishes his readers to acknowledge the factuality of new global realities and "think like globalists."[23] For Friedman, this means that people ought to accept the following "truth" about globalization:

> The driving idea behind globalization is free-market capitalism—the more you let market forces rule and the more you open your economy to free trade and competition, the more efficient your economy will be. Globalization means the spread of free-market capitalism to virtually every country in the world. Therefore, globalization also has its own set of economic rules—rules that revolve around opening, deregulating and privatizing your economy, in order to make it more competitive and attractive to foreign investment.[24]

Asserting that, for the first time in history, "virtually every country in the world has the same basic hardware—free-market capitalism," Friedman predicts that globalization will result in the creation of a single global marketplace. He informs his readers that this feat will be achieved by means of the "Golden Straitjacket"—the "defining political–economic garment of this globalization era."[25] Stitched together by Anglo-American neoliberal politicians and business leaders, the Golden Straitjacket forces every country in the world to adopt the same economic rules:

> [M]aking the private sector the primary engine of its economic growth, maintaining a low rate of inflation and price stability, shrinking the size of its state bureaucracy, maintaining as close to a balanced budget as possible, if not a surplus, eliminating and lowering tariffs on imported goods, removing restrictions on foreign investment, getting rid of quotas and domestic monopolies, increasing exports, privatizing state-owned industries and utilities, deregulating capital markets, making its

currency convertible, opening its industries, deregulating its economy
to promote as much domestic competition as possible, eliminating
government corruption, subsidies and kickbacks as much as possible,
opening its banking and telecommunications systems to private ownership and competition and allowing its citizens to choose from an array
of competing pension options and foreign-run pension and mutual
funds. When you stitch all of these pieces together you have the
Golden Straitjacket.[26]

Friedman concludes his pitch for the liberalization and global integration of markets by pointing out that today's global market system is
the result of "large historical forces" that gave birth to a new power
source in the world—the "Electronic Herd." Made up of millions of
faceless stock, bond, and currency traders sitting behind computer
screens all over the globe, the Electronic Herd also includes the executive officers of large TNCs who shift their production sites to the most
efficient, low-cost producers. In order to succeed in the new era of
globalization, countries not only have to put on the Golden Straitjacket,
but they also have to please the Electronic Herd. Friedman explains:

> The Electronic Herd loves the Golden Straitjacket, because it embodies
> all the liberal, free-market rules the herd wants to see in a country.
> Those countries that put on the Golden Straitjacket are rewarded by
> the herd with investment capital. Those that don't want to put it on
> are disciplined by the herd—either by the herd avoiding or withdraw-
> ing its money from that country.[27]

A critical discourse analysis of the globalist claim that globalization
is about the liberalization and global integration of markets must begin
by contrasting the neoliberal rhetoric of liberty with Friedman's depic-
tion of globalization proceeding by means of the Golden Straitjacket. If
the liberalization of trade and markets depends upon coercive measures employed by the dominant powers, then this form of liberty
comes dangerously close to Jean-Jacques Rousseau's famous idea that
in only obeying the "general will"—even under duress—a person is
truly free. Yet, for Rousseau, in order to count as a truly universal expression, the general will must come from *all* citizens, and not merely
from a partisan Electronic Herd that seeks to impose its market ideology on the rest of the world. In selling their will as the general will,
globalists disregard local ways of organizing the economy. Their project of "opening up economies" is advocated as an endeavor of univer-

sal applicability, for it supposedly reflects the dictates of human freedom in general. Thus it must be applied to all countries, regardless of the political and cultural preferences expressed by local citizens. As former U.S. Undersecretary Stuart Eizenstat put it: "All nations—developed or developing—must maintain a solidly pro-growth, open-market orientation which supports trade liberalization."[28] However, such efforts to stitch together a neoliberal economic straitjacket—one size fits all countries—are hardly compatible with a process of globalization that is alleged to contribute to the spread of freedom, choice, and openness in the world.

Secondly, as Friedman concedes, the globalist message of liberalizing and integrating markets is only realizable through the *political* project of engineering free markets. In order to advance their enterprise, globalists must be prepared to utilize the powers of government to weaken and eliminate those social policies and institutions that curtail the market. Since only strong governments are up to this ambitious task of transforming existing social arrangements, the successful liberalization of markets depends upon the *intervention* and *interference* by centralized state power. Former Undersecretary Joan Spiro's assertion that governments can best contribute to the process of market liberalization by simply "getting out of the way" represents, therefore, a clear example of ideological distortion. Another such example can be found in a recent bestseller on the subject written by two British correspondents of the *Economist*. The authors insist that globalization remains detached from political initiatives: "As we have indicated, globalization is fundamentally a commercial rather than a political phenomenon, driven by currency traders and entrepreneurs rather than by politicians and bureaucrats."[29]

Such remarks reflect a neoliberal idealization of the limited role of government, which stands in stark contrast to government's role in the actual social arena. In truth, globalists do expect governments to play an extremely active role in implementing their political agenda. The activist character of neoliberal administrations in the United States, the United Kingdom, Australia, and New Zealand during the 1980s and 1990s attests to the importance of strong governmental action in engineering free markets.[30] Indeed, promarket governments serve as indispensable catalysts of what Richard Falk calls "globalization from above." In their pursuit of market liberalization and integration, neoliberal political and economic elites violate their own principles of decentralization, limited government, and negative liberty.

Finally, the neoliberal claim that globalization is about the liberalization and global integration of markets serves to solidify as "fact" what is actually a contingent political initiative. Globalists have been successful because they have persuaded the public that their neoliberal account of globalization represents an objective or at least neutral diagnosis rather than a contributor to the emergence of the very conditions it purports to analyze. To be sure, neoliberals may indeed be able to offer some "empirical evidence" for the "liberalization" of markets. But does the spread of market principles really happen because there exists an intrinsic, metaphysical connection between globalization and the expansion of markets? Or does it occur because globalists have the political and discursive power to shape the world largely according to their ideological formula.

LIBERALIZATION + INTEGRATION OF MARKETS = GLOBALIZATION?

Moreover, this economistic-objectivist representation of globalization detracts from the multidimensional character of the phenomenon. Ecological, cultural, and political dimensions of globalization are discussed only as subordinate processes dependent on the movements of global markets. Even if one were to accept the central role of the economic dimension of globalization, there is no reason to believe that these processes must necessarily be connected to the deregulation of markets. An alternative view might instead suggest linking globalization to the creation of a global regulatory framework that would make markets accountable to international political institutions.

In either case, the setting of a successful political agenda always occurs simultaneously with concerted efforts to sell to the public the general desirability of a particular system of ideas. Globalism is no exception. Like all ideologies, its values and beliefs are conveyed through a number of justificatory claims, usually starting with one that establishes what the phenomenon is all about. As international-relations expert Edward Luttwak points out, there is a good reason why the spectacular advance of "turbo-capitalism" in the world is accompanied by so much talk about globalization in the public arena. For business interests, the presentation of globalization as an enterprise that liberates and integrates global markets as well as emancipates individuals from governmental control is the best way of enlisting the public in their struggle against those laws and institutions they find most restrictive.[31] As long as globalists succeed in selling their neoliberal understanding of globalization to large segments of the population, they will be able to maintain a social order favorable to their own interests. By engineering popular consent, globalists are only rarely forced to resort to open forms of coercion. The Golden Straitjacket will do splendidly to keep the global South in line. For those who remain skeptical, globalists have another claim up their sleeves: Why doubt a process that proceeds with historical inevitability?

Claim No. 2: Globalization Is Inevitable and Irreversible

At first glance, the belief in the historical inevitability of globalization seems to be a poor fit for a globalist ideology based on neoliberal principles. After all, throughout the twentieth century, liberals and conservatives have consistently criticized Marxism for its determinist claims that devalue human free-agency and downplay the ability of non-economic factors to shape social reality. In particular, neoliberals have attacked the Marxist notion of history as a teleological process that unfolds according to "inexorable laws" that hasten the demise of capitalism, ultimately leading to the emergence of a classless society on a global scale.

However, a close study of the utterances of influential globalists reveals their reliance on a similar monocausal, economistic narrative of historical inevitability. While disagreeing with Marxists on the final goal of historical development, globalists nonetheless share with their ideological opponents a fondness for such terms as "irresistable," "inevitable," and "irreversible" to describe the projected path of globalization. As Ulrich Beck points out: "In a way, neoliberal globalism thus resembles its archenemy: Marxism. It is the rebirth of Marxism as a management ideology."[32] By focusing on the "logic" of technology and markets, globalists minimize the role of human agency and individual choice—the centerpiece of liberal thought from John Locke and John Stuart Mill to Milton Friedman.

According to the globalist perspective, globalization reflects the spread of irreversible market forces driven by technological innovations that make the global integration of national economies inevitable.

In fact, globalism is almost always intertwined with the deep belief in the ability of markets to use new technologies to solve social problems far better than any alternative course.[33] When, years ago, British Prime Minister Margaret Thatcher famously pronounced that "there is no alternative," she meant that there existed no longer a theoretical and practical alternative to the expansionist logic of the market. In fact, she accused those nonconformists who still dared to pose alternatives as foolishly relying on anachronistic, socialist fantasies that betrayed their inability to cope with empirical reality. Governments, political parties, and social movements had no choice but to "adjust" to the inevitability of globalization. Their sole remaining task was to facilitate the integration of national economies in the new global market. States and interstate systems should, therefore, serve to ensure the smooth working of market logic.[34] Indeed, the multiple voices of globalism convey to the public their message of inevitability with tremendous consistency. Below are some examples.

In a speech on U.S. foreign policy, President Clinton told his audience: "Today we must embrace the inexorable logic of globalization—that everything from the strength of our economy to the safety of our cities, to the health of our people, depends on events not only within our borders, but half a world away."[35] On another occasion he emphasized that "globalization is irreversible. Protectionism will only make things worse."[36] Clinton's Undersecretary Eizenstat echoed the assessment of his boss: "Globalization is an inevitable element of our lives. We cannot stop it anymore than we can stop the waves from crashing on the shore. The arguments in support of trade liberalization and open markets are strong ones—they have been made by many of you and we must not be afraid to engage those with whom we respectfully disagree."[37]

Frederick W. Smith, chairman and CEO of FedEx Corporation, suggests that "globalization is inevitable and inexorable and it is accelerating. . . . Globalization is happening, it's going to happen. It does not matter whether you like it or not, it's happening, it's going to happen."[38] Journalist Friedman comes to a similar conclusion: "Globalization is very difficult to reverse because it is driven both by powerful human aspiration for higher standards of living and by enormously powerful technologies which are integrating us more and more every day, whether we like it or not."[39] But Friedman simply argues by asserting that there is something inherent in technology that requires a neoliberal system. He never considers that, for example, new digital-communication technologies could just as easily be used to enhance public-service media as it can be utilized in commercial, profit-making enterprises. The choice depends on the nature of the political will exerted in a particular social order.

Neoliberal elites in non-Western countries faithfully echo the globalist language of inevitability. For example, Rahul Bajaj, a leading Indian industrialist, insists that "we need much more liberalization and deregulation of the Indian economy. No sensible Indian businessman disagrees with this. . . . Globalization is inevitable. There is no better alternative." He adds that "India and Indian companies have to recognize that the forces of globalization are irreversible. I think the agenda for India is not whether globalization is on, but what to do about it, what are the implications of networking and alliances."[40] Manuel Villar, the Philippines Speaker of the House of Representatives, agrees: "Of course, we cannot simply wish away the process of globalization. It is a reality of a modern world. The process is irreversible."[41] Masaru Hayami, governor of the Bank of Japan, concurs: "The essence of globalization is the integration of markets worldwide and the deepening of various interdependent relations. . . . Thus, the move toward globalization is an inevitable reality, and not likely to be reversed."[42]

The neoliberal portrayal of globalization as some sort of natural force, like the weather or gravity, makes it easier for globalists to convince people that they must adapt to the discipline of the market if they are to survive and prosper. Hence, the globalist claim of inevitability serves a number of important political functions. For one, it neutralizes the challenges of antiglobalist opponents by depoliticizing the public discourse about globalization: Neoliberal policies are above politics, because they simply carry out what is ordained by nature. This view implies that, instead of acting according to a set of choices, people merely fulfill world-market laws that demand the elimination of government controls. There is nothing that can be done about the natural movement of economic and technological forces; political groups ought to acquiesce and make the best of an unalterable situation. Since the emergence of a world based on the primacy of market values reflects the dictates of history, resistance would be unnatural, irrational, and dangerous.

As John Malott, U.S. Ambassador to Malaysia, puts it: "Some people think that the debate about globalization is whether it is good or bad. To me, globalization just *is*. We cannot stop it; we have to accept it, and adjust to it. Those countries, those companies, those people who adjust to a changing world will do better. Those who resist will suffer." For Malott, "adjustment" refers to the implementation of deregulatory policies that allow for "less rather than more government control and influence over business decision-making."[43] Thus globalists utilize the idea of the historical inevitability of globalization in order to advance better their thoroughly political project of implementing neoliberal economic policies. For the masses, however, globalists prescribe an attitude of political passivity in the face of inevitability. This makes it easier for globalists to admonish the general public to "share the burdens of globalization." In short, globalist ideology constitutes high politics while presenting itself in nonpolitical garb.

The narrative of inevitability also helps globalists to justify the creation and execution of governmental austerity measures. Following Paul Ricoeur's understanding of ideology functioning as legitimation, this globalist claim legitimizes public-policy choices directed at the dismantling of the welfare state and the deregulation of the economy. It allows globalists to portray these measures as a rational response to objective historical pressures rather than the self-interested agenda of particular political interests. The idea of inevitability also supports the excuse often utilized by neoliberal politicians: "It is the market that made us cut social programs." As German President Roman Herzog put it in a nationally televised appeal, the "irresistible pressure of global forces" demands that "everyone will have to make sacrifices."[44] To be sure, President Herzog never spelled out what kinds of sacrifices will await large shareholders and corporate executives. In fact, historical evidence suggests that it is much more likely that sacrifices will have to be borne disproportionately by those workers and employees who lose their jobs or social benefits as a result of neoliberal trade policies or profit-maximizing practices of "corporate downsizing."

By turning the market into a natural force, globalists suggest that human beings are at the mercy of external imperatives they cannot control. As the neoliberal economist Alain Lipietz emphasizes, the modern market economy is an autonomous realm that is "defined by immutable economic laws, behaviors and tendencies."[45] The strategy seems to be working. Even prolabor voices such as David Smith, AFL-CIO Director of Public Policy, have accepted the globalist claims of inevitability and irreversibility: "Globalization is a fact. . . . We're not going to turn these tides back. We shouldn't want to turn these tides back; even if we wanted to, we couldn't."[46]

In a lucid article that appeared in the *Atlantic Monthly*, theologian Harvey Cox argues that the globalist claim of market inevitability bears a striking resemblance to religious narratives found in Genesis, St. Paul's Epistle to the Romans, and St. Augustine's *City of God*. According to Cox, Christian stories of human origins and the fall from grace, as well as doctrines of sin and redemption find their contemporary expression in neoliberal discourses about the creation of wealth, the seductive temptations of statism, captivity to economic cycles, and, ultimately, salvation through the advent of the global free market. Both narratives are sustained by a belief in an inner meaning of human history determined by the unalterable will of a transcendental force. Endowing it with the divine attributes of omnipotence, omniscience, and omnipresence, globalists assign to "The Market" a "comprehensive wisdom that in the past only the gods have known. . . . It has risen above these demigods and chthonic spirits to become today's First Cause." Of course, the divine attributes of "The Market" are not always completely evident to mortals, but must be trusted and affirmed by neoliberal faith. "Further along," an old gospel song says, "we'll understand why."[47]

Ulrich Beck echoes Cox's assessment, emphasizing that globalism is "a kind of economic New Ageism, a revivalist movement whose apostles and prophets, instead of handing out leaflets at underground stations, preach salvation of the world in the spirit of the marketplace."[48] Conversely, market infidels and agnostics such as Beck argue that the market is neither an ahistorical nor an asocial manifestation of blind natural forces working behind people's backs. Markets are the creation of human interactions; they do not dictate policy. Global economic integration is not a natural process. Rather, it is driven by decisions of governments that have removed barriers to cross-border movements of capital and goods. People who are organized in powerful social groups facilitate the process of neoliberal globalization. They demand—in the name of "The Market"—the implementation of economic policies favorable to their interests.

Finally, the claim that globalization is inevitable and irresistible is inscribed within a larger evolutionary discourse that assigns a privileged position to those nations that are in the forefront of "liberating" markets from political control. For example, Lorenzo Zambrano, the Mexican CEO of CEMEX Corporation, the world's third-largest cement producer, strongly supports this idea: "I agree that globalization is inevitable and that it may be inherent to the evolution of a civilization and that it has been brought about by progress in telecommunications allowing instantaneous contact to be established."[49]

Some American globalists are more culturally explicit than Zambrano. For them, the United States and its philosophy of free-market capitalism is spearheading the inevitable historical progress toward the creation of a global "market civilization." Francis Fukuyama represents an extreme perspective on this issue. He insists that globalization is really a euphemism that stands for the irreversible Americanization of the world: "I think it has to be Americanization because, in some respects, America is the most advanced capitalist society in the world today, and so its institutions represent the logical development of market forces. Therefore, if market forces are what drives globalization, it is inevitable that Americanization will accompany globalization."[50] Thomas Friedman, too, ends his book on globalization with a celebration of America's unique role in a globalizing world:

> And that's why America, at its best, is not just a country. It's a spiritual value and role model. . . . And that's why I believe so strongly that for globalization to be sustainable America must be at its best—today, tomorrow, all the time. It not only can be, it must be, a beacon for the whole world.[51]

These statements reveal the existence of a strong link between the globalist claim of inevitability and the American pursuit of global cultural hegemony. As John Gray observes, neoliberal forces have successfully "appropriated America's self-image as the model for a universal civilization in the service of a global free market."[52] History looks kindly upon the "shining city on the hill," because it has been listening to the voice of the market. As a reward, objective market forces have chosen the United States to point all other nations in the right direction. In what appears to be the globalist version of the old American theme of manifest destiny, U.S. political and business leaders proclaim to the rest of the world: Adopt our neoliberal policies and you, too, can become "America."

By activating what Paul Ricoeur calls the ideological function of integration, globalists favor the creation of an American-style market identity that is designed to eclipse most other components of personal, group, or class identity. As Steven Kline points out, global marketing efforts particularly attempt to provide young people with the identity of the consuming global teenager. Coca-Cola, Levi-Strauss, McDonald's, and Disney "have become the source of endless campaigns to enfranchise youth in the globalizing democracy of the market."[53] Why should mere consumers be interested in strengthening civic ties and work for global justice if such endeavors aren't profitable? Why show moral restraint and solidarity if "we," the consumers, are incessantly told that we can have it all? As Benjamin Barber emphasizes, by broadly endorsing happiness that comes with shopping and consuming, this market identity takes on distinct cultural features, because "America" and "American culture" are best-selling commodities in the global marketplace. American films, American television, American software, American music, American fast-food chains, American cars and motorcycles, American apparel, and American sports—to name but a few of those cultural commodities—are pervading the world to such an extent that even ordinary Indonesians have become convinced that they also can become "cool" by drinking Coke instead of tea. In Budapest, people are breathlessly watching *The Cosby Show* on reruns, and the Russian version of *Wheel of Fortune* offers lucky winners Sony VCRs into which they can load their pirated versions of wildly popular American films.[54]

And so it appears that globalist forces have been resurrecting the nineteenth-century paradigm of Anglo-American vanguardism propagated by Herbert Spencer and William Graham Sumner. The main ingredients of classical market liberalism are all present in globalism. We find inexorable laws of nature favoring Western civilization, the self-regulating economic model of perfect competition, the virtues of free enterprise, the vices of state interference, the principle of *laissezfaire*, and the irreversible, evolutionary process leading up to the survival of the fittest. Indeed, globalism merely provides new verbiage for these old liberal themes. As some globalists put it: "Globalization offers the chance to fulfill (at least come considerably closer to fulfilling) the goals that classical liberal philosophers first identified several centuries ago and that still underpin Western democracy."[55] Equipped with a quasi-Marxist language of historical inevitability, globalists look forward to the final realization of their free-market utopia. They are confident that history will end on a positive note—in spite of some undeniable risks and conflicts inherent in the process of globalization.

Claim No. 3: Nobody Is in Charge of Globalization

Globalism's deterministic language offers another rhetorical advantage. If the natural laws of "The Market" have indeed preordained a neoliberal course of history, then globalization does not reflect the arbitrary agenda of a particular social class or group. In other words, globalists merely carry out the unalterable imperatives of a transcendental force much larger than narrow partisan interests. People are not in charge of globalization; markets and technology are. Certain human actions might accelerate or retard globalization, but in the last instance (to paraphrase none other than Friedrich Engels), the invisible hand of the market will always assert its superior wisdom. As the prominent economist Paul Krugman puts it: "Many on the Left dislike the global marketplace because it epitomizes what they dislike about markets in general: the fact that nobody is in charge. The truth is that the invisible hand rules most domestic markets, too, a reality that most Americans seem to accept as a fact of life."[56] Robert Hormats, vice chairman of Goldman Sachs International agrees: "The great beauty of globalization is that no one is in control. The great beauty of globalization is that it is not controlled by any individual, any government, any institution."[57]

In the early part of *The Lexus and the Olive Tree*, Thomas Friedman imagines himself engaged in a spirited debate with the prime minister of Malaysia, who had accused Western powers of manipulating markets and currencies during the 1997–1998 Asian crisis in order to destroy the vibrant economies of their overseas competitors. Friedman tells his readers how he would respond to Prime Minister Mahatir Mohamad's charge:

> Ah, excuse me, Mahatir, but what planet are you living on? You talk about participating in globalization as if it were a choice you had. Globalization isn't a choice. It's a reality. . . . And the most basic truth about globalization is this: *No one is in charge.* . . . We all want to believe that someone is in charge and responsible. But the global

marketplace today is an Electronic Herd of often anonymous stock, bond and currency traders and multinational investors, connected by screens and networks.[58]

Of course, Friedman is right in a formal sense. There is no conscious conspiracy orchestrated by a single evil force to disempower Asian nations. But does this mean that nobody is in charge of globalization? Is it really true that the liberalization and integration of global markets proceeds outside the realm of human choice? Does globalization, therefore, absolve businesses and corporations from social responsibility? A critical discourse analysis of Friedman's statement reveals how he utilizes a realist narrative to sell to his audience a neoliberal version of globalization. He implies that anyone who thinks that globalization involves human choice is either hopelessly naïve or outright dangerous. Such persons might as well apply for permanent residency on Prime Minister Mohamad's alien planet.

For Friedman, the real player in the global marketplace is the Electronic Herd. But he never offers his readers a clear picture of the Herd's identity. Throughout his book, he portrays the Herd as a faceless crowd of individual profit-maximizers whose human identity remains hidden behind dim computer screens. Apparently, these traders and investors are solely interested in moneymaking; they don't seem to be part of any politically or culturally identifiable group. Although they wield tremendous power, they are not in charge of globalization. Ah, excuse me, Tom, but where is the "realism" in your description?

Writing about the importance of unfettering financial markets in the emerging global economic order, Steward Brand, the co-founder of California-based Global Business Network, also asserts that "nobody is in charge of globalization." According to Brand, there exists "no policy body nor even an agreed-on body of theory to constrain the activity of world markets; the game continues to evolve rapidly, with none of the players ever quite sure what the new rules are."[59] Notice how this statement denies the existence of antiglobalist challengers who propose the regulation of markets. Moreover, Brand's argument implies that the "players" of the globalization "game" do not make the rules themselves. Presumably, they merely adjust to the new rules dictated to them by the impersonal logic of evolving markets.

Social thinkers Michael Hardt and Antonio Negri remind their readers that it is important to be aware of the two extreme conceptions of global authority that reside on the opposite ends of the ideological spectrum. One is the globalist notion that nobody is in charge, because globalization somehow rises up spontaneously out of the natural workings of the hidden hand of the world market. The other is the antiglobalist idea that a single evil power dictates to the world its design of globalization according to a conscious and all-seeing conspiratorial plan. Both conceptions are distortions.[60]

Still, even some neoliberal commentators concede that the globalist initiative to integrate and deregulate markets around the world is sustained by asymmetrical power relations. Backed by powerful states in the North, international institutions such as the WTO, the IMF, and the World Bank enjoy the privileged position of making and enforcing the rules of the global economy. In return for supplying much-needed loans to developing countries, the IMF and the World Bank demand from their creditors the implementation of neoliberal policies that further the material interests of the First World. Unleashed on developing countries in the 1990s, these policies are often referred to as "Washington Consensus." It consists of a ten-point program that was originally devised and codified by John Williamson, formerly an IMF adviser in the 1970s. The program was mostly directed at countries with large remaining foreign debts from the 1970s and 1980s. Its purpose was to reform the internal economic mechanisms of debtor countries in the developing world so that they would be in a better position to repay the debts they had incurred. In practice, the terms of the program spelled out a new form of colonialism. The ten areas of the Washington Consensus, as defined by Williamson, required Third World governments to enforce the following reforms.

1. A guarantee of fiscal discipline, and a curb to budget deficits.
2. A reduction of public expenditure, particularly in the military and public administration.
3. Tax reform, aiming at the creation of a system with a broad base and with effective enforcement.
4. Financial liberalization, with interest rates determined by the market.
5. Competitive exchange rates, to assist export-led growth.
6. Trade liberalization, coupled with the abolition of import licensing and a reduction of tariffs.

7. Promotion of foreign direct investment.
8. Privatization of state enterprises, leading to efficient management and improved performance.
9. Deregulation of the economy.
10. Protection of property rights.[61]

To call this program "Washington Consensus" is no coincidence. The United States is by far the most dominant economic power in the world, and the largest transnational corporations are based in the United States. As the British journalist Will Hutton points out, one of the principal aims of the Economic Security Council set up by President Clinton in 1993 was to open up ten countries to U.S. trade and finance. Most of these "target countries" are located in Asia.[62] Again, this is not to say that the United States is in complete control of global financial markets and, therefore, rules supremely over this gigantic process of globalization. But it *does* suggest that both the substance and direction of economic globalization are, indeed, to a significant degree shaped by American foreign and domestic policy.

Substantiation of this claim comes from no less an observer than Thomas Friedman, who, in later passages of his book, surprisingly contradicts his previous account of a leaderless, anonymous Electronic Herd. Speaking in glowing terms about the global leadership of the United States, he suddenly acknowledges the existence of a captain at the helm of the global ship:

> The Golden Straitjacket was made in America and Great Britain. The Electronic Herd is led by American Wall Street Bulls. The most powerful agent pressuring other countries to open their markets for free trade and free investments is Uncle Sam, and America's global armed forces keep these markets and sea lanes open for this era of globalization, just as the British navy did for the era of globalization in the nineteenth century.[63]

Toward the end of his book, the *New York Times* journalist becomes even more explicit:

> Indeed, McDonald's cannot flourish without McDonnell Douglas, the designer of the U.S. Air Force F-15. And the hidden fist that keeps the world safe for Silicon Valley's technologies to flourish is called the U.S. Army, Air Force, Navy, and Marine Corps. And these fighting forces and institutions are paid for by American taxpayer dollars.[64]

In other words, global neoliberalism does not rely blindly on a hidden hand of the self-regulating market. When the chips are down, globalism seems to prefer the not-so-hidden fist of U.S. militarism.

Yet Friedman is not the only globalist who oscillates between the claim that "nobody is in charge" and the admission that "America is in control" (or that it should be). After telling a U.S. Congressional subcommittee that globalization proceeds in a neutral arena allowing access to "many players," Joseph Gorman, chairman and CEO of TRW Inc., a large Cleveland-based manufacturing and service company of high-tech products, urges his audience to strengthen the leadership role of the United States. His ten-page statement[65] is divided into sections that bear the following titles:

- "To win in the global economy, the United States must lead liberalization efforts."
- "International trade and investment agreements are still needed to open foreign markets for American companies and their workers."
- "If the United States is not at the table, it can't play and it can't win."
- "Success in the global economy is critical for the American economy, its companies, and its workers."
- "The global economy is real, and the United States is part of it."
- "Because the United States is the world's most competitive nation, we have the most to gain from the global economy and from trade and investment liberalization."
- "Developing countries in particular hold huge promise."

The interpretive possibilities arising from a critical discourse analysis of Gorman's testimony are almost limitless. Images of the world as a gambling table that can only be accessed by the best "players" are as telling as his neoimperialist desire to cash in on "promising" developing nations. As far as the integrative, identity-giving function of ideology is concerned, Gorman's testimony seeks to persuade its audience that one's loyalty to market principles allows one to be both a patriot defending American interests and a globalist. Although class conflicts continue to be a very real phenomenon in the daily world of commodity production, the market rhetoric of globalism nonetheless conjures up a harmonious common identity. Business people, workers, and farmers of the world unite around your consumer identity!

But if nobody is in control of globalization, why does Gorman try so hard to make a case for U.S. leadership? Why does U.S. National Security Adviser Samuel Berger seek to convince his large audiences that the United States ought to become a "more active participant in an effort to shape globalization"?[66] One obvious answer is that the claim of a leaderless globalization process does not reflect social reality. Rather, the idea that nobody is in charge serves the neoliberal political agenda of defending and expanding American global hegemony. Like the globalist rhetoric of historical inevitability, the portrayal of globalization as a leaderless process seeks to both depoliticize the public debate on the subject and demobilize antiglobalist movements. The deterministic language of a technological progress driven by uncontrollable market laws turns political issues into scientific problems of administration. Once large segments of the population have accepted the globalist image of a self-directed juggernaut that simply runs its course, it becomes extremely difficult for antiglobalists to challenge what Antonio Gramsci calls the "power of the hegemonic bloc." As ordinary people cease to believe in the possibility of choosing alternative social arrangements, globalism gains strength in its ability to construct passive consumer identities. This tendency is further enhanced by globalist assurances that globalization will bring prosperity to all parts of the world.

Claim No. 4: Globalization Benefits Everyone

This claim lies at the very core of globalism because it provides an affirmative answer to the crucial normative question of whether globalization represents a "good" or a "bad" phenomenon. Globalists frequently connect their arguments in favor of the integration of global markets to the alleged benefits resulting from the liberalization and expansion of world trade. At the 1996 G7 Summit in Lyon, France, the heads of state and government of the seven major industrialized democracies issued a joint communiqué that contains the following passage:

> Economic growth and progress in today's interdependent world is bound up with the process of globalization. Globalization provides great opportunities for the future, not only for our countries, but for

all others too. Its many positive aspects include an unprecedented expansion of investment and trade; the opening up to international trade of the world's most populous regions and opportunities for more developing countries to improve their standards of living; the increasingly rapid dissemination of information, technological innovation, and the proliferation of skilled jobs. These characteristics of globalization have led to a considerable expansion of wealth and prosperity in the world. Hence we are convinced that the process of globalization is a source of hope for the future.[67]

The public discourse on globalization reverberates with such generalizations. Here are some more examples. Former U.S. Secretary of the Treasury Robert Rubin asserts that free trade and open markets provide "the best prospect for creating jobs, spurring economic growth, and raising living standards in the United States and around the world."[68] Former Undersecretary Joan Spiro agrees with her colleague, emphasizing that free trade and the opportunity of investment on a global scale ensure that "the benefits of globalization will spread to all corners of the world and to all sectors of society."[69] Denise Froning, trade-policy analyst at both the Center for International Trade and Economics and the Heritage Foundation, suggests that "societies that promote economic freedom create their own dynamism and foster a wellspring of prosperity that benefits every citizen."[70] Alan Greenspan, chairman of the U.S. Federal Reserve Board, insists that "there can be little doubt that the extraordinary changes in global finance on balance have been beneficial in facilitating significant improvements in economic structures and living standards throughout the world."[71]

Similarly, Peter Sutherland, chairman of the Overseas Development Council, chairman and managing director of Goldman Sachs International, and chairman of British Petroleum, argues that "globalization's effects have been overwhelmingly good. Spurred by unprecedented liberalization, world trade continues to expand faster than overall global economic output, inducing a wave of productivity and efficiency and creating millions of jobs." To resist these developments would not only be futile but positively dangerous, since "the costs of being left behind by globalization are usually much greater than the losses caused by instability."[72] George David, CEO of United Technologies, shares Sutherland's opinion: "The wealth generation in emerging markets is going to happen whether we like it or not." Insisting that we need to "ensure the continued success of this globalizing agenda," David assures his audiences that

> we are at an optimistic time in our world: the barriers between nations are down, economic liberalism is decidedly afoot and proven to be sound, trade and investment are soaring, income disparities between nations are narrowing, and wealth generation globally is at record high levels, and I believe likely to remain so.[73]

However, neither of the persons cited above addresses the ideological assumptions behind their key concepts. Who exactly is "*we*"? Who "*proved*" liberalism "*sound*"? What does "*sound*" mean? As will be discussed in more detail in chapter 4, antiglobalist forces have offered solid evidence that income disparities between nations are actually widening at a quicker pace than ever before in recent history. For example, Jay Mazur, the president of the U.S. Union of Needletrades, Industrial, and Textile Employees, argues that

> the benefits of the global economy are reaped disproportionately by the handful of countries and companies that set rules and shape markets. . . . Of the 100 largest economies in the world, 51 are corporations. Private financial flows have long since surpassed public-development aid and remain remarkably concentrated.[74]

There are many indications that the global hunt for profits actually makes it more difficult for poor people to enjoy the benefits of technology and scientific innovations. Consider the following story. A group of scientists in the United States recently warned the public that economic globalization may now be the greatest threat to preventing the spread of parasitic diseases in sub-Saharan Africa. They pointed out that U.S.-based pharmaceutical companies are stopping production of many antiparasitic drugs because developing countries cannot afford to buy them. For example, the U.S. manufacturer for a drug to treat bilharzia, a parasitic disease that causes severe liver damage, has stopped production because of declining profits—even though the disease is thought to affect over 200 million people worldwide. Another drug used to combat damage caused by liver flukes has not been produced since 1979, because the "customer base" in the Third World does not wield enough "buying power."[75]

While globalists typically acknowledge the existence of unequal global-distribution patterns, they nonetheless insist that the market itself will eventually correct these "irregularities." As John Meehan, chairman of the U.S. Public Securities Association, puts it, while such "episodic dislocations" are "necessary" in the short run, they will eventually give way to "quantum leaps in productivity."[76] Although he admits that problems of global and domestic inequality created by such dislocations constitute a "legitimate concern," the former speaker of the U.S. House of Representatives, Newt Gingrich, is quick to add that the "reality" of globalization is made visible in "a rising general standard of living for everybody." Ignoring the glaring contradiction arising from his recognition of global inequality, while at the same time including "everyone" in the pool of globalization's beneficiaries, Gingrich launches into a masterpiece of globalist distortion:

> That is people overall are generally better off than they have ever been—but in the short run, in a period of great transition those who are more successful pull away, and get even wealthier faster. But the historical pattern is that everybody else begins to catch up over time, and I think if you know what you are doing you don't become a "have not," and if you don't know what you are doing transferring welfare to you does not solve the problem. We've got to find a way to have more people understand the information age and participate in it.[77]

In the end, Gingrich justifies the real human costs of globalization as the short-term price of economic liberalization. Such ideological statements are disseminated to large audiences by what Benjamin Barber calls the profit-oriented "infotainment telesector." Television, radio, and the Internet frequently place existing economic, political, and social realities within a neoliberal framework, sustaining the claim that globalization benefits everyone through omnipresent affirmative images and sound bites. As a popular television commercial suggests, "the whole world is Ford country." Globalist ideology appears as "videology," the product of popular culture driven by commercial interests that incessantly instills in its audience the values, needs, and desires required for the expansion of markets.[78] The alleged benefits of globalization are also touted on television and in film. Shopping malls and theme parks glorify the new global market as enhancing consumer choice and facilitating individual self-realization. The last few years have seen an enormous expansion of the celebrity "gossip market," which represents viewers and readers with the riveting private lives and heart-rending troubles of global celebrities such as the late Princess

Diana, Britney Spears, Leonardo DiCaprio, and Kobe Bryant. These stories have become more real and newsworthy than the persistence of poverty, inequality, displacement, and environmental degradation.

Actual economic and social conditions matter little; TNCs that control global information and communications can conjure up an ideal world of the global village inhabited by beautiful people who live long and fulfilling lives as mindless consumers. In fact, globalists such as Thomas Friedman even pretend to know beyond the shadow of a doubt that the poor in developing countries are itching to assume the identity of Western consumers: "[L]et me share a little secret I've learned from talking to all these folks [in the Third World]: With all due respect to revolutionary theorists, the 'wretched of the earth' want to go to Disney World—not the barricades. They want the Magic Kingdom, not *Les Misérables*."[79]

In short, globalists do their best to convince their audiences that the liberalization of trade and the integration of global markets serve the interests of everyone. Some writers seem to be completely oblivious to the fact that only a small minority of the world's population can actually take advantage of the alleged opportunities provided by globalization:

> Globalization increases people's freedom to shape their identities, independent of those of their ancestors; to sharpen their talents by pursuing education anywhere in the world. The same global bazaar that allows consumers to buy the best that the world can offer also allows producers to find the best partners.[80]

Business executives such as Robert Hormats emphasize how globalization fosters new market "opportunities":

> In my view, globalization is primarily about opportunity. It's about the opportunity to sell in many markets. It's about the opportunity to raise capital in many markets. . . . I think that globalization has dramatically increased the opportunities of people around the world. . . . In many parts of the world a lot of people are a lot better off because of a global market in which they can sell their goods. And consumers are a lot better off because they have access to goods from all around the world.[81]

When asked by a reporter to respond to the charge that corporate strategies are responsible for the rise of child labor and appalling sweatshop conditions in developing countries, Hormats replied with a personal story:

I was in Pakistan several years ago and saw an example of very young kids—I don't know—10- or 11-year-old kids who were working, helping their mothers to make rugs during the day. They did this after school. They went to school six hours and worked for four hours with their mothers to make rugs, which is their only source of income. Well, to me, that was not abuse of those children. That was the only way their parents were going to get money and they were going to eat was if the kids helped their mothers make rugs. There are a number of societies where the only way people can earn enough money to live is to work at menial jobs, jobs in very large factories. They don't get paid much, that's true. But are we going to go in there and try to legislate what the workplace should be like or what wages should be like in these other countries? It would be nice if their lives could improve, if they could get more money but I don't think that's proper for American legislation or coercive pressures.[82]

The picture of globalization Hormats seeks to convey is clear: Americans shouldn't worry about child labor in the Third World. Kids are simply helping out their mothers. Their wages may not be great, but if the global markets are left alone, everybody will eventually reap the benefits of globalization. Most importantly, business should not be expected to meet social obligations that cut into their profits. Praising the establishment of a new America Online service center in the Philippines that pays 900 young local technicians less than a third of the wage of comparable American workers, Friedman comes to a similar conclusion:

The AOL call center here is but one example of the simple truth that the best hope for alleviating poverty around the world is through more globalization, not less, and by encouraging governments to put into place the market-friendly policies, institutions, and environmental protections that will attract global investment and jobs.[83]

Neoliberal attempts to strengthen the belief of lawmakers and the general public in the benefits of economic globalization are particularly evident in statements made at large conferences and public hearings on the subject. For example, at the 2000 Annual Meeting of the World Economic Forum in Davos, Phil Knight, the chairman and CEO of Nike Corporation, emphasized that developing nations had taken great strides toward the alleviation of poverty, "thanks to free trade and sound economic policies."[84] In a 1999 hearing before the powerful U.S.

Subcommittee on Trade of the House Committee on Ways and Means, Phil Condit, speaking as the chairman of the Business Roundtable Task Force on Trade and Investment, testified to the "enormous benefits" resulting from the "integration of global markets for capital." He urged lawmakers around the world to join business in its role as a "force for positive change in the global economy" and work for a trade agenda based upon a set of fundamental [neoliberal] principles.[85] Speaking for the World Bank before a global symposium on globalization, managing director Caio K. Koch-Weser mixed his lecture on the benefits on the "globalizing markets" with thinly veiled warnings directed at "transition countries" in the former Eastern Bloc:

> The challenge will be for them to take advantage of the favorable climate to move ahead with some of the tough reform measures that need to be taken to establish the basis for robust and sustained growth. . . . The message from early reformers and from elsewhere in the world is loud and clear: Good policies pay off.[86]

Apparently, "good policies" are those that attracted foreign investments regardless of the dire consequences of such policies reflected in rising unemployment, welfare cuts, and general human suffering.

Globalists who deviate from the official portrayal of globalization as benefiting everyone must bear the consequences of their criticism. For example, Joseph Stiglitz, chief economist of the World Bank, was severely attacked for publicly criticizing the neoliberal economic policies created by his institution. He argued that the structural-adjustment programs imposed on developing countries by both the World Bank and the IMF often lead to disastrous results. Moreover, he noted that "market ideologues" had used the 1997–1998 Asian economic crisis to discredit state intervention and to promote more market liberalization. At the end of 1999, Stiglitz decided to resign from his position. Five months later, his consulting contract with the World Bank was terminated.[87]

In June 2000, Ravi Kanbur, the principal author of the World Bank's 2000 World Development Report, also resigned from his post after being pressured by U.S. Secretary of the Treasury Larry Summers to change the language of the draft report. Noting the rise of global poverty in developing countries (except for China) during the 1990s, Kanbur suggested that market liberalization does not affect all countries in the same way. In particular, he argued that poor people in the

Third World do not have the resources or the access to participate in markets and reap material benefits. Thus excessive liberalization may actually exacerbate global inequality, ultimately leading to financial volatility, economic instability, and social crisis. Kanbur concluded that the World Bank's neoliberal philosophy should be revised in the direction of recommending more government regulation and oversight.

Kanbur's assessment echoes similar sentiments expressed in the 1999 U.N. Development Report. The report states that global economic inequality has increased dramatically as a direct result of economic globalization and the current rules of world trade: "When the market goes too far in dominating social and political outcomes, the opportunities and rewards of economic globalization spread unequally and inequitably—concentrating power and wealth in a select group of people, nations, and corporations, marginalizing the others."[88]

The U.N. General Assembly recently discussed why the number of people living in absolute poverty has gone up from 1 billion in 1995 to 1.2 billion in 1999 despite increasing globalization. Juan Somavia, Director-General of the U.N. International Labor Organization, concluded that business, governments, and international organizations had not done enough to alleviate poverty in the world: "We can no longer give globalization the benefit of the doubt. The results are in and it flunked."[89]

It seems that Secretary Summers strongly objected to the idea that developing countries need to be more careful and conditional about the way they approach market liberalization. Joseph Stiglitz's publicly expressed doubts about the effects of the free-market panacea and Ravi Kanbur's critical draft report clearly undermined the central globalist claim that globalization benefits everyone. While neither man can be considered as a political "radical" by any standard, their consistent concern for the world's poor proved to be incompatible with the globalist agenda.

Claim No. 5: Globalization Furthers the Spread of Democracy in the World

This globalist claim is anchored in the neoliberal assertion that *free markets* and *democracy* are synonymous terms. Persistently affirmed as common sense, the compatibility of these concepts often goes unchallenged in the public discourse. The most obvious strategy by which neoliberals generate popular support for the equation of democracy and the market is through a discreditation of traditionalism and socialism. The contest with both precapitalist and anticapitalist forms of traditionalism such as feudalism has been won rather easily because the political principles of popular sovereignty and individual rights have been enshrined as the crucial catalyst for the technological and scientific achievements of modern market economies. The battle with socialism turned out to be a much tougher case. As late as the 1970s, socialist thinkers provided a powerful critique of the elitist, class-based character of liberal democracy, which, in their view, revealed that a substantive form of democracy had not been achieved in capitalist societies. Since the collapse of communism in Eastern Europe, however, the ideological edge has shifted decisively to the defenders of a neoliberal perspective who emphasize the relationship between economic liberalization and the emergence of democratic political regimes.

Francis Fukuyama, for example, asserts that there exists a clear correlation between a country's level of economic development and successful democracy. While globalization and capital development do not automatically produce democracies, "the level of economic development resulting from globalization is conducive to the creation of complex civil societies with a powerful middle class. It is this class and societal structure that facilitates democracy."[90] Praising the economic transitions towards capitalism in Eastern Europe, U.S. Senator Hillary Rodham Clinton told her Polish audience that the emergence of new businesses and shopping centers in former communist countries should be seen as the "backbone of democracy." Clinton insisted that

> choosing the path of democracy, free markets, and freedom required
> great vision, courage, and moral leadership. Ten years ago it was not
> the obvious choice, nor was it easy. But today in so many of your
> countries, there is no question that the path of free markets and
> democracy is the right choice.[91]

Fukuyama and Clinton agree that the globalization process strengthens the existing affinity between democracy and the free market. Their argument hinges on a limited definition of democracy that emphasizes formal procedures such as voting at the expense of the direct participation of broad majorities in political and economic decision-making. This "thin" definition of democracy is part of what William I. Robinson has identified as the Anglo-American neoliberal project of "promoting polyarchy" in the developing world. For Robinson, the concept of polyarchy differs from the concept of "popular democracy" in that the latter posits democracy as both a process and a means to an end—a tool for devolving political and economic power from the hands of elite minorities to the masses. Polyarchy, on the other hand, represents an elitist and regimented model of "low intensity" or "formal" market democracy. Polyarchies not only limit democratic participation to voting in elections, but also require that those elected be insulated from popular pressures, so that they may "effectively govern."[92]

This focus on the act of voting—in which equality prevails only in the formal sense—helps to obscure the conditions of inequality reflected in existing asymmetrical power relations in society. Formal elections provide the important function of legitimating the rule of dominant elites, thus making it more difficult for popular movements to challenge the rule of elites. The claim that globalization furthers the spread of democracy in the world is largely based on a narrow, formal-procedural understanding of "democracy." Neoliberal economic globalization and the strategic promotion of polyarchic regimes in the Third World are, therefore, two sides of the same ideological coin. They represent the systemic prerequisites for the legitimation of a full-blown world market. The promotion of polyarchy provides globalists with the ideological opportunity to advance their neoliberal projects of economic restructuring in a language that ostensibly supports the "democratization" of the world.

Friedman's discussion of the democratic potential of globalization represents another clear example of such ideological maneuvers. Assuring his readers that globalization tends to impose democratic standards (like voting) on undemocratic countries, he argues that the integration of countries such as Indonesia and China into the global capitalist system has shown that the global market forces upon authoritarian regimes the rules-based business practices and legal standards they cannot generate internally. Friedman coins the term "globalution" to refer to today's "revolutionary process" by which the powerful Electronic Herd contributes to building the "foundation stones of democracy":

The Electronic Herd will intensify pressures for democratization generally, for three very critical reasons—flexibility, legitimacy, and sustain-
ability. Here's how: The faster and bigger the herd gets, the more
greased and open the global economy becomes, the more flexible you
need to get the most out of the herd and protect yourself from it. While
one can always find exceptions, I still believe that as a general rule the
more democratic, accountable, and open your governance, the less
likely it is that your financial system will be exposed to surprises.[93]

It is not difficult to notice the instrumentalist tone of Friedman's
argument. Devoid of any moral and civic substance, democracy represents for Friedman merely the best shell for the imperatives of the market. His use of the term "accountability" hardly resonates with the
democratic idea of civic participation. Rather, he equates accountability with the creation of social and economic structures conducive to
the business interests of the Electronic Herd. Moreover, he uses "flexibility" as a code word for deregulatory measures and privatization
efforts that benefit capitalist elites but threaten the economic security
of ordinary citizens. Granted, the "flexibility" of labor markets may
well be an important factor in attracting foreign investment, but it is
hardly synonymous with the successful creation of popular-democratic
institutions in developing nations.

Friedman's claim that globalization furthers the spread of democracy in the world stands in stark contrast to the results of empirical
research, most of which point in a rather different direction. Even
media outlets that faithfully spread the gospel of globalism occasion-
ally concede that large TNCs often prefer to invest in developing countries that are not considered "free" according to generally accepted
political rights and civil liberties standards. For example, the *Chicago
Tribune* recently cited a report released by the New Economic Information Service that suggests that democratic countries are losing out in
the race for American export markets and American foreign investments. In 1989, democratic countries accounted for more than half of
all U.S. imports from the Third World. Ten years later, with more democracies to choose from, democratic countries supplied barely one-
third of U.S. imports from the Third World: "And the trend is growing.
As more of the world's countries adopt democracy, more American
businesses appear to prefer dictatorships." These findings raise the important question of whether foreign purchasing and investment deci-

sions by U.S. corporations are actually undermining the chances for the survival of fragile democracies. Why are powerful investors in the rich Northern countries making these business decisions? For one, wages tend to be lower in authoritarian regimes than in democracies, giving businesses in dictatorships a monetary advantage in selling exports abroad. In addition, lower wages, bans on labor unions, and relaxed environmental laws give authoritarian regimes an edge in attracting foreign investment.[94]

Toward the end of his chapter on democratization, Friedman seems to be less clear on the role of globalization in creating open societies. While he still emphasizes that the Electronic Herd and the influential financial "Supermarkets" in New York, London, and Frankfurt will be important contributors to democratization, he also concedes that they might also create the opposite effect. As he puts it, "they will contribute to a widespread feeling, particularly within democracies, that even if people have a democracy at home they have lost control over their lives, because even their elected representatives have to bow now to unelected market dictators." In fact, Friedman even acknowledges that "the biggest challenge for political theory in this globalization era is how to give citizens a sense that they can exercise their will, not only over their own governments but over at least some of the global forces shaping their lives." Regrettably, however, the *New York Times* journalist shies away from suggesting a solution to this problem. Instead, he ends his discussion of the postulated link between democracy and globalization with another troubling question: "How do we deal with a world where the Electronic Herd gets to vote in all kinds of countries every day, but those countries don't get to vote on the herd's behavior in such a direct and immediate manner?"[95]

This question raises the important issue of what kind of democratic governing mechanisms can be attached to economic globalization. Globalists have consistently suggested that globalization can be harnessed to democratic processes by utilizing existing global and regional institutions such as the World Trade Organization (WTO). In their view, globalization promotes democratic forms of international cooperation while at the same time combating virulent forms of ethnonationalism. For example, Mike Moore, Director-General of the WTO, emphasizes that his organization is a "member-driven organization" that encourages the representatives of all member states to express their opinions freely on all matters of international trade. According to Moore, the WTO can be characterized by "democratic transparency," because its decision-making process is based on the "consensus principle." In other words, consensus is "at the heart of the WTO" because it represents a "fundamental democratic guarantee."[96]

However, Moore's representation of the "consensus principle" leaves out important information. Consensus, in the WTO, is typically managed by a handful of powerful nations led by the United States, Japan, the European Union, and Canada. Decisions are arrived at informally via oligarchical caucuses convoked by the big trading powers in the organization's corridors and in "green-room" negotiations during the WTO ministerial meetings. The formal plenary sessions, which in representative democracies are the central arena for decision-making, are reserved for prescripted speeches. Consensus usually functions as a cloak to render nontransparent a process where smaller, weaker countries are pressured to conform to decisions made in advance by powerful countries. With surprising candor, former U.S. Trade Representative Charlene Barshefsky openly admitted to the undemocratic character of the WTO procedures:

> The process, including even at Singapore as recently as three years ago [1996 WTO ministerial meeting], was a rather exclusionary one. All meetings were held between 20 and 30 key countries. . . . [T]his led to an extraordinarily bad feeling that they were left out of the process and that the results even at Singapore had been dictated to them by the 25 or 30 privileged countries who were in the room.[97]

During the raucous 1999 WTO meeting in Seattle, the vast majority of the developing countries were shut out of the negotiation process. They were not even informed which meetings were held or what the topics for discussion were. Confronted with assurances that a "consensus" was being worked on, many delegates from the Third World reacted with open defiance. For example, the African ministers issued a strong statement that there was "no transparency" in the meetings, and African countries had been systematically excluded from the process: "Under the present circumstances, we will not be able to join the consensus required to meet the objectives of this Ministerial Conference." Similar statements were issued by the Caribbean Community ministers and by some Latin American countries.[98]

Given the WTO's continued efforts to expand the neoliberal economic order, the prospect for genuine international cooperation on the basis of democratic principles appears to be slim. It seems that the inequalities resulting from the rapid globalization of markets can only be tackled by a commensurable globalization of political and civic institutions that are committed to "thick" participatory forms of democracy. As Benjamin Barber notes,

> the democratic world is out of control because the instruments of benign control—democratic governing institutions—simply do not exist in the international setting, where markets in currency, labor, and goods run like engines without governors. Happily, the rising internationalism of transnational institutions and social movements promises a measure of countervailing power in the international arena.[99]

Conclusion

The five globalist claims discussed in this chapter show that globalism is sufficiently comprehensive and systematic to count as a new ideology. As capitalism has been restructuring itself in the last decade, it has largely drawn on the central ideas of nineteenth-century free-market philosophers. It is the ability of globalists to connect these old arguments to the twenty-first-century framework of globality that bestows new currency upon their antiquated vision. Thus it appears that the Anglo-American framers of globalism have grasped the political advantage of utilizing the concept of "globalization" as a vehicle for the solidification and further expansion of their market paradigm. Presented to the public as a leaderless, inevitable juggernaut that will ultimately produce benefits for everyone, globalism has emerged as the dominant ideological vision of our time. It provides much of the conceptual and cultural glue that sustains the social and political power of neoliberal elites throughout the world. Its well-publicized promises of material well-being and social mobility often sustain consensual arrangements of rule, thus providing the foundation of what Antonio Gramsci has called "hegemony."

However, to argue that globalism has become a hegemonic discourse does not mean that it enjoys undisputed ideological dominance. There exists a multiplicity of stories about globalization that aim to provide authoritative accounts of what the phenomenon is all about. Globalism's claims are increasingly contested by nationalist-protectionist forces of the political Right and egalitarian-communitarian cohorts of the political Left. It is the task of the next chapter to examine the counter-arguments advanced by the challengers of globalism.

ANTIGLOBALIST CHALLENGERS FROM THE POLITICAL LEFT AND RIGHT

The Left/Right Distinction

The distinction between the political left and right originated in the French National Assembly at the outset of the revolutionary period. Those representatives favoring radical change in the direction of more-equal social arrangements congregated on the left side or "wing" of the chamber, whereas those arguing for the traditional status quo gathered on the right wing. The French deputies supporting only moderate change sat in the center. Yet the political landscape in the world has changed dramatically since 1789, and the reliance on the left/right metaphor as an indicator for main ideological differences has been subject to growing criticism.

In the mid-1990s, Norberto Bobbio defended the continued significance of this political distinction in *Left & Right*, an enormously successful book that sold hundreds of thousands of copies in Europe. The

Italian political thinker argued that the attitude of political groups toward the ideal of equality constitutes the most important criterion in distinguishing between the left and the right. According to Bobbio, members of the political left had historically shown support for the idea that political and social institutions are socially constructed. Hence, they emphasized the power of human reason to devise workable schemes for the reduction of social inequalities such as power, wealth, educational opportunity, and so on. But this does not mean that all members of the left have favored the complete elimination of all forms of inequality; only *extreme* leftists have embraced such a radical position.

Representatives of the political right, on the other hand, have been more reluctant to support policies that reduce existing social inequalities. They hold that many of these inequalities are legitimate because they are anchored in a largely unalterable "natural order." Skeptical of the power of reason to change social arrangements without seriously undermining social stability, they have affirmed existing social arrangements based on custom, tradition, and the force of the past. Only *extremist* members of the right have been opposed to all social change; others have supported change, provided that it occurs in slow, incremental fashion over a long period of time. Thus Bobbio suggested that the distinction between left and right concerns values, whereas the contrast between extremism and moderation pertains to the method of social change.[1]

Although the Italian thinker conceded that the line dividing the left and the right always has been shifting with changing historical circumstances, he nonetheless emphasized that this distinction—anchored in two fundamentally different perspectives on equality—retains its significance even in our postcommunist era of globalization:

> The communist left was not the only left; there was—and still is—another left within the capitalist horizon. The distinction has a long history which goes back long before the contrast between capitalism and communism. The distinction still exists, and not, as someone jested, simply on road signs. It pervades newspapers, radio, television, public debates, and specialized magazines on economics, politics, and sociology in a manner which is almost grotesque. If you look through the papers to see how many times the words "left" and "right" appear, even just in headlines, you will come up with a good crop.[2]

Consciously linking his analysis of the left–right distinction to today's condition of globality, sociologist Anthony Giddens arrives at a somewhat different conclusion. He suggests that "right" and "left" have come to mean different things in different social and geographical contexts. For example, Giddens maintains that it is very problematic to label neoliberalism as a right-wing ideology. After all, neoliberal programs tend to undermine the sanctity of tradition and custom by supporting radical processes of change stimulated by the incessant expansion of markets. On the other hand, neoliberalism *does* depend upon the persistence of some traditional values for its legitimacy. Its attachment to conservative norms is particularly obvious in the areas of religion, gender, and the family. Likewise, this fuzzy boundary between the political left and right is also reflected in the eclectic value structures of new social movements such as environmentalism and feminism. Hence, Giddens concludes that the left–right metaphor retains only limited validity in the contemporary political discourse:

> No doubt, the differentiation of left and right—which from the beginning has been a contested distinction in any case—will continue to exist in the practical contexts of party politics. Here its prime meaning, in many societies at least, differs from what it used to be, given that the neoliberal right has come to advocate the rule of markets, while the left favors more public provision and public welfare: straddling the ground of left and right, as we know, is a diversity of other parties, sometimes linked to social movements. But does the distinction between left and right retain any core meaning when taken out of the mundane environment of orthodox politics? It does, but only on a very general plane. On the whole, the right is more happy to tolerate the existence of inequalities than the left, and more prone to support the powerful than the powerless. This contrast is real and remains important. But it would be difficult to push it too far, or make it one of overriding principle.[3]

In this chapter, I classify globalism's challengers in accordance with the traditional left–right distinction. Indeed, my typology owes much to the insights of both Bobbio and Giddens. I agree with the Italian thinker that conflicting political worldviews—particularly on the issue of global equality—justify the drawing of a general distinction between left and right antiglobalists. But I also recognize that the respective arguments advanced by these two political camps sometimes share common themes and similar concepts. For this reason, I believe that

Giddens is correct when he highlights the difficulty of maintaining absolute lines of demarcation. Moreover, as I will argue in more detail in the final chapter, there has been a surprising convergence of left and right antiglobalist positions in recent years. Still, I conclude that the existing differences between these two camps are significant enough to distinguish between two antiglobalist groups: The nationalist-protectionists on the political right, and the internationalist-egalitarians on the political left.

Members of the nationalist-protectionists tend to blame globalization for most of the social, economic, and political ills afflicting their home countries.[4] Threatened by the slow erosion of old social patterns and traditional ways of life, they denounce free trade, the increasing power of global investors, and the neoliberal internationalism of multinational corporations as unpatriotic practices that have contributed to falling living standards and moral decline. Fearing the loss of national self-determination and the destruction of a circumscribed national culture, they pledge to protect the integrity of their nation from those "foreign elements" that they identify as responsible for unleashing the forces of globalization. Antiglobalists on the right are more concerned with the well-being of their own citizens than with the construction of a more-equitable international order based on global solidarity.

In the United States, Patrick Buchanan and other economic nationalists represent a good example of this position. In Europe, national-populist parties such as Jörg Haider's Austrian Freedom Party, Jean-Marie Le Pen's French National Front, Gerhard Frey's German People's Union, or Gianfranco Fini's Italian National Alliance have expressed their opposition to "American-style globalization" and its alleged tendency to produce a multicultural "New World Order." In developing countries, one finds similar voices on the right that blame globalization and the expansion of unregulated capital markets for triggering economic crises and undermining national autonomy. Hugo Chávez's Venezuelan brand of national populism represents a good example of such antiglobalism in the South.

The internationalist-egalitarian camp includes not only progressive political parties whose members envision more equitable relationships between the global North and the global South, but also a growing number of nongovernmental organizations and transnational networks concerned with the protection of the environment, fair trade and international labor issues, human rights, and women's issues. Challenging the central claims of globalism discussed in the previous chapter, these groups point to the possibility of constructing a new international economic and political framework based on a global redistribution of wealth and power. Internationalist-egalitarians claim to be guided by the ideals of equality and social justice for all people in the world, not just the citizens of their own countries. They accuse globalist elites of pushing neoliberal policies that are leading to greater global inequality, high levels of unemployment, environmental degradation, and the demise of social welfare. Calling for a "globalization from below" that would empower the marginalized and poor, they seek to transform current corporate strategies of subjecting the world by a "globalization from above."

In the United States, the consumer advocate and Green party presidential candidate Ralph Nader has emerged as the leading critic of the neoliberal corporate agenda. In particular, Nader argues that economic globalization has undermined the democratic accountability of transnational corporations. He also denounces the WTO, IMF, and World Bank as undemocratic institutions that engage in imperialist forms of exploitation. In Europe, the spokespersons for established Green parties have long suggested that unfettered economic globalization has resulted in serious ecological problems such as global warming, the mass extinction of species, the depletion of the earth's ozone layer, and the pollution of oceans and rivers.

In developing countries, democratic-popular movements of resistance against neoliberal policies such as the Zapatista rebellion in Mexico, the Chipko movement in India, or Haitian President Jean-Bertrand Aristide's poor people's movement have received some attention, even in Western media. Many of these Third World social movements have forged close links to antiglobalist nongovernmental organizations such as the International Forum on Globalization, Global Exchange, and Focus on the Global South. Such transnational alliances seek to draw people's attention to the deleterious effects of economic globalization, especially on the Southern Hemisphere.

The Nationalist-Protectionist Right

Patrick Buchanan's Economic Nationalism

Associated with the right wing of the Republican party since the early 1960s, Patrick J. Buchanan served as an aide and speechwriter for President Nixon from 1966 to 1974. After Nixon's resignation, he became a successful newspaper columnist and popular TV talk-show host. In the mid-1980s, he briefly interrupted his media career to serve as President Reagan's Director of Communications. Buchanan has been credited with scripting Reagan's controversial remarks that German SS soldiers buried in Bitburg Veterans' Cemetery in Germany were victims, "just as surely as the victims in the concentration camps." In 1992, Buchanan mounted an impressive challenge to President George Bush for the presidential nomination of the Republican party. Four years later, he defeated Senator Robert Dole in the important New Hampshire Republican presidential primary. Although Buchanan ultimately lost the primary contest, he received almost a quarter of the national Republican primary vote. By the mid-1990s, Buchanan had emerged as the most prominent leader of right-wing populism in the United States.

Political theorist Margaret Canovan defines *populism* as a political ideology that articulates antielitist positions involving some kind of exaltation of "the people" mixed with appeals to people's "common sense" and "moral decency."[5] Right-wing populists such as Buchanan demonize transnational corporate elites while at the same time launching xenophobic attacks against domestic "social parasites." Rather than endorsing fundamental social change in the direction of greater equality, right-wing populists maintain and intensify existing systems of social privilege. As political scientist Chip Berlet points out, populist movements are fueled by people's legitimate grievances against existing forms of domination, but they "deflect popular discontent away from positive social change by targeting only small sections of the elite or groups falsely identified with the elite." Moreover, right-wing populists channel the brunt of people's anger against ethnic minorities, recent immigrants, and welfare recipients. These oppressed and marginalized groups offer easier and more vulnerable targets than political and economic elites. Berlet refers to this practice of scapegoating undesirable Others as "producerism"—a doctrine that ostensibly champions the middle-class and working-class "producers" in society against "unproductive" and "treacherous" elites as well as against subordinate groups defined as "lazy," "immoral," or "foreign."[6]

After serious disagreements with leading Republicans on issues of free trade and immigration, Buchanan left the Republican party to pursue the presidential nomination of the Reform party. Although he eventually achieved his goal, his positions on a variety of social and economic issues proved to be highly controversial with many party delegates. While Buchanan accepted the Reform party nomination in the summer of 2000, a sizeable splinter group held a rival conference and nominated a different candidate for president. It took a formal ruling by the Federal Election Commission to confirm Buchanan as the official Reform party nominee. This allowed him to gain access to the disputed $12.6 million federal subsidy that went with the Reform party's presidential nomination.

The Reform party emerged in the mid-1990s as the brainchild of Texas billionaire H. Ross Perot. Tapping into a public mood of growing dissatisfaction with the country's two major political parties, Perot founded the nationwide antiestablishment organization "United We Stand." In 1992, he ran a maverick presidential campaign as an independent candidate, capturing an astonishing 19 percent of the national vote. Perot's candidacy demonstrated the considerable appeal of national populism to large segments of the American public. Between 1992 and 1996—the year he received the Reform party's presidential nomination—Perot used his reputation as a self-made entrepreneur to project the image of an independent, straight-talking patriot. He claimed to defend the interests of the common people against the corrupting influence of internationalist financial and political elites in the United States and abroad. Perot built the Reform party on an ideological platform that combined familiar populist themes with strong nationalist-protectionist appeals to protect the economic national interest and reduce the exploding trade deficit.

Most famously, Perot opposed the expansion of the regional free-trade agreement between the United States and Canada. Convinced that NAFTA carried the "virus of globalism," he argued that the inclusion of Mexico would lead to a massive flight of manufacturing capital to the South in search of cheap labor. Emerging as one of the principal spokespersons of the anti-NAFTA campaign, Perot forged tactical alliances with organized labor, environmentalists, and import-competing agricultural and industrial interests. His public utterances on the subject often conveyed thinly veiled anti-immigration sentiments. For example, the platform of the Reform party reflects Perot's conviction that more stringent immigration controls would help to "unite all Americans in spirit and purpose."[7] Although Congress passed the southward expansion of NAFTA in 1993 by a comfortable margin, Perot's protectionist arguments had made a lasting impression on the American public. In the following years, GATT and its successor organization, the WTO, came under severe criticism by an odd coalition of old-style liberals and right-wing politicians led by Buchanan and North Carolina's Senator Jesse Helms. During 1997–1998, this left–right alliance of free-trade opponents won a major battle on trade policy by defeating strong globalist initiatives to secure a so-called "fast-track" trade-negotiating authority for President Clinton.

When Buchanan inherited the remains of the Reform party in the summer of 2000, he had already succeeded Ross Perot as the chief spokesperson of the antiglobalist right in the United States. His best-selling books and his fiery campaign speeches conveyed his fierce opposition to a "Darwinian world of the borderless economy, where sentiment is folly and the fittest alone survive. In the eyes of this rootless transnational elite, men and women are not family, friends, neighbors, fellow citizens, but 'consumers' and 'factors of production.'" Turning the ideological table on free-trade Republicans who were dismissing his arguments as "antiquated protectionism," Buchanan reminded his former comrades of the Republican party's traditional perspective on trade policy. "For not only was the party of Lincoln, McKinley, Theodore Roosevelt, Taft, and Coolidge born and bred in protectionism, it was defiantly and proudly protectionist."[8]

Buchanan referred to his antiglobalist position as "economic nationalism"—the view that the economy should be designed in ways that serve the nation. Indeed, he defined economic nationalism as

> tax and trade policies that put America before the Global Economy, and the well-being of our own people before what is best for "mankind." . . . Our trade and tax policies should be designed to strengthen U.S. sovereignty and independence and should manifest a bias toward domestic, rather than foreign, commerce.[9]

Buchanan claimed that his economic nationalism espoused not only those patriotic sentiments that "carried Lincoln to the presidency," but also reflected the noble ideas that "Washington, Hamilton, and Madison had taken to Philadelphia and written into the American Constitution, and that Henry Clay had refined to create 'The American System' that was the marvel of mankind."[10]

Buchanan's 1998 address to the Chicago Council on Foreign Relations represents the most concise outline of his economic nationalism.[11] He begins his speech by expressing his conviction that there exists at the core of contemporary American society an "irrepressible conflict between the claims of a New American nationalism and the commands of the Global Economy." Assuring his audience that he considers himself a strong proponent of a free-market system operating within a national context, he insists that global markets must be harnessed in order to work for the good of the American people. This means that the leaders of the United States must be prepared to make economic decisions for the benefit of the nation, not in the interests of "shameless cosmopolitan transnational elites" who are sacrificing "the interests of their own country on the altar of that golden calf, the Global Economy."

For Buchanan, American economic nationalism is anchored in the resolute rejection of the European ideology of free trade—an "alien import, an invention of European academics and scribblers, not one of them ever built a great nation, and all of whom were repudiated by America's greatest statesmen, including all four presidents on Mt. Rushmore."[12] Buchanan argues that the greatness of modern nations such as the United States has always been built upon a staunchly nationalist economic philosophy that favors low taxes and prescribes high tariffs on imports in order to protect domestic manufacturers. After all, he asserts, the United States experienced its greatest economic successes when antifree-trade sentiments prevailed in the Protectionist Era of 1865 to 1913 and during the 1920s.

Mirroring the strategy of his globalist opponents, the Reform party leader relies on an endless stream of "hard data" to make his case to the public. Referring to his numbers as a "read-out of the electrocardiogram of a nation in decline," Buchanan utilizes his information as evidence against the globalist claim that globalization benefits everyone.[13] Arguing that globalization benefits only the wealthy transnational elites, he notes that since the onset of globalization in the late 1970s, real wages of working Americans have fallen by as much as 20 percent. By the mid-1990s, top CEO salaries skyrocketed to 212 times over an average worker's pay, and corporate profits more than doubled between 1992 and 1997.

Bemoaning the loss of independence and national sovereignty as a result of free-trade policies, Buchanan becomes nostalgic: "America was once a self-reliant nation; trade amounted to only 10 percent of GNP [gross national product]; imports only 4 percent. Now, trade is equal to 25 percent of GNP, and the trade surpluses we ran every year from 1900 to 1970 have turned into trade deficits for all of the last 27 years." In typical populist fashion, he highlights the devastating effect of globalization on the country's industrial workers: "In 1965, 31 percent of the U.S. labor force had manufacturing-equivalent jobs. By 1997, it was down to 15 percent, the smallest share in 100 years." The result of corporate globalization is that other countries have mounted a successful challenge to the economic leadership of the United States: "Americans no longer make their own cameras, shoes, radios, TVs, toys. A fourth of our steel, a third of our autos, half of our machine tools, two-thirds of our textiles are foreign-made. We used to be the world's greatest creditor nation; now, we are its greatest debtor."

Buchanan's focus on the treacherous activities of the neoliberal "Washington Establishment" serves as the foundation for his rejection of the globalist claim that nobody is in charge of globalization. In his view, "greedy global mandarins who have severed the sacred ties of national allegiance" head the Council on Foreign Relations and the Business Roundtable. Their elitist conspiracy has eroded the power of the nation-state and replaced it with a neoliberal New World Order.[14] In Buchanan's view, most mainstream American politicians are beholden to transnational corporate interests that are undermining the sovereignty of the nation by supporting the WTO and other international institutions. The Reform party leader accuses the Washington Establishment of channeling billions of dollars to the IMF and the World Bank for the purpose of bailing out undeserving developing countries in Africa, Latin America, and Asia. Evoking the wrath of "the American taxpayer" who is saddled with the costs of these bailouts, Buchanan demands severe punishment for the "global socialists" at the helm of the IMF and the World Bank.

Expanding on the subject of nefarious foreign influences, Buchanan also turns against the Organization of Petroleum Exporting Countries (OPEC). As president, he would "smash the price-fixing conspiracy called OPEC once and for all. If Americans are paying two dollars a gallon for their gas price in June [of 2000], it will be because of the lack of political courage and vision of Clinton and Gore, and their placing globalism ahead of patriotism."[15] Denouncing the "phony internationalism" of the two major parties, Buchanan calls for a massive tax increase on consumer imports, including a "social tariff" on Third World manufactured goods. These measures would not only add billions of dollars to the U.S. treasury, but they would also protect American industry against "unfair competition" from low-wage countries.

Finally, Buchanan accuses the nation's "liberal advocates of multiculturalism" of opening the doors to millions of immigrants. "Since the free-trade era began, four thousand new factories have been built in northern Mexico, and 35 million immigrants, most of them poor, have come into the United States—among them five million illegal aliens, mostly from Mexico. Free trade is not free." In his view, trade deals should be judged solely by nationalist-protectionist standards: whether they maintain U.S. sovereignty, protect vital economic interests, and ensure a rising standard of living for the American worker.[16]

Buchanan's fundamentally inegalitarian message is especially obvious in his persistent scapegoating of immigrants from developing countries. In his view, such immigrants are responsible for the economic and moral decline of the United States. Criticizing what he considers to be "astronomical levels of immigration," Buchanan suggests that this "invasion of legal and illegal immigrants" is eroding "our tax base, swamping social services, undermining the social cohesion of the Republic."[17] He assures his audiences that he would

> strengthen the Border Control, lengthen the "Buchanan Fence" on the southern frontier, repatriate illegals, and repair the great American melting pot. The twenty-seven million who have come into our nation since the 1970s shall be assimilated and Americanized, introduced fully into our history, culture, the English language, and American traditions.[18]

Although he grudgingly accepts the globalist claim that globalization is about the liberalization and global integration of markets, Buchanan challenges the alleged inevitability and irreversibility of this process. Citing the defeat of the campaign for presidential fast-track trade authority and the emergence of a global antifree-trade movement, he suggests that globalization is not inevitable and irreversible:

> Is this steady attrition of America's independence and sovereignty irreversible? My answer is *no*. For the balance of power in America has begun to shift. . . . A majority of Americans no longer believe these trade deals are good for America, and a majority of the House now agrees with them. The force is with us. Neither NAFTA nor GATT would pass today.[19]

Although Buchanan greatly exaggerates the decline of globalism as the dominant ideology in the United States, he nonetheless makes an important point when he predicts an intensifying ideological battle over the future direction of globalization: "[There will be] a struggle of nationalism against globalism, and it will be fought out not only among nations, but within nations." Banking on the victory of economic nationalism, he believes that there are already clear signs of globalism's imminent demise:

> The first is the tidal wave of imports from Asia about to hit these shores. When all those manufactured goods pour in, taking down industries and killing jobs, there will arise a clamor from industry and labor for protection. If that cry goes unheeded, those who turn a stone face to the American workers will be turned out of power.[20]

Buchanan's economic nationalism appeals to parochial, conservative elements in both the business community and organized labor—the "old" constituencies of the Republican and Democratic parties. As far as business is concerned, Buchanan calls for the replacement of the new internationalist-globalist outlook with "the old corporate mind set [that] was nationalist-protectionist." In other words, U.S.-based corporations ought to be pressured to show their patriotic loyalty by "putting America first."[21] Citing President Andrew Jackson's nativist outlook, he urges the business community to abandon its globalist faith: "We have been too long subject to the policy of foreign merchants. We need to become more Americanized, and instead of feeding the paupers and laborers of Europe . . . feed our own, or in a short time . . . we shall all be rendered paupers ourselves. America First, and not only first, but second and third as well."[22] However, Buchanan always makes sure to couple his idealistic appeals to patriotic loyalty with the more tangible assurance that old-style protectionism will produce profits for business and workers alike.

With regard to labor issues, Buchanan claims to embrace major parts of the antiglobalist agenda espoused by union leaders such as John Sweeney, the president of the AFL-CIO, and James Hoffa, the leader of the Teamsters. Echoing the same concerns of the old industrial working class, Buchanan's slogans are tailored to fit the backward-looking mood of his blue-collar audience. His arguments for greater social equality in America rest on the willingness to tolerate high levels of international inequality. In addition, his inegalitarian tendencies are reflected in stump speeches that abound with racist and anti-Semitic allusions. For example, Buchanan told a crowd of American steelworkers that "Asian invaders" were dumping devalued steel on American markets in a concerted effort to destroy the U.S. steel industry. In permitting these "illegal practices" to continue, the Washington Establishment had turned a blind eye to the "wholesale sacrifice of the United Steelworkers of America" in order "to make the world safe for Goldman Sachs." During the April 2000 anti-IMF protests in Washington, D.C., Buchanan told cheering members of the Teamsters Union that, as president, he would tell the Chinese to either shape up or "you guys have sold your last pair of chopsticks in any mall in the United States." He also assured the appreciative crowd that he would pick their boss, James Hoffa, as America's top trade negotiator.[23] In spite of his prolabor rhetoric, however, Buchanan owns a long record of refusing to endorse such basic workers' demands as raising the minimum wage.

A number of writers have suggested that the global surge of right-wing populism can be explained as an extreme reaction against both the structural and institutional development of twentieth-century capitalism. With the onset of globalization in the 1970s, mid-twentieth-century American industrial-welfare capitalism was rapidly transformed into the postindustrial individualized capitalism of the early twenty-first century. A similar transformation also occurred on the cultural level with the spread of multiculturalism and the rise of a postmodern culture whose central features include the collapse of *high* into *mass* culture, increased advertising and commercialization, and the individualization of choice and lifestyle.[24]

According to this interpretation, then, the antiglobalist voices of the nationalist-protectionist camp represent an antiquated authoritarian response to the economic hardships and dislocations brought about by globalization. Experiencing considerable anxiety over the dissolution of secure boundaries and familiar orders, groups such as industrial workers and small farmers are losing their former privileged status in traditional social hierarchies. As people's old identities are subjected to a growing sense of fragmentation and alienation, one possible response to the new challenges of the postmodern world lies in assigning blame to internal and external Others for the desecration of the familiar.

Buchanan and other successful right-wing populists present themselves to these sectors of "globalization losers" as strong traditional leaders who are prepared to halt the erosion of traditional social bonds and environments. Insisting on the possibility of reversing the mighty dynamic of globalization, they capitalize on people's sense of powerlessness in the face of massive structural change. Thus they give voice to the authoritarian longing for a bygone world of cultural uniformity, moral certainty, and national superiority. Mark Worrell notes that although right-wing populist leaders wear an egalitarian label and valorize the power of the grass-roots democracy, they actually contribute to the decline of participatory democracy: "Buchananism does not promise collective and democratic participation, but redemption by the hero."[25] Championing the simplistic idea of social change through the deeds of great men, Buchanan attacks globalism as the doctrine of hedonistic economic determinists who lack not only the motive but also the will and courage to resist the forces of globalization. Promising to lead America's struggle against neoliberal internationalism, Buchanan told the Daughters of the American Revolution:

> It is time Americans took their country back. Before we lose her forever, let us take America back from the global parasites of the World Bank and the IMF who siphon off America's wealth for Third World socialists and incompetents. And, let us take her back from the agents of influence who occupy this city [Washington, D.C.] and do the bidding of foreign powers.[26]

Although Buchanan received only 1 percent of the national vote in the 2000 presidential election, variations on his nationalist-protectionist message continue to resonate with a significant segment of the U.S. population. In fact, there has been a rise in the number of nationalist organizations in America whose antiglobalist rhetoric is even more extreme than Buchanan's right-wing populism. Groups such as the John Birch Society, the Christian Coalition, the Liberty Lobby, and so-called patriot and militia movements are convinced that globalization lies at the root of an incipient anti-American New World Order. Regarding neoliberal internationalism as an alien and godless ideology engulfing the United States, they fear that globalism is relentlessly eroding individual liberties and the "traditional American way of life."[27]

For example, Pat Robertson, the undisputed leader of the million-member Christian Coalition, published in the early 1990s a best-selling book that describes globalization as part of a diabolical conspiracy among transnational corporate elites to create "a new order for the human race under the domination of Lucifer and his followers."[28] This antiglobalist agenda of right-wing populist groups in the United States finds its equivalent across the Atlantic in a growing number of extremist European parties on the right.

Gerhard Frey's German Right-Wing Extremism

In recent years, the European right has toned down its earlier celebration of free-market economics and the capitalist system. Instead, right-wing parties have warmed up to the rhetoric of economic nationalism, which makes it easier for them to both exploit and fuel the public anxieties over the economic and cultural consequences of globalization. As Hans-Georg Betz points out, the European right's new targets of resentment are international bankers and currency traders, "footloose" capital and transnational corporations, as well as the European Union (EU) bureaucracy in Brussels. Considering globalization as a new threat to national sovereignty and self-determination, right-wing populist parties from Spain to Russia are advocating protectionist measures and the re-regulation of international financial markets. Economic nationalist rhetoric is a particularly effective weapon when combined with the so-called "foreigner problem."

For many years, the issues of immigration, imported laborers, and the general *Überfremdung* ("over-foreignization") of the *Heimat* (home country) have been important catalysts for radical right-wing mobilization in Germany and other European countries, because these themes point to an easily identifiable enemy who is seen as a threat to the cultural heritage and identity of the host countries. In addition, immigrants and resident aliens have been charged with taking jobs away from native workers, as well as driving down wages and exploiting the welfare system.[29] The German People's Union (*Deutsche Volksunion* [DVU]) represents a prime example of a European right-wing party that disseminates old xenophobic ideas in the new garments of antiglobalist populism.

The DVU was founded in Bavaria in 1971 as a right-wing umbrella group by Dr. Gerhard Frey, a neofascist millionaire publisher who has been providing most of the party's funding. Frey owns the *Deutsche National Zeitung* and the *Deutsche Wochenzeitung*, Germany's two largest nationalist weeklies with a combined estimated circulation of about 150,000. Frey's papers regularly feature anti-American and anti-Semitic articles that, among other topics, question the official death toll of the Holocaust and place "Jewish financiers" at the center of a conspiratorial circle of international capitalists who have unleashed the forces of globalization. Every autumn, the DVU hosts a lavish party rally in Passau, Bavaria, which attracts thousands of sympathizers. The event usually ends with Chairman Frey's two-hour keynote speech lambasting foreigners and the evils of internationalism.

Although its active membership is estimated at less than 25,000, the DVU utilizes Frey's extensive publishing contacts and relies on massive direct mailings to disseminate its political message to a national audience. After some initial electoral success in the early 1990s, when it entered the state parliaments of Bremen and Schleswig-Holstein with over 5 percent of the vote, the DVU staggered through several years of electoral setbacks brought on by the rise of a competing right-wing party, the Republicans (*Republikaner* [REP]). Benefiting from a protracted internal leadership struggle in the REP, the DVU has managed to again establish itself as the leading right-wing party in the country. During the mid-1990s, it surpassed even the REP's most spectacular electoral success. By winning 13 percent of the vote in the former East German state of Sachsen-Anhalt, the DVU achieved in 1998 the strongest electoral showing of any right-wing extremist party in Germany since 1945. In the fall of 1999, the party gained five seats in the state parliament of Brandenburg by garnering over 5 percent of the vote.

The DVU's electoral success coincided with a steep rise of right-wing violence and the number of right-wing organizations in Germany.[30] In 2000, German far-right crime soared to its highest levels since World War II. The total number of offenses—which include such acts as the illegal display of neo-Nazi symbols and propaganda materials—rose to almost 20,000, an increase of 59 percent over 1999.[31] German mainstream political parties have condemned criminal right-wing activity in public, and the country's highest court is considering a government request to ban the neo-fascist National Democratic party. Still, the most common political response in Germany is to call for a more "civilized solution" to the foreigner problem, thus indirectly legitimating the xenophobic outlook of the DVU.

Many commentators consider the successful demonization of globalization as one of the leading causes for the growth of right-wing extremism in Germany and other European countries. The DVU in particular has found an effective way to insinuate that mainstream politicians have abandoned the concerns of "hard-working Germans," because they have been bribed to look out for "the interests of stock gamblers, banks, and big business." The party's official statement of its "aims and principal policies" forcefully attacks the globalist claim that globalization is inevitable and irreversible. Echoing Buchanan's populist language, the DVU document suggests that strong political leaders, backed by popular referenda on key social issues, would be capable of halting the neoliberal juggernaut:

> We adamantly oppose any cuts in social spending and strongly resist the neoliberal agenda to turn Germany into a low-wage class society like Britain and the USA. An increasing number of people in these countries have to cope with "Third World"-style living conditions while a small minority of billionaires and multimillionaires are earning more money than they could possibly spend. [German Chancellor] Schröder wants to introduce this perverse culture to Germany too. There is no way we will ever tolerate this.[32]

The DVU document encourages "resolute German leaders" to accept the challenge and spearhead the popular struggle against globalization. Citing the party's cardinal principle—"Germany first," the document calls upon patriots from all walks of life to elect leaders who will defend the "vital interests of the German people." To honor their "sacred duty" and stand by the fatherland means that Germans must ensure that their *Heimat* will never become a country of immigration lest its own people "become a minority in their own country." Presenting itself as the guardian of traditional norms and values, the DVU seeks to convey to its audiences that those in charge of globalization must be identified in order to stop neoliberal internationalism. However, the alleged identification of these groups by members of the radical right involves acts of ideological distortion in which old, nationalistic images of the pernicious Other are modified to match the new global context: "Our firms and companies must not become prey of Anglo-American take over gambling [sic]; our cities must not become the home of Russian mobsters. The German army must not be used for the aims of ruthless U.S. imperialism."

At the same time, however, the DVU document concedes that Germany on its own would be too weak to "oppose the power of international banks and multinational corporations." Hence, the party endorses the development of a regional European strategy to protect the interests of "ordinary European citizens" against "the international dictatorship of the Anglo-American bank and big-business World Empire." United in their opposition to a neoliberal internationalism, sovereign European nations would voluntarily cooperate to form an "anti-imperialist" bloc against the further spread of American-style globalization. Moreover, those countries belonging to an ideologically nationalist-protectionist "Fortress Europe" would actively "support popular movements in many [other] countries [of the world] against so-called 'globalization,' which is in fact an Americanization of the world."[33]

Such antiglobalist and protectionist statements can be found on the websites of all major European right-wing populist parties. In all cases, there exists a strong agreement that the dominant claims of globalism must be attacked from a nationalist-protectionist perspective. Confronted with economic competition from low-wage countries in Eastern Europe and the developing world, even the previously promarket Austrian Freedom party has recently come out in support of selective "protectionist measures for industry in the interest of the preservation of work places."[34]

Its antiglobalist rhetoric notwithstanding, however, the European right has not managed to extricate itself from the forces of globalization it so denounces. In fact, the antiglobalist right is being increasingly internationalized. Recent trends show a remarkable convergence of radical right-wing ideas and activities on both sides of the Atlantic. Having increased personal and virtual contacts through better travel connections and sophisticated electronic media, right-wing groups in Europe and North America have begun to look and sound very similar. As Leonard Weinberg notes, although a common Euro-American radical right has not yet emerged, one certainly appears to be on the horizon.[35] Indeed, such similarities reach even to South America, where Venezuela's charismatic President Hugo Chávez embodies the qualities of an ideal antiglobalist leader envisioned by the national-populist right.

Hugo Chávez's Bolivarian National Populism

Born in 1954, the son of provincial school teachers, Hugo Chávez joined the Venezuelan military forces at the age of seventeen. He spent the next twenty years fighting ultra-leftist guerillas, teaching sports and history at the military academy in Caracas, and serving as a military aide in the national security council. A keen observer of politics who cultivated personal connections to important figures on both the left and the right, Chávez ultimately came to the conclusion that the traditional Venezuelan party system was too corrupt to be reformed. Taking advantage of his new assignment as the commanding officer of a parachute regiment close to the capital, Chávez conspired in 1992 with other mid-career officers to overthrow the democratically elected social-democratic government of President Carlos Andres Perez.

Although his coup attempt failed within a few hours, Colonel Chávez's nationally televised appeal to his fellow officers to accept defeat made him a popular martyr for the nationalist cause. Pardoned only two years later by the newly elected center left President Rafael Caldera, Chávez left prison prepared to continue his former activities. As he expanded his contacts to pivotal military and civilian figures, he pondered his political future. Rejecting the arena of electoral politics as irredeemably corrupt, he refused to run for president. However, when it became clear that large segments of the population supported his national populism, he changed his mind. Assuming the leadership of Patriotic Pole, a peculiar left–right political alliance, Chávez embarked on a vigorous election campaign. In December 1998, he was elected president with 56 percent of the vote. He immediately issued a decree for a national referendum on elections for a national constituent assembly that would be given the task of drafting a new constitution. The referendum passed with 88 percent of the vote, clearing the way for the adoption of the new constitution a year later. On July 30, 2000, Chávez was elected to a six-year term as the first president of the renamed

"Bolivarian Republic of Venezuela." His victory was further sweetened by the electoral success of his political alliance, which won a majority of seats in the new single-chamber legislative body.[36]

Chávez's astonishing popularity with Venezuelans—particularly the middle and lower classes—has been credited to his charismatic personality and his antiglobalist, national-populist rhetoric. This message resonates with the vast majority of ordinary people in Latin America who suffered greatly when the neoliberal reforms of the early 1990s swept the region. Although Venezuela is a country blessed with vast natural resources, its considerable oil wealth has been poorly managed, being more often used for political patronage than for a fair distribution among its 23 million inhabitants. By the 1980s, Venezuela's foreign debt had skyrocketed, giving the IMF the opportunity to link further loans to the implementation of a comprehensive economic program that included strong deregulation measures and drastic austerity budgets. The implementation of this neoliberal agenda led to significant price increases for basic goods and services, ultimately sparking large urban riots in 1989 and 1996, during which police forces and military troops killed thousands of demonstrators. Throughout the 1990s, neoliberal globalization filled the coffers of Venezuela's tiny wealthy elite, whereas the vast majority of citizens experienced a noticeable drop in their living standard. By the time Chávez campaigned for president, nearly 80 percent of Venezuelans lived in poverty, unemployment held steady at almost 20 percent (with 50 percent of the workers languishing in the "informal economy"), and the violent crime rate had exploded to 50 murders per weekend in the capital city of Caracas alone.[37]

Chávez's political message took aim at two targets: Venezuela's elitist and corrupted political system perpetuated by the established parties, and the "savage neoliberalism unleashed on the South by Northern globalist forces." As Richard Gott puts it in his biography of the Venezuelan leader, Chávez stirred up the nationalist passions of his country's population with a good dose of revolutionary rhetoric: "He has tried to combat the unquestioning acceptance of neoliberalism and globalization with the revival of radical nationalism, drawing on the words and actions of Venezuela's pantheon of nineteenth-century heroes."[38] Criticizing the globalist faith in the power of unfettered market forces, the Venezuelan leader instead supported an economic nationalism through which the state would actively seek to promote Venezuela's internal development, using its own resources and whatever planning mechanisms might be necessary.[39] Insisting that "Venezuela always comes first," Chávez prom-ised his people that he would protect them from the forces of "predatory globalization." His recently established "Project Bolivar 2000" represents an initiative designed to improve the quality of life of the nation by bringing the armed forces and civilian volunteers together to rebuild and improve the conditions in the countryside.

Vowing to complete his social revolution within the next few years, the Venezuelan president regularly takes aim at the claims of globalism. In particular, he routinely challenges the notion that globalization is inevitable and ultimately beneficial to developing nations. Strongly influenced by the neofascist ideas of his former advisor, Argentine sociologist Norberto Ceresole, Chávez believes that Latin American countries should forge economic and military alliances with nations in the Middle East and Asia in order to counterbalance the power of glob-alism most evident in the U.S.-based "Jewish financial mafia."[40] To this end, Chávez has sought warmer relations with the political leaders of China, Libya, Iraq, and Iran. During his 1999 visit to China, the Vene-zuelan president made a special effort to point out that the collapse of Soviet power did not mean that "neoliberal capitalism has to be the model followed by the people of the West."[41] He also warned that U.S.-led corporate globalization would further heighten conditions of social inequality and mass poverty in Latin America. Consequently, he called upon Cuba, Colombia, Ecuador, and other countries in the region to lock arms against globalism: "The only way we can fight neoliberalism is to unite."[42]

On occasion, Chávez has admitted that his aim is nothing less than to realize the old dream of the nineteenth-century "liberator" Simon Bolivar: The political and economic union of the peoples of Latin America and the Caribbean. In Chávez's view, the creation of such a modern "Gran Colombia" would be an important foundation from which to challenge the hegemony of the United States and the Euro-pean Union.[43] Propagating his nationalist vision of a strong Latin American bloc under his leadership, the Venezuelan president has emerged as a firm opponent of the United States who does not hesitate to undercut U.S. foreign policy whenever an opportunity presents itself. For example, he opposed Washington's decision to use billions of dollars to support Colombia's government in its war against guerillas and drug dealers. Convinced that the involvement of the United States would only lead to "the Vietnamization of the entire Amazon region," he refused to allow American planes monitoring drug trafficking to fly over Venezuelan airspace.

Most importantly, Chávez has been extremely successful in using oil as an important instrument of his anti-American foreign policy. He recently signed a major deal with Fidel Castro that allows Cuba to buy half of its imported oil from Venezuela on favorable terms. In the summer of 2000, he organized the 40th-anniversary summit of OPEC in Caracas. In his keynote address, Chávez argued in favor of keeping oil prices as high as possible in order to put pressure on the North: "For a century, they [Northern countries] took millions of barrels of oil at giveaway prices. How nice it would be if they also lowered the prices of computers, medicine, and cars, and the interest rates on foreign debt."[44] Promising to make OPEC one of the main pillars in his overall "strategy against globalization," Chávez cleverly arranged to have Venezuela's energy minister named the president of this organization. The latter's immediate goals for the future include the founding of an OPEC university, the creation of an OPEC bank, and the building of an OPEC technological institute.[45] The United States is clearly irked by Chávez's rising influence in world affairs. Warning that it might "get tougher on Venezuela's leader," the incoming Bush administration signaled its willingness to challenge Chávez's antiglobalist course, particularly his "distortion of the free-market model advocated by Washington."[46]

Some commentators have suggested that Chávez's antiglobalist Bolivarian ideology should be seen as a genuine leftist alternative to Anglo-American globalism.[47] In my view, however, his brand of antiglobalism fits squarely in the nationalist-protectionist camp of the populist right, for the main reason that his egalitarian aspirations rarely reach beyond a limited geographic area. To be sure, I agree with Jorge Castaneda and other experts that it is not an easy task to draw a sharp line of demarcation between the left and the right in the Latin American context.[48] Moreover, one can find in Chávez's program some ideological and political preferences that link it to some causes espoused by the Latin American populist left during the 1960s and 1970s. He is also clearly dedicated to improving the living conditions of the lower classes in Venezuela. These indicators seem to give some credence to the image of Chávez as a man of the left.

On the other hand, however, the Venezuelan leader has always insisted that his revolutionary ideology is "neither leftist nor rightist."[49] Orthodox Marxists in Latin America have condemned his disdain for the left's cardinal principle of internationalism. Chávez's antiglobalism shows some of the same characteristics discussed in my exposition of Buchananism and European right-wing populism. Like these two ideologies, Bolivarian national populism harbors a deeply hierarchical and paternalistic streak that projects the image of a super-masculine, charismatic leader who, as the unchallenged "tribune of the people," relies on his special ties to the populace in his virtuous struggle against a corrupt domestic system and pernicious alien influences.

As a career military officer, Chávez is very comfortable with an inegalitarian, top-down process of decision-making that merely allows the masses to endorse forgone conclusions. Although formally operating on a democratic platform, Bolivarian national populism relies on constant referenda, plebiscites, and other forms of "direct democracy" to legitimate authoritarian rule in the name of "common sense." For example, Chávez has accused leaders of the Venezuelan Workers' Confederation who opposed some of his policies of representing "an elite that has betrayed the working class." Announcing that he intended to crush the union, the president immediately proposed that a national referendum be held on this issue. Clearly, his intent was to have his supporters provide him with the "democratic" backing to dismantle all of Venezuela's 9,000 unions and instead establish a single, government-dominated labor union.

In addition, Chávez has already moved aggressively to restrict the activities of those civic groups that are not affiliated with his movement.[50] In this regard, Chávez's actions hardly fit the aspirations of an egalitarian leftist, but rather follow in the footsteps of such right-wing populist leaders as Juan Domingo Peron, Juan Velasco, Saddam Hussein, and Benito Mussolini. Indeed, if one accepts that the protection of a nationalist or regionalist framework against the internationalist logic of globalization constitutes the core of the antiglobalist enterprise of the right, then Bolivarian national populism clearly belongs in the latter category. This conclusion is borne out in Chávez's open celebration of the "global renaissance of nationalism":

> I think we are living through a period in which nationalism is being re-born. You can see this in the conflict in Chechenia [sic] against the

Russians. It's like the return of history, just as the old nations came back after the First World War. . . . What we have now is world disorder. There is no order, and there is not a single superpower. The future will have many centers, and we shall see the formation of [regional] alliances and blocks.[51]

The Internationalist-Egalitarian Left

Ralph Nader's Left Populism

For the last few decades, Ralph Nader has been one of the most prominent spokesperson for the democratic left in the United States. Recently, *Life* magazine named him one of the hundred most-influential people of the twentieth century. Born in Connecticut to Lebanese immigrants, Nader showed extraordinary intellectual promise as a student. He received his B.A. degree (magna cum laude) from Princeton University, and his law degree from Harvard University. In 1963, he abandoned a conventional law practice for a consulting job with the Department of Labor's assistant secretary, Daniel Patrick Moynihan. The young lawyer also freelanced as a journalist, writing regular articles for left-liberal journals such as the *Nation* and progressive newspapers such as the *Christian Science Monitor*. In 1965, he published his best-selling book, *Unsafe at Any Speed: The Designed-In Dangers of the American Automobile*, in which he targeted the American auto industry for covering-up serious safety hazards in order to protect their profits. After prevailing in an ensuing lawsuit involving General Motors, Nader used the settlement money he received to launch the modern consumer movement in America.

His reputation as a relentless critic of corporate America grew over the next decades as Public Citizen, his major nonprofit organization, successfully lobbied Congress for the passage of new consumer-protection laws. By the 1990s, more than 150,000 people were actively involved in Public Citizen's six major divisions. One of these branches, Global Trade Watch, is dedicated to educating the American public about the negative impact of neoliberal economic globalization on job security, the environment, public health and safety, and democratic accountability. Founded in 1993 as a direct response to the passage of NAFTA in Congress, Global Trade Watch has emerged as a leading watchdog organization monitoring the activities of the IMF, the World

Bank, and the WTO. Nader has established himself as one of the principal left critics of these organizations, arguing that their main purpose lies in promoting a neoliberal, corporatist agenda at the expense of the interests of ordinary citizens all over the world.

After his botched presidential campaign of 1996, Nader ran again as the Green party presidential candidate four years later. This time, he and his party managed to put together a vigorous national campaign. On Election Day 2000, the antiglobalist consumer advocate received 3 percent of the national vote, which amounted to about 3 million votes nationwide. Many political pundits argued that Nader's candidacy in such hotly contested states as Florida and New Hampshire ultimately lost the election for the Democratic presidential candidate, Vice President Al Gore.

In his official statement announcing his candidacy for the Green party's nomination for president, Nader presents himself as a "new populist" who defends democratic principles against the "neoliberal forces of globalism."[52] Unlike Buchanan's nationalist version, however, Nader's left brand of populism refuses to stoke the fires of popular resentment against ethnic minorities, recent immigrants, or welfare recipients. On these issues, Nader always invokes the inclusive spirit of the Green party platform, which "opposes those who seek to divide us for political gain by raising ethnic and racial hatreds, blaming immigrants for social and economic problems."[53] The left dimension of Nader's populism is also evident in his conscious attempt to avoid the right's exaggerated patriotism. In spite of his occasional tendency to play to the chauvinistic passions of his campaign audiences by defending the "self-determination of nations" against the "domination of global corporations," Nader regularly returns to the idea that globalism must be opposed by an international alliance of egalitarian forces. For example, in his acceptance speech at the 2000 Green party convention, he notes that the values of "deep democracy" and social justice, the elimination of poverty, and the protection of the environment constitute moral imperatives that ought to transcend the narrow conceptual framework of nationalism or regionalism.[54]

With regard to the role of corporate elites, however, Nader's and Buchanan's respective brands of populism find a common enemy. In a joint on-line interview given to *Time* magazine on the evening of the 1999 Seattle anti-WTO protests, both men affirmed that underlying their antagonistic ideological positions was a common understanding of the globalist agenda as undermining the power of the people.[55] Time and again, Nader directs the brunt of his populist message against the globalist claims that nobody is in charge of globalization and that globalization furthers the spread of democracy in the world. For the consumer advocate, globalization is driven by powerful corporate elites who subordinate human rights, labor rights, consumer and environmental rights, and democratic rights to the imperatives of global trade and investment. As he points out, of the top 100 economic entities in the world, 51 are corporations and only 49 are countries. Moreover, the gross annual sales of such huge TNCs as General Motors exceed the GDP of countries such as Norway, South Africa, or Saudi Arabia. Shaping the globalization of commerce and finance in an authoritarian fashion, these multinational companies contribute to a widening "democracy gap" between ordinary people and their political institutions:

> The global corporatists preach a model of economic growth that rests on the flows of trade and finance between nations dominated by giant multinationals—drugs, tobacco, oil, banking, and other services. The global corporate model is premised on the concentration of power over markets, governments, mass media, patent monopolies over critical drugs and seeds, the workplace, and corporate culture. All these and other power concentrates homogenize the globe and undermine democratic processes and their benefits.[56]

In Nader's view, the implementation of the "corporate model of globalization" goes hand-in-hand with the creation of autocratic institutions of political governance that push a neoliberal agenda of economic development. For example, the establishment of the WTO signifies a landmark formalization and strengthening of corporate power. For Nader, institutions such as the WTO were designed by globalist forces in order to eliminate "the oppositional factors we call democracy—to have an international system of autocratic governance that undermines open judicial courts and replaces them with [the] secret tribunals [of the WTO]." In this way,

> corporate globalization establishes supranational limitations and impinges deeply on the ability of any nation to control commercial activity with democratically enacted laws. Globalization's tactic is to eliminate democratic decision-making and accountability over matters as intimate as the safety of food, pharmaceuticals and motor vehicles,

or the way a country may use or conserve its land, water and minerals, and other resources. What we have now in this type of globalization is a slow-motion coup d'etat, a low-intensity war waged to redefine free society as subordinate to the dictates of international trade—i.e., big business *über alles*.[57]

Noting the rise of political-action committees in the United States from 400 in 1974 to about 9,000 in 2000, Nader claims that this "huge, beefed up corporate-lobby presence in Washington" successfully pressured Congress and the president to stay on a neoliberal course. A "massive avalanche of [corporate] money" has buried the democratic system of the United States:

Government has been hijacked to a degree beyond anything we have seen in the last 70 years. It's been hijacked by corporate power, the multinationals mostly. They have their own people in government. They run their own people, they appoint their own people, they get corporate lawyers to agree to become judges. And when that happens you no longer have a countervailing force called government arrayed against excesses of what Jefferson called "the moneyed interest." Instead, you have this convergence, almost a phalanx, of business controlling government and turning it against its own people.[58]

If even the world's sole remaining superpower has been captured by corporate interests, Nader concludes, then one should not be surprised to see the growth of unaccountable corporate power all over the world. Rather than living up to their globalist claim of stimulating the spread of democratic values, Western corporatist governments have propped up authoritarian, oligarchic regimes in the developing world that ensure social conditions conducive to foreign direct investment. Pitting states against each other, powerful TNCs have created a "race to the bottom" in which governments attempt to attract foreign investment by lowering wage levels, imposing the lowest pollution standards, and cutting business taxes to an absolute minimum. Thus American standards of living and the standards of justice have been pulled down "to the level of other countries that happen to be authoritarian and dictatorial. That is why, for example, globalization does not ban trade produced by child labor. That's why it does not ban trade produced by brutalizing working conditions."[59]

Responding to neoliberal figures that suggest a worldwide rise in living standards, Nader employs his own data effectively against the globalist claim that globalization benefits everyone. Referring to rising levels of inequality in America alone, Nader notes that the United States ranks 37th among nations in the world regarding the quality of health care. Forty-seven million workers, over one-third of the U.S. workforce, make less than $10 per hour and work 160 hours longer per year than did workers in 1973. The low U.S. unemployment rate in the 1990s, often cited by globalists as evidence for the economic benefits of globalization, is masked by low wages and millions of part-time laborers who are registered as employed if they work 21 hours a week and cannot get a full-time job. At the same time, the average salary of a CEO employed in a large corporation has exploded. In 2000, it was 416 times higher than that of an average worker. The financial wealth of the top 1 percent of American households exceeds the combined wealth of the bottom 95 percent, reflecting a significant increase in the last twenty years.[60]

Nader also makes certain to address the increase of global inequalities brought on by corporate globalization. Some of the numbers he uses are readily available from recent editions of the United Nations' Human Development Report. For example, the world income distribution among households in the last ten years has shown a sharp rise in inequality. The economic gap between rich and poor is widening in most countries. At the same time, economic growth has stagnated in many developing countries, leading to an increase in income disparities between rich and poor countries by orders of magnitude out of proportion to anything previously experienced. Just before the onset of globalization in 1973, the income ratio between the richest and poorest countries was at about 44 to 1. Twenty-five years later it had climbed to 74 to 1. In the period since the end of the cold war, the number of persons subsisting below the international poverty line rose from 1.2 billion in 1987 to 1.5 billion today, and, if current trends persist, will reach 1.9 billion by 2015. This means that, at the dawn of the twenty-first century, the bottom 25 percent of humankind lives on less than $140 a year. Meanwhile, the world's 200 richest people have doubled their net worth to more than $1 trillion between 1994 and 1998. The assets of the world's top three billionaires are worth more than the combined GNP of all least-developed countries and their 600 million people.[61]

Despite the seemingly hopeless social dynamic expressed in these statistics, the Green party leader refuses to accept the globalist claim that globalization equals the liberalization and integration of markets and that this dynamic is inevitable and irresistable. But a successful challenge to the concentration of global corporate power over governments requires a "revitalized citizen democracy in the United States and movement building across national borders."[62] Rather than emphasizing the central role of strong political leaders, Nader invokes the memory of countless social-justice movements in the world where ordinary people struggled together to overcome steep concentrations of undemocratic power. He also points to recent, worldwide mass mobilizations against globalism and its institutions as evidence for ordinary people's ability to halt, reverse, or redirect the allegedly inexorable march of the globalist juggernaut.

Time and again, Nader challenges his audience to participate in open forms of resistance against the corporatist order. He attempts to delegitimize the ideological claims of globalism by drawing on the central elements of the popular-democratic tradition of the previous two centuries: citizen participation, grass-roots democracy, racial and gender equality, ecological balance, community-based economics, and economic justice. But he is not above fighting the ideological distortions of globalism with equally contorted images of a "selfish corporate oligarchy" responsible for all the ills in society, including economic decline, the debasement of politics, and the betrayal of the democratic heritage.[63]

On the other hand, Nader's ideological enterprise also contains a constructive, integrative function that seeks to transform people's one-dimensional consumer identities. At the heart of his struggle for the creation of a new identity lies his moral commitment to "putting human values first." Emphasizing the importance of ethical ideals guiding political action, Nader directs his antiglobalist message especially at young people:

> I say, beware of being trivialized by the commercial culture that tempts you daily. I hear you saying often that you're not turned on to politics. The lessons of history are clear and portentous. If you do not turn on to politics, politics will turn on you. The fact that we have so many inequalities demonstrates this point. Democracy responds to hands-on participation. And to energized imagination. That's its essence. We need the young people of America to move into leadership positions to shape their future as part of this campaign for a just society.[64]

The Internationalization of Antiglobalist People's Movements

Ralph Nader's organizational empire in the United States is part of an emerging framework of nongovernmental organizations (NGOs) also referred to by such terms as "international civil society" or "international advocacy networks." While representing a diversity of local concerns and issues, many of these grass-roots initiatives contest corporate "globalization from above" by working together across national boundaries. As neoliberal policies generate rising levels of inequality, people at the grass roots around the world seek to impose their needs and interests on the process of corporate globalization. Indeed, the spread of the globalist agenda is generating a worldwide movement of antiglobalist resistance evident in the internationalization of egalitarian peoples' movements and organizations. Some commentators have referred to such wide-ranging collaborative efforts to combat the agenda of globalism as "grass-roots globalization" or "globalization from below."[65]

Candido Grzybowski, the executive director of the Brazilian Institute for Social and Economic Analysis, notes that one of the most fundamental responses to economic globalization has been the internationalization of civil society. "Civil society" refers to the realm of voluntary associations located between the state and the family. Grzybowski argues that the world's civil societies have already begun to view themselves within the framework of globalization, increasingly enabling people to assume a more cosmopolitan identity. One of the primary goals of globalization from below is to produce a counterhegemonic discourse that challenges the dominant deterministic claims of globalism and contributes to the emergence of an egalitarian global consciousness. Grzybowski believes that people at the grass roots can affect the course of globalization, but only by means of forging transnational alliances that reach across geographic, ethnic, and class boundaries:

> Forging another kind of globalization within civil society is possible. To do that we must reaffirm the primacy of the ethical principles constituting democracy: Equality, freedom, participation, and human diversity and solidarity. They are capable of touching the hearts and minds of civil society's different groups and sectors. These principles should regulate power and market and be upheld and practiced throughout the world. The priority task is to counterpose a deepening process of global

democracy and of planetary-scale cultural change to worldwide neo-liberal disorder.[66]

Today, there exist thousands of antiglobalist NGOs in all parts of the world. Some consist only of a handful of activists while others attract a much larger membership. Here are four examples of such influential international advocacy networks.

Third World Network (TWN). The Third World Network is a non-profit international network of organizations based in Malaysia, with regional offices on all five continents. Its objectives are to conduct research on development issues pertaining to the South, to publish books and magazines, to organize seminars, and to provide a platform representing antiglobalist perspectives at international forums. Secretary Martin Khor emphasizes that the members of TWN are particularly concerned about the social consequences of corporate globalization and the deregulation of markets. He views as the central task of his organization the mounting of an effective international campaign to change the nature and consequences of present neoliberal globalization trends.[67]

International Forum on Globalization (IFG). The International Forum on Globalization is a nonprofit alliance of activists, scholars, economists, researchers, and writers formed to stimulate an internationalist-egalitarian response to globalism. Representing over 60 organizations in 25 countries, IFG associates develop alternative ideas and strategies that might reverse the current globalization trend and redirect actions toward a revitalizing of local communities within a new international institutional framework. Emphasizing that globalization from above is neither historically inevitable nor desirable, IFG associates recognize that a major part of their educational activities must be directed at challenging the public discourse of globalism, especially the claim that the liberalization and integration of global markets will eventually "lift all boats."[68] The organization's many publications, seminars, and teach-ins make available to the public important information about the undemocratic governing structures and policies of the WTO, the IMF, and the World Bank.

Global Exchange (GEX). Global Exchange is a nonprofit research, education, and action center dedicated to promoting people-to-people ties between the global North and South. Headquartered in California, the organization strives to increase global awareness among the U.S.

public while building international partnerships with grass-roots initiatives around the world. GEX maintains six main programs, including campaigns against the inegalitarian policies of globalist financial institutions, and a "fair-trade program" that seeks to build economic justice from the bottom up by educating First World consumers about the social conditions existing in developing countries where many products are made. In addition, GEX produces publications and visual materials to increase coverage of international issues from an antiglobalist perspective. The organization also provides small grants and technical assistance to community-initiated development projects in the South.[69]

GEX also managed to organize a coalition of over a dozen prominent U.S. women's organizations to take a common stance against sweatshops and other exploitative labor practices. Mainstream women's groups in the United States have only recently begun to pay more attention to the gendered critiques of globalism offered by many women's movements outside of North America. Diane Elson, Isabella Bakker, and other feminist economists in the International Association of Feminist Economists have exposed the male bias in globalist discourse.[70] Given the fact that many victims of neoliberal structural-adjustment programs are women in the global South, it is not surprising to witness the rapid spread of new international feminist alliances.[71] According to political sociologist Valentine Moghadam, transnational feminist networks are informal or formal organizations whose members are individual women or women's groups from three or more countries that unite around a common agenda, typically pertaining to women's rights or a feminist critique of economic policy. Seeing themselves as agents of social change, transnational feminist networks have been in the forefront of the ongoing struggle to resist the globalist agenda.[72]

Focus on the Global South (FOCUS). Focus on the Global South is a Bangkok-based research, analysis, and advocacy program on North–South issues. This organization aims to create distinct and cogent links between local, community-based programs of development and a global paradigm of popular democracy. Such "micro–macro linking programs" concentrate on analyzing and counteracting the impact of globalization from above. According to FOCUS co-director Walden Bello, the ultimate goal of his organization is to re-empower people through a process of "deglobalization." This does not mean that he endorses local strategies of total withdrawal from the international economy. Rather, Bello advocates a reorientation of market economies to benefit the people at the grass roots. At the same time, he acknowledges that such a gigantic project of global wealth redistribution can only succeed "if it takes place within an alternative system of global economic governance." Envisioning such an alternative paradigm, he tells his audiences that all forms of globalization are human-made. Since globalist claims of inevitability are designed to paralyze political resistance, globalization from below must emphasize the possibility of successful collective resistance:

> Let us put an end to this arrogant globalist project of making the world a synthetic unity of individual [consumerist] atoms shorn of culture and community. Let us herald, instead, an internationalism that is built on, tolerates, respects, and enhances the diversity of human communities and the diversity of life.[73]

* * *

Having sprung from a wide range of movements reflecting specific concerns, globalization from below has begun to converge around a common internationalist-egalitarian agenda. In spite of their attempts to develop a constructive program for an internationalist-egalitarian left, the spokespersons of globalization from below are often criticized for failing to go beyond their focus on resistance. As Jan Nederveen Pieterse notes, resistance is not always an enabling position, analytically or politically. The articulated strategies often do not go beyond "just saying no" to globalization.[74] Such tendencies to disconnect, or "delink," the antiglobalist camp from the "system" sometimes lead to the adoption of a parochial, communitarian agenda that separates local concerns from cosmopolitan issues. In fact, a number of antiglobalist communitarian thinkers have voiced suspicions about the viability of any internationalist perspective, thereby making it easier for representatives of the right to find recruits in the communitarian camp. Moreover, social-communitarian agendas often relate only obliquely to the deeper political problems or do not address in sufficient detail how people at the grass-roots level are to tackle the concrete political and economic obstacles encountered while transforming neoliberal institutional arrangements.[75]

Finally, many grass-roots organizations lack the financial means to sustain their efforts. Perpetually exposed to the tremendous power differential between themselves and the forces of globalism, a number of antiglobalist NGOs let themselves be captured by elite interests and serve as their agents. The temptation to accept funding from neoliberal sources is often great, because support is greatly needed and the attached strings are not readily apparent. For example, World Bank president James Wolfensohn emphasizes that his institution has made great efforts to "give NGOs a seat at the table." Today, over 70 NGO policy specialists work in the Bank's offices worldwide, and half of the Bank's projects have some direct NGO involvement.[76] Indeed, the nongovernmental status of social organizations does not guarantee that they will work for social justice and greater equality.

All major international advocacy networks of the left started out as small, seemingly insignificant groups of like-minded people. Many of them learned important theoretical and practical lessons from antiglobalization struggles in developing countries, particularly from Mexico's Zapatista rebellion. On January 1, 1994, the day NAFTA went into effect, a small band of indigenous rebels calling themselves the Zapatista Army of National Liberation (EZLN) captured four cities in the Chiapas region of Southeast Mexico. Engaging in a number of skirmishes with the Mexican army and police over the next few years, the Zapatistas continued to protest the implementation of NAFTA and what their leader Subcomandante Marcos called the "global economic process to eliminate that multitude of people who are not useful to the powerful." In addition, the EZLN leadership put forward a comprehensive antiglobalist program that pledged to reverse the destructive consequences of neoliberal free-market policies. Although the Zapatistas insisted that a major part of their struggle related to the restoration of the political and economic rights of indigenous peoples and the poor in Mexico, they also emphasized that the fight against neoliberalism had to be waged globally.

Cognizant of the importance of forging lasting transnational linkages to sympathetic global NGOs, as well as to similar protest movements in the South, the EZLN organized in August 1996 the "Intercontinental Gathering for Humanity and Against Neoliberalism." This international conference attracted more than 5,000 delegates and, most importantly, involved 600 press representatives who carried Subcomandante Marcos's antiglobalist message to their respective audiences all over the world:

We declare: First. That we will make a collective network of all our particular struggles and resistances. An intercontinental network of resistance against neoliberalism, and intercontinental network of resistance for humanity. This intercontinental network of resistance, recognizing differences and acknowledging similarities, will search to find itself with other resistances around the world. This intercontinental network of resistance will be the medium in which distinct resistances may support one another. This intercontinental network of resistance is not an organizing structure; it doesn't have a central head or decision-maker; it has no central command or hierarchies. We are the network, all of us who resist.[77]

Marcos's constructive project of resistance to neoliberalism assigns to intellectuals the special role of public educators to tirelessly debunk the political interests behind the claims of globalism: "Progressive thinkers must start to use ideas as weapons in the battle against the big-business-backed dogma that 'the globalization economy is inevitable.' . . . The problem is not why the global economy is inevitable, but why almost everyone agrees that it is." The Zapatista leader accuses neoliberal intellectuals of solidifying the hegemonic position of globalism. In his view, they have failed to live up to their moral responsibility of criticizing global inequality and social injustice. In exchange for "a place in the sun and the support of certain media and governments," these intellectuals "cast off their critical imagination and any form of self-criticism and espouse the new, free-market creed." Instead of presenting the public with a critical perspective on globalism, neoliberal intellectuals have "become remarkably pragmatic, echoing the advertising slogans that flood the world's markets."[78]

Marcos's message not only influenced many members of antiglobalist NGOs, but also resonated with a number of left-wing political leaders in the global South who are reluctant to embrace globalism as a development philosophy. For example, Jean-Bertrand Aristide has referred to the Zapatista struggle against neoliberalism and racism in his public speeches. During his first tenure as president of Haiti, Aristide noted that the neoliberal policies of structural adjustment had failed to benefit the masses in his country. In a recent book, he offers many examples of globalist measures that led to the collapse of his nation's agricultural economy. In all cases, he blames large corporations and neoliberal institutions such as the IMF and the World Bank for putting commercial interests over human values: "The neoliberal strategy is to weaken the state in order to have the private sector replace the state."[79] Before he was reelected as president of Haiti in November 2000 with almost 92 percent of the vote, Aristide set up the Aristide Foundation for Democracy—his personal attempt to contribute to the process of globalization from below.

Conclusion

The strategy of antiglobalist challengers on both the right and left is to challenge globalism with an attractive counterhegemonic discourse that would motivate people to end their expressed or tacit support of the dominant globalization regime. Throughout much of the 1990s, it seemed as though such antiglobalist efforts were no match for the dominant neoliberal paradigm. However, in the last few years, globalization from below scored a number of symbolic victories, some of them significant enough to alarm even the Washington Consensus. The massive anti-WTO protests in Seattle in December 1999 represent an important milestone in the emerging ideological struggle of the new century. Even mainstream newspapers acknowledged that globalism had come under sustained attack by well-organized opponents:

> The surprisingly large protests in Seattle by critics of the World Trade Organization point to the emergence of a new and vocal coalition . . . [that included] not just steelworkers and auto workers, but antisweat-shop protesters from colleges across the nation and members of church groups, consumer groups, the Sierra Club, Friends of the Earth, and the Humane Society.[80]

After an examination of several mass demonstrations against corporate globalization, the following chapter analyzes a variety of globalist responses to these events. A careful consideration of these recent developments is indispensible for my concluding speculation on possible future trajectories of the ideological confrontation between globalism and its challengers.

THE "BATTLE OF SEATTLE" AND ITS AFTERMATH

IN THE FIRST CHAPTER OF THIS STUDY, I suggested that ideologies represent systems of ideas, values, and beliefs that make simplified claims about social reality. Putting before the public a specific agenda of things to discuss, various groups in society seek to advance their particular interests. I also emphasized that ideology should not be reduced to a nebulous construct floating in thin air above more material political or economic processes. Ideals, power interests, and physical entities all converge in concrete social practices that are both "mental" and "material." In our age, this interdependent matrix of social activity has assumed the form of globalism. As the dominant ideology of our time, globalism has chiseled into the minds of many people around the world a particular understanding of globalization, which, in turn, is sustained and reconfirmed by the reigning institutional framework of neoliberalism.

Still, no single social formation ever enjoys absolute dominance. Even the strongest ideological edifice contains small fissures that threaten to turn into dangerous cracks when a recalcitrant social environment refuses to behave according to the dominant ideological claims and pronouncements. Growing gaps between claim and experience may usher in a long-term crisis for the hegemonic paradigm. At the same time, this crisis also represents a golden opportunity for social groups that propagate new ideas, beliefs, practices, and institutions.

As the 1990s were drawing to a close, antiglobalist arguments began to receive more play in the public discourse on globalization, perhaps aided by a heightened awareness of how extreme corporate-profit strategies were leading to widening global disparities in wealth and well-being. But it was not until the final years of the waning century that the simmering contest between globalism and its ideological challengers erupted in open street confrontations during the WTO's Third Ministerial Conference, held between November 30 and December 3, 1999. Growing to maturity in the tear-gas-shrouded streets of Seattle, a new type of political activism inspired another wave of demonstrations in major cities around the world. From Seattle and Prague to Chiang Mai and Melbourne, antiglobalist protesters were accumulating valuable practical experience.

The "Battle of Seattle"

It is important to note that the "Battle of Seattle" did not start the antiglobalist protest movement. As Canadian activist Naomi Klein observes, Seattle was really about American groups joining an international movement that had been growing for at least a decade.[1] As was pointed out in the previous chapter, antiglobalist organizations on the political left and right had been drawing increased media attention throughout the 1990s. A clear indication of an impending, large-scale confrontation between globalism and its opponents came on June 18, 1999, when various labor, human rights, and environmental groups organized international protests known as "J18" to coincide with the G8 Economic Summit in Cologne, Germany. Financial districts of cities in North America and Europe were subjected to well-orchestrated direct actions that included large street demonstrations, as well as to more than 10,000 "cyber-attacks" perpetrated by sophisticated hackers against the computer systems of large corporations. In London, a march of 2,000 protesters turned violent, causing dozens of injuries and significant property damage.

Six months later, 40,000 to 50,000 people took part in the anti-WTO protests in Seattle. In spite of the predominance of North American participants, there was also a significant international presence. In fact, the transnational character of the Seattle demonstrations was a central feature that distinguished it from other mass protests in the recent past. Activists such as José Bové, a French sheep farmer who became an international celebrity for thrashing a McDonald's outlet, marched shoulder-to-shoulder with Indian farmers and leaders of the Philippines peasant movement. Clearly articulating internationalist-egalitarian concerns, this eclectic alliance of antiglobalists included consumer activists, labor activists (including students demonstrating against sweatshops), environmentalists, animal-rights activists, advocates of Third World debt relief, feminists, and human-rights proponents. Especially criticizing the WTO's neoliberal position on agriculture, multilateral investments, and intellectual-property rights, this impressive crowd represented more than 700 organizations and groups, including organizations such as Direct Action Network, The Ruckus Society, IFG, GEX, and the Rainforest Action Network.

Alongside the political left, however, there also marched a number of people who championed the nationalist perspective of the radical right. For example, Pat Buchanan called on his supporters to join his protectionist cause against the WTO. He appealed particularly to labor unionists to "put America first" and take part in the demonstrations.[2] Similarly, hard-edged soldiers of neofascism such as Illinois-based "World Church of the Creator" founder Matt Hale encouraged their followers to come to Seattle and "throw a monkey wrench into the gears of the enemy's machine." The dangerous neo-Nazi group "National Alliance" was represented as well. White supremacist leader Louis Beam praised the demonstrators, emphasizing that the "police state goons" in Seattle were paid by international capital to protect "the slimy corporate interests of 'free trade' at the expense of free people." In the sea of signs bearing leftist slogans there were occasional posters bitterly denouncing the "Jewish Media Plus Big Capital" and the "New World Order."[3] Nonetheless, it is safe to say that the vast majority of the demonstrators who gathered in Seattle advanced left–progressive criticisms of free-market capitalism and corporate globalization. Their main message was that the WTO had gone too far in setting global rules that supported corporate interests at the expense of developing countries, the poor, the environment, workers, and consumers.[4] The "Battle of Seattle" received extensive news coverage, ultimately making headlines in both the United States and abroad. For the purposes of this study, it suffices to provide a brief summary of the unfolding events.[5]

Most commentators agree that both the WTO and Washington State officials severely underestimated both the quantitative strength and organizational skill of the protesters. On the opening day of the WTO meeting, large groups of demonstrators interrupted traffic in the city center and managed to block off the major entrances to the convention center by forming human chains. Many demonstrators had been trained in nonviolent methods of resistance and acted in accordance with a nonviolent strategy that called for blocking key intersections and entrances in order to shut the WTO meeting down before it even started. As delegates were scrambling to make their way to the conference center, Seattle police stepped up their efforts to clear the streets. Equipped with gas masks, commando boots, leg guards, combat harnesses, disposable plastic cuffs, slash-resistant gloves, riot batons, rubber-bullet stingers, tear-gas grenades, ballistic helmets, and body armor, the city's police force was indeed a frightening sight to behold. Soon it launched tear-gas cans into the crowds—even into throngs of people who were peacefully sitting on streets and pavements. Next, the force fired rubber bullets at some protesters. Having failed to accomplish its goal by early afternoon, the Seattle police force began to use batons and pepper-spray stingers against the remaining demonstrators.

To be sure, there were perhaps 200 individuals who, having declined to pledge themselves to nonviolent direct action, delighted in smashing storefronts and turning over garbage cans. Most of these youthful protesters belonged to the anarchist Black Bloc, an Oregon-based political organization ideologically opposed to free-market capitalism and the centralized state power of modern nation-states. Wearing dark hoods and black jackboots, the spokespersons of the Black Bloc would later defend their actions by emphasizing that they were not senseless vandals but political resisters acting according to a strategic plan worked out in advance. They insisted that anarchist youths had been instructed to move only against corporations that had been identified as engaging in extremely callous business practices. For example, they spared a Charles Schwab outlet, but smashed the windows of Fidelity Investments for maintaining high stakes in Occidental

Petroleum, the oil company most responsible for violence against indigenous people in Colombia. They moved against Starbucks because of the company's nonsupport of fair-traded coffee, but not against Tully's. They stayed away from REI stores, but inflicted damage on GAP outlets because of the company's heavy reliance on sweatshops in Asia.[6]

By late afternoon, Seattle mayor Paul Shell declared a civic emergency in the city. Only one step away from martial law, this measure allowed Seattle's police chief to impose a rigid 7:00 P.M. to 7:00 A.M. curfew and create generous "no protest zones" that included a 25-square-block area in downtown. The closure appeared to be in stark violation of the 1996 U.S. Court of Appeals (9th Circuit) decision in the case of *Collins v. Jordan*, which compels municipal governments to permit protests close enough so that they can be heard and seen by the intended audience. In addition, there were some indications that the U.S. Army's Delta Force was present in Seattle. If this observation were true, it would mean that the Clinton administration violated the Posse Comitatus Act of 1887, forbidding the U.S. military any role in domestic law enforcement.[7]

When it became clear that many demonstrators refused to obey these emergency orders, police actions became even more extreme. Some police officers resorted to using their thumbs to grind pepper spray into the eyes of their victims and kicking nonviolent protesters in the groin. Moreover, there were more than 300 reports of beatings and other acts of brutality against protesters inside Seattle's jails.[8] In the early morning hours of December 1st, the last remaining demonstrators were finally forced to vacate the city center. However, by the next morning, several thousand had regrouped in the Capitol Hill area, ready to march to the conference center. But National Guard units and police armed with AR-15 assault rifles made clear that they were no longer limiting themselves to rubber bullets. A police officer told a demonstrator that, this time, they should expect the "real thing."[9] Not only did the police prevent protesters from entering the restricted areas, they also arrested people outside these spaces for such "incendiary" actions as handing out anti-WTO leaflets. Altogether, the police arrested over 600 persons. Significantly, the charges against over 500 of them were eventually dismissed. Only fourteen cases actually went to trial, ultimately yielding ten plea bargains, two acquittals, and only two guilty verdicts.[10]

Negotiations inside the conference center did not proceed smoothly either. Struggling to overcome the handicap of a late start, the WTO delegates soon deadlocked over such important issues as international labor and environmental standards. Many delegates of developing countries refused to support an agenda that had been drafted behind closed doors by the major economic powers. Caught between two rebellions, one inside and one outside the conference center, the Clinton administration sought to put a positive spin on the events. Downplaying the street demonstrations as "a rather interesting hoopla," the president agreed to meet with opposition leaders from moderate labor unions and environmental organizations.[11] While emphasizing the "obvious benefits of free trade and globalization," Clinton nonetheless admitted that the WTO needed to implement "some internal reforms." In the end, the Seattle meeting ended without the traditional joint communiqué. In her improvised closing remarks, U.S. Trade Representative Charlene Barshefsky conceded that "we found that the WTO has outgrown the processes appropriate to an earlier time. . . . We needed a process which had a greater degree of internal transparency and inclusion to accommodate a larger and more diverse membership."[12]

Ironically, the "Battle of Seattle" showed that many of the new technologies hailed by globalists as the true hallmark of globalization could also be employed in the service of antiglobalist forces and their political agenda. For example, the Internet has enabled the organizers of events such as Seattle to arrange for new forms of protest such as a series of demonstrations held in concert in various cities around the globe. Individuals and groups all over the world can utilize the Internet to readily and rapidly recruit new members, establish dates, share experiences, arrange logistics, identify and publicize targets—activities that only fifteen years ago would have demanded much more time and money. Other new technologies such as cell phones allow demonstrators not only to maintain close contact throughout an event, but also to react quickly and effectively to shifting police tactics. This enhanced ability to arrange and coordinate protests without the need of a central command, a clearly defined leadership, a large bureaucracy, and significant financial resources has added an entirely new dimension to the nature of street demonstrations. Moreover, cheap and easy access to global information raises the protesters' level of knowledge and sophistication. Antiglobalist teach-ins and street-theater performances, organized by various groups via the Internet, have been particularly successful in recruiting college students for international antisweatshop campaigns. Organizations such as the California-based Ruckus Society used the video capacities of the World Wide Web to train potential Seattle protesters in the complex techniques of nonviolent direct action.

Finally, the "Battle of Seattle" also vindicated the old vision of forging nonhierarchical alliances among progressive groups—even among those who share a rather antagonistic history. Perhaps the best example of this new spirit of coalition-building on the left is the willingness of labor unions and environmental groups to advance a common antiglobalist agenda. There were many signs of this new cooperation in Seattle. For example, when a longshoreman from Tacoma hoisted up a banner that read "Teamsters and Turtles Together at Last," marching environmentalists enthusiastically responded with their own chant, "Turtles Love Teamsters." Likewise, the Alliance for Sustainable Jobs and the Environment—a coalition of environmental activists and steelworkers—made its presence felt in the streets of Seattle.[13] Although there remains a strong presence of protectionist voices in organized labor, it also appears that a number of American and European union leaders have learned the crucial lesson of Seattle: The best way of challenging the established framework of globalism is to build a broad international support network that includes workers, environmentalists, consumer advocates, and human-rights activists. As the representatives of this new alliance insist, any trade system of the future must be anchored in fair international rules supportive of extensive labor rights, environmental protections, and human rights.[14]

The Specter of Seattle Stalks the World: More Antiglobalist Protests

In the months following the events in Seattle, several large-scale demonstrations against neoliberal globalization took place in rapid succession all over the world. In February 2000, the annual meeting of the World Economic Forum (WEF) in the Swiss ski resort of Davos was targeted by thousands of protesters denouncing the globalist vision and neoliberal policies advocated by most delegates. After transforming itself from a body concerned with bland management issues into a dynamic political forum in the late 1980s, the WEF managed to attract to its annual meeting hundreds of the world's most powerful business executives and senior policymakers. The WEF also generates dozens of publications, including a yearly index that measures the economic competitiveness of all the world's countries. The annual conference in Davos provides unparalleled opportunities for global corporate elites and politicians (including dozens of heads of state and government) to streamline social and economic policies. Employing strategies similar to the participants in the "Battle of Seattle," anti-WEF protesters clashed with police forces in the streets of the small Swiss alpine village. Surprised by the size and organizational strength of the demonstrations, Swiss security forces struggled for several days to disperse the crowds. The disturbing images of these fierce street battles featured prominently in national and international news reports, attesting to the considerable extent of the existing backlash against globalism.

In mid-April 2000, between 15,000 and 30,000 antiglobalist activists from around the world attempted to shut down the semiannual meetings of the IMF and the World Bank in Washington, D.C. Planning to march into the heart of the city and protest the neoliberal policies imposed by these institutions on developing countries, the demonstrators found the entire downtown area blocked off. Forced into the northwest part of town, they attempted several times to break through the menacing phalanx of thousands of police and National Guard troops. The demonstrators' efforts to get closer to the conference center were greeted by clouds of tear gas and pepper spray. Several protesters were injured by club-wielding police officers. No doubt, District of Columbia authorities had paid close attention to the events in Seattle. As Police Chief Charles Ramsey put it, his force was "fully prepared" and "ready to defend the city." In fact, his strategic decision to shut down the city in order to guard the meetings more effectively was backed up by significant monetary commitments. In anticipation of the demonstrations, Ramsey had requested and received millions of dollars for overtime pay and new riot equipment.[15]

Police officers politely ushered conference delegates to waiting buses and escorted them to their meetings. At the same time, they shut down the protesters' headquarters, declaring that it was a "fire hazard." Overall, the police arrested about 1,200 protesters on a variety of charges, including "parading without a permit" and "obstructing traffic." After two days of clashes, the police finally claimed victory. "We didn't lose the city," Chief Ramsey announced proudly to throngs of journalists. Mayor Anthony A. Williams insisted that the police had acted with "appropriate force" and that the mass arrests of peaceful protesters the night before were justified as a "matter of prudence."[16] Dutifully, most of the next day's morning papers reported that city officials had "done their job" and demonstrators had "failed" in their goals. Unfazed, the remaining protesters staged a victory party in the streets, celebrating the meteoric rise of their antiglobalist movement. After all, the impressive images and sounds of their "failure" in the District of Columbia had been broadcast worldwide, leaving millions of viewers and listeners with the distinct impression that the "Battle of Seattle" had not been an isolated event.

After similar protests against both the Asian Development Bank in Chiang Mai, Thailand, and the Asia-Pacific Summit of the WEF in Melbourne, the struggle against globalism shifted in the autumn of 2000 to Prague. The capital of the Czech Republic had been chosen as the site for the annual meeting of the IMF and the World Bank. Many antiglobalist organizations encouraged their sympathizers to travel to Prague in order to participate in a series of demonstrations against the neoliberal policies devised by these Bretton Woods institutions. Although Czech border authorities denied entry to many would-be protesters with arrest records from previous antiglobalist rallies, over 10,000 demonstrators, most of them Europeans, managed to make their way to the Czech capital. "This is our Seattle," a young German union activist told a television reporter; "Seattle was the most amazing thing I have ever seen—people uniting to shut down a global institution."[17]

Having prepared for this occasion for weeks, an astonishing number of Czech police officers—11,000, along with advisers from the FBI and Britain's Special Branch were armed with pistols, attack dogs, and water cannons. Indeed, the police force outnumbered the demonstrators. In addition to guarding the 31 hotels occupied by delegates, the task of the Czech police was to keep protesters from reaching the Congress Center, where most of the weeklong sessions were held. Large areas of the city were closed to traffic, and most urban shopkeepers closed early. Authorities advised citizens to stock up on food and then bolt their doors and stay inside. Indeed, the U.S. State Department even warned Americans to avoid "unnecessary" travel to the

Czech capital for the week of the meetings.[18] Although almost all of the 200 planned protests were organized as avowedly peaceful events, the chief security coordinator for the Czech police emphasized the presence of potentially violent groups such as the neofascist skinheads and the radical anarchists. In order to justify the size of the security operation, he claimed that as many as 20 percent of the demonstrators could be aggressive. "The foreigners are the worst," he added. "We're afraid they're teaching the Czechs their violent methods."[19]

On September 26, 2000, street demonstrations turned violent after some protesters had been injured in confrontations with the police. Some groups pelted police with a hail of bottles and stones, while others deluged them with Molotov cocktails. In response, police in armored personnel carriers raced into position to close off the streets, showering the demonstrators with more tear gas, water canons, and stun grenades. Soon, the narrow cobblestone streets of Prague's Old Town were flooded and the air was filled with dense clouds of smoke. Most marchers, however, refused to abandon their commitment to nonviolence, instead hurling at attacking police officers antiglobalist slogans such as "Stop the economic terror now," and "Our world is not for sale." As a result of the fierce street battles, the convention was ended a day before its scheduled conclusion. Over 100 people, half of them police officers, had been injured, and 420 protesters had been arrested.[20]

Although Prague protest organizers distanced themselves from extremist groups, they conceded that acts of violence and destruction were detracting from the political message of the internationalist-egalitarian left. While blaming the media for focusing excessively on fringe-group activities, many antiglobalists were beginning to realize that their demonstrations were providing cover for groups that championed entirely different causes. This usurpation of the antiglobalist agenda by extremist groups was particularly apparent during the European Union Summit in December 2000. Hundreds of Basque separatists, French anti-immigration groups, and Italian communists mingled with antiglobalist demonstrators to battle police in the streets of Nice, France. Attacking banks, looting shops, and wrecking cars, these groups rampaged through the famous Riviera resort without showing much concern for a constructive solution to the problem of global inequality.[21]

At the same time, however, the "Battle of Seattle" and the subsequent series of antiglobalist demonstrations had also served as a convenient excuse to radicalize police forces all over the world. The increasing brutality and arbitrariness of police actions became especially evident at the January 2001 WEF meeting in Davos. Determined to prevent a repetition of the "embarrassing events" of the year before, Swiss authorities pledged to keep protesters out of the alpine village. In what has been described as the country's largest security operation since World War II, Swiss border units refused entry to thousands of people—often merely on the suspicion that these individuals might be participating in anti-WEF demonstrations. Police and military units set up dozens of roadblocks on all streets leading to Davos. They halted all train services to the town, and placed thousands of police and military troops on alert.[22]

Notwithstanding these drastic measures, demonstrators and police *did* finally confront each other in Davos and Zurich. These street battles led to dozens of injuries and hundreds of arrests. At times, Swiss police even arrested demonstrators merely for handing out anti-WEF leaflets, singing protest songs, or dressing up in "fat cat" costumes with conference-style identification cards around their necks reading "Frank Suisse," "Dave Dollar," and "Mark Deutsch."[23] As in Seattle, a significant part of the Swiss protests was performative, featuring puppets, colorful costumes, and even some giant kites and paper sculptures.

The harsh treatment of peaceful protesters received intense criticism from within Switzerland and abroad. The Swiss Social Democratic Party publicly accused authorities of violating the demonstrators' right to free speech as well as encroaching on other "basic principles of democracy." Swiss newspapers denounced the police for using "methods just like a dictatorship."[24] But in the aftermath of Seattle, such disproportionate official responses to antiglobalist demonstrations had become a common occurrence. This raises the discomforting possibility that an escalating ideological struggle over the meaning and direction of globalization could encourage the further extension of existing police powers as well as the militarization of the police force. If democratic governments continue to accept this new role of serving the globalist agenda by suppressing or isolating large demonstrations, a new wave of authoritarianism may just be around the corner.

Globalist Responses

Reacting with increased levels of repression toward largely nonviolent antiglobalist protesters proved to be a common response among governments that faced mass demonstrations in the months following the "Battle of Seattle." One must keep in mind, however, that relying on overwhelming physical intimidation represents only one among a variety of options available to globalist forces. Indeed, as Antonio Gramsci has pointed out, the maintenance of social control by means of open coercion is the path least favored by ruling elites, for it makes visible to the public a serious loss of legitimacy on the part of the hegemonic ideology. As political theorist Hannah Arendt aptly put it, "violence appears where power is in jeopardy."[25] As the crisis of the dominant ideology deepens, its spokespersons must seek to regain the active consent of subordinate groups in society—without risking the further destabilizing of the situation through the excessive use of force. Yet it is precisely in times of mounting ideological challenges that the use of force against counterideological social movements is most required.

Caught on the horns of this dilemma, the representatives of the dominant worldview often struggle to find a more moderate defense of their position. Typically, their willingness to deploy large numbers of police is balanced by the launching of multipronged public-relations campaigns in the media that showcase new or revised ideological claims. This media blitz is designed to prop up crumbling forms of popular consent and continue the old logic of social domination. The standardized set of globalist responses to Seattle and its aftermath attests to the importance of the existing commercial-media system for the globalist project. This is not to say that the media were entirely uncritical of globalism or showed themselves to be entirely partisan on the subject. After all, as Robert McChesney points out, the genius of the commercial-media system is the general lack of overt censorship.[26] Lacking any necessarily conspiratorial intent and acting on their own bottom-line interest, the mainstream media in the United States nonetheless disseminated remarkably similar stories about the nature and meaning of the events in Seattle.

This homogenization of news reports about antiglobalist protests makes sense in the context of the "new economy." Given that news is less than half as profitable as entertainment, media firms are increasingly tempted to pursue higher profits by ignoring journalism's much-vaunted separation of newsroom practices and business decisions. Partnerships and alliances between news and entertainment companies are fast becoming the norm, making it more common for publishing executives to press journalists to cooperate with their newspapers' business operations. The attack on the professional autonomy of journalism is, therefore, part of the neoliberal transformation of media and communication.[27]

A number of communication scholars have pointed out that a small group of very large TNCs dominate global markets for entertainment, news, television, and cinema. In 1999, for example, just 12 media corporations accounted for more than half of the $250 billion in yearly worldwide revenues generated by the communications industry.[28] In the first half of 2000, the volume of merger deals in global media, Internet, and telecommunications totaled $300 billion, triple the figure for the first six months of 1999, and exponentially higher than the figure from ten years earlier.[29]

Such astounding figures highlight the growing power of what Benjamin Barber calls the global "infotainment telesector" directed by the likes of AOL-Time Warner, Disney, Sony, Viacom, Vivendi, Bertelsmann, and the News Corporation. None of these giant companies existed in their present form as media companies as recently as fifteen years ago. In 2001, nearly all of them rank among the largest 300 nonfinancial firms in the world. These transnational media enterprises imbue global cultural reality with consumerist values as their ubiquitous advertisements and television images shape people's self-images and structure of wants. For example, a few companies control 85 percent of the global music market. Christopher Dixon, media analyst for the investment firm Paine Webber, concedes that the recent emergence of a global commercial-media market amounts to the "creation of a global oligopoly. It happened to the oil and automotive industries earlier this century; now it is happening to the entertainment industry."[30]

In his careful study of 57 reports and editorials on the Seattle protests published in the *Los Angeles Times* and the *New York Times*, Rutgers University journalism professor William Solomon found that these articles generally convey a neoliberal perspective. Solomon's fine analysis suggests that the corporate media imposed on the events and participants of Seattle a set of "standardized assumptions" supportive of the reigning globalist paradigm.[31]

One of these standardized globalist narratives consisted of showering the demonstrators with scorn and ridicule. For example, during the protests in Seattle, ABC News anchor Peter Jennings commented that "it seems as though every group with every complaint from every corner of the world is represented in Seattle." Similar statements appeared in the major newspapers and magazines. *U.S. News* dismissed the protesters as "causists and all-purpose agitators," and the *Philadelphia Inquirer* referred to them as "the terminally aggrieved" with "a stew of grievances so confusing that they drowned any hope of broad public support."[32] Editorials in the *Economist* described the protesters as a "travelling circus" and a "rag-tag mob." The *Chicago Tribune* editors asserted that the main activity of the demonstrators was to "run around in Seattle and scream: Down with prosperity! . . . Their message, like the weather in Seattle, is all wet."[33] In his *New York Times* column of December 1, 1999, Thomas Friedman went even further, calling the Seattle demonstrators "a Noah's ark of flat-earth advocates, protectionist trade unions and yuppies looking for the 1960s fix" who had been duped by "knaves like Pat Buchanan."

The main purpose of denigrating the protesters was to convey to millions of viewers and readers that the demonstrators could be dismissed as a meaningless movement of malcontents whose antiglobalist views were extreme, even outright dangerous. After all, if the suggested marginality and "kookiness" of the protesters were repeated often enough, large segments of the public would be less likely to critically engage the basic claims and assumptions of globalism. But the attempts of globalists to construct marginal identities for the protesters were much broader than the idea that they were just plain "crazy." They included suggestions that people who expressed their concern for the lack of accountability and transparency of global economic institutions were "naïve New Agers," "cultists," "pseudo-idealists," "bleeding-heart liberals," "mouthpieces of special-interest groups," and "lawless environmentalists."[34]

Unsurprisingly, the advocates of globalism delighted in conjuring up the specter of "communism" by associating their opponents with the "failed Marxist ideology" of a bygone era. It seemed that beating up on the corpse of the Soviet Union represented a favorite globalist strategy for avoiding or detracting from more substantive and issue-oriented globalization debates. For example, former Wyoming senator Malcolm Wallop ended his article on the subject in *Investor's Business Daily* on the following note: "It's necessary to look at the endgame of these [antiglobalist] groups—a utopian, pollution-free, socialist world—and decide whether to fight for your business or let the radicals destroy it, issue by issue."[35]

Another standard response to the antiglobalist demonstrations offered by neoliberal market ideologists consisted of turning up the volume on the five globalist claims for the alleged purpose of educating the public (including the ignorant demonstrators) about the "real" meaning and consequences of globalization. As Richard McCormick, president of the International Chamber of Commerce, emphasized: "It's time for business to move the debate away from the cheap sloganeering and mindless vandalism of the protesters in the streets and stand up and proclaim the benefits of globalization."[36] Caio Koch-Weser, Germany's deputy finance minister, agreed with this assessment: "If we do not succeed in making clear to citizens that globalization is to their benefit, we run a big political risk. . . . People are afraid of losing jobs to the whims of multinationals. We need to bring Wall Street to Main Street."[37]

Bringing Wall Street to the people meant enhancing the visibility of globalist claims in the public discourse. In the months following Seattle, globalist forces in the United States stepped up their efforts to mobilize more people behind a neoliberal agenda. For example, a number of business executives led by Cargill Inc. CEO Warren Staley pledged additional funds for already-existing proglobalization education programs for employees, politicians, and fellow executives. Policy analysts at the conservative Cato Institute's Trade Center announced new initiatives to "educate the public about the economic and moral benefits of free trade, and conversely, the costs of protectionism." Federal Reserve Board Chairman Alan Greenspan joined the chorus, arguing that "we should not hesitate to remind our fellow citizens of the manifest net benefits of free trade in goods, services, and assets, benefits that accrue not only to all trading partners on average but also especially to some of the least fortunate within those trading societies." Carl Ware, Coca-Cola's executive vice president of public affairs, noted that the greatest challenges for the international business community following the "debacle in Seattle" was to demonstrate to the entire world that transnational corporations such as Coca-Cola played an important role as "an engine for growth and development."[38]

A third globalist response to Seattle and its aftermath was to admit to the validity of "some concerns" raised by the protesters and promise modest reforms that would put a "human face" on globalization. As President Bill Clinton repeatedly put it during the last days of his administration, some of the problems identified by the protesters ought to be addressed by "a very serious attempt to put a human face on the global economy and to direct the process of globalization in a way that benefits all people."[39] While insisting that "globalization is a fact of life," U.N. Secretary-General Kofi Annan nonetheless warned global business leaders and politicians at the 2001 WEF conference in Davos that globalization had to be made to work for all, otherwise it would end up working for none. He asserted that people do not wish to reverse globalization, but that they *do* aspire to a different and better kind than we have today. "The unequal distribution of benefits, and the imbalances in global rule-making," Annan emphasized, "inevitably will produce backlash and protectionism. And that, in turn, threatens to undermine and ultimately to unravel the open world economy that has been so painstakingly constructed over the course of the past half-century."[40] The secretary-general also announced that he would seek to strengthen "Global Compact," a recent U.N. program designed to persuade transnational corporations to endorse a binding set of human rights, environmental, and labor principles, and to allow private groups to monitor their compliance. So far, almost 50 companies have signed up, pledging their allegiance to the vision of globalization with a human face—as long as it remained anchored in "sound market principles."

Surprised by the strength of the antiglobalist protests, several prominent business leaders openly conceded the need for a comprehensive reassessment of their previous approach. In an issue devoted to the topic of global reforms, neoliberal journalists speculated whether the backlash against globalization had marked the end of its "naïve, euphoric beginning" and the "start of a more complex stage in its evolution."[41] While reaffirming the overall desirability of global capitalism, some globalist voices even admitted that "market liberalization by itself does not lift all boats, and in some cases, it has caused severe damage to poor nations. What's more, there's no point denying that multinationals have contributed to labor, environmental, and human-rights abuses as they pursue profit around the globe."[42] This is not to say that all globalists have suddenly embraced a mildly reformist model. The prominent Columbia University political economist Jagdish Bhagwati best expresses the reluctance on the part of many neoliberals when he asserts that reformers have given in too easily to antiglobalist demands. There is no need for reforms, Bhagwati emphasizes, since "globalization already has a human face."[43]

Journalist Friedman argues for a middle position on the issue of reform. Although he affirms the continued validity of the central globalist claims, he nonetheless considers himself an "integrationist social-safety-netter"—that is, a pragmatic adherent to "a politics and ethics of sustainable globalization." He explicitly praises the contribution of "Thatcherites" and "Reaganites" in preparing the world for the "current era of globalization," while condemning those who remain wedded to the old "paternalism of the welfare state." Friedman proceeds to describe his own vision of "sustainable globalization" in very general terms. He pays lip service to the need for mild democratic reforms, but never deviates fundamentally from the basic ideological framework of globalism.[44] Indeed, most proposals for the reform of global institutions by the heads of the WTO and the IMF have remained equally vague and noncommittal. The final chapter of this study speculates on whether such mild reformism advanced by some globalists under the slogan "globalization with a human face" might actually amount to more than a calculated strategy of staving off further antiglobalist direct action.

Conclusion

Reflecting on the impact of Seattle and its aftermath almost two years later, it is difficult to make a conclusive assessment. Some commentators have argued that these events marked the crucial moment when antiglobalist forces finally emerged from the ideological sidelines and imprinted their claims and demands on the mainstream consciousness.[45] According to this rather optimistic interpretation, Seattle represents a milestone in the history of antiglobalist transnational social movements and their evolution toward a more egalitarian global civil society. As Luis Hernandez Navarro, editor of the radical Mexican daily *La Jornada*, put it: "[T]he ideology of neoliberal globalization has produced a new transnational political actor: The globalized. The Revolt of Seattle is an announcement that his—and her—hour has arrived."[46]

More cautious observers do not necessarily view the "Battle of Seattle" as the first stage in a global popular revolution.[47] Voicing their skepticism about the lasting significance of Seattle and similar protests, they question the ability of antiglobalist movements to develop into a well-organized global civil society capable of challenging the hegemonic neoliberal paradigm. Other commentators point to considerable philosophical differences and tactical cleavages separating various antiglobalist groups, particularly with regard to the ultimate political goal of the movement.[48] Is it to reform the existing system and its global institutions, or is it to smash them altogether? Is it to strengthen nation-states or transcend them? Is it to advocate localization and disengagement from the global economy, or is it to support a limited form of global capitalism?

I believe that we will begin to receive some answers to these questions during the next few years. Particular agendas will be strengthened as more linkages are forged by a growing number of organizations across different political and cultural zones. We are already witnessing the emergence of huge transnational networks such as the North American-based network "50 Years Is Enough" and the European-based alliance, the "Association for the Taxation of Financial Transactions for the Aid of Citizens." As the contacts among antiglobalist groups intensify they will learn from one another, perhaps developing a comprehensive global direct-action network that further challenges the legitimacy and authority of the globalist worldview.

Organizations such as the World Social Forum (WSF)—founded as the counterpart to the WEF—have already emerged as a viable foundation from which to develop such antiglobalist policy proposals as the cancellation of Third World debt and the taxation of international capital flows. The 2001 WSF summit in Porto Alegre, Brazil, was attended by about 10,000 activists and politicians who pledged to design a common platform of principles and a coherent plan of action. Most importantly, the conference participants emphasized the overriding importance of poking holes in the dominant neoliberal discourse on globalization. As long as most people accept the five central globalist claims as an accurate picture of social reality, the antiglobalist movement will remain a weak competitor relegated to the sidelines. As Bernard Cassen, a French WSF organizer and editor of *Le Monde Diplomatique*, put it: "We are here to show the world that a different world is possible."[49]

FUTURE PROSPECTS

THE STRUGGLE OVER THE MEANING AND DIRECTION of globalization that has culminated in open confrontations on the streets of major world cities belies the grand thesis of an "end of ideology" popularized by Daniel Bell and Francis Fukuyama. Indeed, the spokespersons of various anti-globalist alliances have already announced a new round of urban demonstrations against globalist institutions and neoliberal policy. As of the time of this writing, large antiglobalist protests at the April 2001 Summit of the Americas in Quebec City are underway. Similar protests are planned for the September 2001 Joint Annual General Meetings of the IMF and the World Bank in Washington, D.C. Thus it appears unlikely that serious challenges to globalism will dissipate any time soon. The series of antiglobalist protests that emerged in the last years of the twentieth century appear to mark the beginning of a structural trend that might last well into the new century. In the remainder of this study, I provide a sketch of what I consider to be the three most-likely future trajectories for the ongoing ideological confrontation between globalism and its challengers.

Globalism with a Human Face

The first of these possible future trajectories might best be character-ized as "rhetoric of reform, but business as usual." Having been con-fronted by their opponents with a rather sophisticated and effective strategy of resistance, globalist forces have been contemplating the pur-suit of a less transparent road to their ultimate objective—the creation of a single, global free market. Moreover, the five central globalist claims emerged during a time of relative prosperity in Europe and the United States; recent economic downturns and falling stock prices are beginning to lend more credence to antiglobalist criticisms of neo-liberalism. Indeed, as noted in the previous chapter, globalists have already expanded their public-relations efforts to convince the public that they will make globalization "work better for all people."

But despite their reassurances to put a "human face" on their free-market version of globalization, globalists have generally remained within the parameters of their neoliberal agenda. If implemented at all, their proposed "reforms" are likely to remain largely symbolic in char-acter. But in order to appeal to the public—especially to the increas-ingly worried middle class—globalists advertise their reformist gestures as a conciliatory attempt to engage their opponents and bridge "philo-sophical differences" on the subject. For example, in her speech to the 2000 World Bank conference, Overseas Development Council Board Member Nancy Birdsall argued that business interests ought to unite behind an agenda of moderate reform in order to nurture a "market-friendly middle class" in both developed and developing countries.[1]

In fact, there are additional signs that seem to indicate that global-ist forces are increasingly selecting this rhetoric of mild reformism as their preferred strategy. After the Seattle debacle, for example, repre-sentatives of the wealthy countries joined the WTO secretary-general in assuring audiences worldwide that they would be willing to reform the economic institution's rules and structure in the direction of greater transparency. Almost two years later, however, no concrete steps have been taken to honor these commitments. Granted, the WTO has been holding special general-council sessions to comply with the urgent requests of developing countries to review several of its questionable procedures. However, the spokespersons of the powerful governments in the global North that dominate the WTO have made it clear that they consider existing arrangements as being legally binding. In their view, procedural problems can only be addressed in the context of a new, comprehensive round of multilateral negotiations conducted according to the very rules that are being contested by many developing countries and internationalist-egalitarian organizations.

Thus it appears that the major powers welcome a new round of negotiations not because they wish to address the deplorable lack of democratic accountability and procedural fairness in globalist institutions, but to safeguard their economic interests. Even a cursory perusal of the prospective agenda for this new round of negotiations indicates that it abounds with elaborate proposals for new neoliberal agreements in such important areas as investment, government procurement, intellectual property, competition, labor, and the environment.[2] Moreover, perhaps in a calculated move to avoid large demonstrations, the WTO has decided to hold its November 2001 meeting in the city of Doha in the tiny Persian Gulf country of Qatar. The IMF and the World Bank also have announced that they will hold their 2003 summit meeting in the Persian Gulf country of Dubai. Groups opposed to the WTO will be allowed to send a total of 500 delegates to Qatar to present their views. Consequently, activists such as Kenneth Roth, executive director of Human Rights Watch, accused the WTO of hiding in a country that has no recognizable standards for the protection of civil liberties:

> Holding this meeting in Qatar would shut down any possibility of peaceful protest. The WTO can't avoid public protests by holding a meeting in a country that doesn't allow public protest. That sends the signal that it's O.K. to build the global economy on a foundation of repression—exactly the opposite of the message the WTO should be pronouncing.[3]

Designed to protect globalist business as usual, the rhetoric of reform has found ardent supporters not merely in conservative circles, but also among European social democrats and North American left-liberals. Invoking with gusto the trope of "globalization with a human face," European labor leaders have been taking a page out of former President Bill Clinton's agenda to sell their constituency on a kinder and gentler version of globalism. Prime Minister Tony Blair and Chancellor Gerhard Schröder recently issued a joint manifesto that calls for the replacement of "old social democratic dogmas" with more fashionable centrist views heralded as "The Third Way" in the United Kingdom and "*Die Neue Mitte*" in Germany. The much-publicized document starts with the globalist claim that the liberalization and global integration of markets provides the necessary content and unalterable context of globalization. At the same time, the manifesto still contains some nostalgic references to the labor movement's "timeless values" of "solidarity" and "responsibility to others" that "will never be sacrificed" by upright social democrats. Still, only a few paragraphs later, the two political leaders celebrate the emergence of a "new entrepreneurial spirit at all levels of society" that "makes the individual and businesses fit for the knowledge-based economy of the future."[4]

In less than ten pages, Blair and Schröder present their version of globalism with a human face in calculated phrases that may please political centrists, but nevertheless fail to conceal mutually exclusive theoretical positions. For example, the manifesto emphasizes the importance of differentiating between the virtues of a "market economy" and the evils of a "market society," but it never explains the significance of this distinction. The document declares that the state should make limited efforts to "steer" economic activity, but that it should never attempt to "control" the market. It announces its support for the political agenda of trade unions, while also favoring significant corporate tax cuts. Furthermore, it seeks to convince the reader that it is not too difficult to "marry environmental responsibility with a modern market-based approach." Finally, the Blair–Schröder manifesto declares war on unemployment and poverty, while simultaneously promising to make special efforts to accommodate corporate demands for more "flexibility" on labor issues.

Convinced that socialism is dead and that the "third way" remains the last hope for some sort of "renewal of social democracy," a number of intellectuals on the political left have begun to adopt the central claims of globalism. The leading British social-thinker Anthony Giddens, for example, seems to have genuinely fallen in love with the idea that globalization with a human face will allow all sectors of society to benefit from the unleashing of market forces, while also creating a compassionate world community that cares for those who have fallen behind.[5] Giddens comes dangerously close to adopting the determinist posture of globalism by explicitly referring to Francis Fukuyama's vision of a de-ideologized world as "essentially correct." As the British social-thinker puts it: "At least for the present time, no one can see any effective alternatives to the combination of a market economy and a democratic political system—even though each of these has great deficiencies and limitations."[6]

Although remaining much less sanguine than Giddens in their assessment of the egalitarian potential of the "third way," many neo-Marxist thinkers are equally resigned to embrace some version of Fukuyama's end-of-ideology position. In the January 2000 issue of the new-look *New Left Review*, editor Perry Anderson concedes with surprising candidness that "the [radical] environment in which *NLR* took shape has all but passed away. . . . Socialism has ceased to be a widespread ideal." Thus Anderson notes with a tone of resignation:

> For the first time since the Reformation, there are no longer any significant oppositions within the thought-world of the West; . . . Whatever limitations persist to its practice, neo-liberalism as a set of principles rules undivided across the globe: the most successful ideology in world history.[7]

The "third way," the "new middle," "globalization with a human face," "compassionate conservatism," "pragmatic centrism"—all of these labels have been popularized in recent years. These terms signify the slightly altered ideological garments in which neoliberalism presents itself in the less-triumphant post-Seattle context. But one must remember that these labels have been coined by a powerful phalanx of social forces unwilling to make drastic changes to the neoliberal course of market globalization. Reluctantly stirred into defensive action by antiglobalist demonstrations, globalists permit but marginal adjustments to the dominance of market institutions over society.

Violent Backlash

The new globalist strategy of fortifying its paradigm with a new rhetoric of reform might work for years, perhaps even for decades. But without the implementation of actual social reforms on a global level, national and international disparities in wealth and well-being are likely to widen even further. As globalist policies impose conditions of inequality on billions of people around the globe, neoliberalism will eventually inflict enough damage to social relations and the environment to cause ever-more-severe societal and political reactions against globalism. The specter of such a violent backlash stands at the center of the second possible future trajectory of the struggle between globalism and its opponents. In my view, this rather bleak scenario of persistent economic crisis and chronic social instability harbors the potential to unleash reactionary social forces that dwarf even those responsible for the suffering of millions during the 1930s and 1940s.

Since the rise of industrial society in the early part of the nineteenth century, progressive commentators have been warning against the dire social consequences that might arise from liberal efforts to "free" markets from all forms of social control. Few academic works on the subject, however, have been able to achieve the clarity of analysis that pervades Karl Polanyi's *The Great Transformation* (1944). In this critical study of modern British economic history, the Hungarian–Canadian political economist locates the origins of the social catastrophe that erupted in Europe during the interwar years in the attempt of nineteenth-century British economic liberals to realize their utopia of a self-regulating market system.[8] According to Polanyi, free markets never arise in spontaneous fashion from people's "natural" tendencies to act primarily on the basis of self-interest. Rather, the modern market system represents the outcome of conscious political actions and governmental decisions. As he puts it, "while *laissez-faire* economy was the product of deliberate state action, subsequent restrictions on *laissez-faire* started in a spontaneous way. *Laissez-faire* was planned; planning was not."[9] In other words, Polanyi argues that the social countermovements against a self-regulating free market in the second half of the nineteenth century were spontaneous, undirected by opinion, and reflective of a strongly reformist spirit.

Polanyi also shows in convincing fashion how nineteenth-century efforts to liberalize markets destroyed complex social relations of mutual obligation, leaving ever-larger segments of the British population without an adequate system of social security and communal support. As a result, the "losers" in the marketization process—mostly workers and farmers—eventually organized themselves politically. They were willing to resort to radical measures to protect themselves against the market forces imposed on them by the owning and trading classes. Extending his analysis of British economic and social conditions to the workings of modern capitalism in general, Polanyi extrapolates that all modern capitalist societies contain two organizing principles that are fundamentally opposed to each other:

> The one is the principle of economic liberalism, aiming at the establishment of a self-regulating market, relying on the support of the trading classes, and using largely *laissez-faire* and free trade as its method; the other is the principle of social protection aiming at the conservation of man and nature as well as productive organizations, relying on the varying support of those most immediately affected by the deleterious actions of the market—primarily, but not exclusively, the working and the landed classes—and using protective legislation, restrictive associations, and instruments of intervention as its method.[10]

Referring to these tendencies as "double movement," Polanyi suggests that the stronger the liberal movement becomes, the more it will be able to dominate society by means of a market logic that effectively "disembeds" people's economic activity from their social relations. In other words, the principles of the free market tend to undermine communal values such as civic engagement, reciprocity, and redistribution, not to speak of human dignity and self-respect.[11] Hence, in their polished ideological formulation, the principles of economic liberalism provide a powerful justification for leaving large segments of the population to "fend for themselves." In a capitalist world organized around the notion of individual liberty understood primarily as unrestrained economic entrepreneurship, the market ideal of competition trumps old social conceptions of cooperation and solidarity.

Still, it is important to remember the other half of Polanyi's double movement: The rapid advance of free-market principles also strengthens the resolve of working people to resist the liberal paradigm and struggle against its social effects. In Europe, Polanyi asserts, antiliberal countermovements eventually gave birth to political parties that forced the passage of protective social legislation on the national level. After a prolonged period of severe economic dislocations following the end of World War I, the nationalist-protectionist impulse contained in these people's parties experienced its most extreme manifestation in Italian fascism and German National Socialism. In the end, the classical liberal dream of subordinating society's institutions to the requirements of the free market had generated an equally extreme backlash that turned markets into mere appendices of the totalitarian state.[12]

The applicability of Polanyi's analysis to our own age of globalization seems obvious. Like its nineteenth-century predecessor, today's globalism also represents an experiment in unleashing the utopia of the self-regulating market on society. This time, however, the leading Anglo-American voices of market liberalism are prepared to turn the entire world into their laboratory. So far, their work has been greatly facilitated by the existence of international social and economic institutions that protect neoliberal interests, as well as by their successful co-option of local elites in developing countries. But if Polanyi's analysis is correct, we can safely assume that the apparent rise of globalism is also an indication of the growing vitality of its ideological opposition. In that case, the antiglobalist alliances of the late 1990s would represent but an embryonic first stage in the development of countermovements. While it is difficult to predict with certainty the ultimate form and precise agenda of these new social forces, I would expect them to be much more potent than those we are seeing today. Capable of attracting millions of sympathizers who suffer from the adverse effects of globalist policies, such countermovements would most likely adopt a radical agenda. As a result, they might show a greater willingness to use violent means in order to achieve their political ends.

The potentially disastrous political and cultural consequences of such a violent struggle between globalism and its opponents have been discussed in much detail in Benjamin Barber's *Jihad vs. McWorld* and John Gray's *False Dawn*. In my view, perhaps the most frightening aspect of this violent-backlash scenario is its tremendous potential to bring together the most extreme elements of the left and right in a common movement. United in their rage against the social and environmental changes they associate with globalization, the spokespersons of this new synthesis of neofascism and anarchism would articulate a more eclectic antiglobalist ideology, most likely one that combines forms of ecological localism and nature spiritualism with elements of protectionist populism and racism. There are already some indications that early efforts are underway to build lasting antiglobalist left–right coalitions. For example, a small number of right-wing activists belonging to a growing neofascist movement known as the Third Position have used their Seattle presence to call on members of the radical left to join them in their efforts to "smash capitalism" and protect the environment.[13] Denouncing the message of intolerance emanating from such coalitions, the large Dutch antifascist group *De Fabel van de*

Illegaal ("The Myth of Illegality") decided to quit a transnational alliance of European groups opposed to the WTO. In particular, the Dutch group warned against the growing synthesis of ecological and racist doctrines popularized by antiglobalists such as Edward Goldsmith, the British owner and editor-in-chief of the prominent environmental magazine *Ecologist*.[14]

Moreover, a series of criticisms have been raised against more moderate representatives of the left and right for their willingness to cultivate strategic alliances. For example, the *New Republic* reported that antiglobalist actions in Seattle spearheaded by Ralph Nader's Public Citizen and related organizations had been partially financed by Roger Milliken, a billionaire textile magnate from South Carolina and generous patron of right-wing causes for almost 50 years.[15] Ralph Nader himself has reaffirmed his willingness to maintain his alliance with Patrick Buchanan on a number of pertinent issues, calling this strategy a "cooperation of convictions that we must defend and improve our democracy so that we can agree to disagree freely." Buchanan expressed the same sentiment:

> Ralph and I have been in this battle for almost six years since the great NAFTA fight. And we stand together firmly on one principle, that whatever the decisions about the economic destiny of Americans are, they will be made by the American people and not by the transnational corporations in collusion with this embryonic institution of world government.[16]

It is quite conceivable that conditions of increasing inequality will serve as a catalyst for the formation of additional alliances among various left and right groups, perhaps leading to the development of a joint platform and plan of action.

The possibility that the confrontation between globalism and its opponents might assume a violent trajectory has already become a reality in many parts of the world. For example, in the early part of 2001, the massive antiglobalist protest movement in Ecuador brought the small Andean country to a virtual standstill. Rural indigenous peoples organized by the Confederation of Indigenous Nations of Ecuador (CONAIE) joined forces with urban human-rights activists and environmentalists to demonstrate against IMF-imposed structural-adjustment programs carried out by the Ecuadorian government in exchange for more loans. According to the figures presented by the demonstrators, these neoliberal policies have resulted in the loss of more than 50 percent of Ecuador's budget earmarked for servicing the national debt. In addition, the IMF-imposed policies have burdened the country with the highest rate of inflation, the highest levels of corruption, the most advanced rates of deforestation and environmental degradation, and one of the worst examples of wealth inequality in South America. As of the time of this writing, the ongoing confrontations between police and protesters have led to a rising number of casualties and levels of repression not seen in Ecuador in over 20 years.[17]

In June 2000, Argentina was paralyzed by a mass strike over President Fernando de la Rua's economic-austerity policies. Several million workers joined in a one-day general strike that paralyzed the country's major cities as well as the countryside. Crowds set bonfires, blockaded bridges, and damaged hundreds of buses and taxis. Courts were forced to close down, and even hospital emergency rooms were reduced to skeletal staffing. The government reacted to the violence in the streets by arresting dozens of demonstrators, including nonviolent participants. Representing a cut of $938 million, or 2 percent of the government budget, the austerity package had been designed to meet IMF deficit guidelines and thus retain access to the Fund's $7.2 billion emergency line of credit. Unsurprisingly, the brunt of the package was to be borne by national government workers in the form of layoffs as well as cuts in salaries, pensions, and fringe benefits. "What the people want is work," pleaded Rudolfo Daer, head of the General Labor Confederation, the nation's largest union. "What the government needs to understand is that people are demanding a change in policy direction."[18]

These are but two recent examples that attest to the potential of a worldwide violent backlash against globalism. Indeed, the 1997–1998 East Asia economic crisis, the French mass strikes in the winter of 1998, and the Russian currency crisis a few months later sent economic shock waves around the globe that led to the collapse of large American and European investment funds. These events prompted George Soros—one of the entrepreneurial icons of globalism—to warn his readership against the potentially devastating effects of the "prevailing ideology of market fundamentalism." Pointing to the "inherent instability" of global markets, the billionaire investor scolded market fundamentalists for continuing to pursue their economic self-interest by means of abolishing democratic decision-making and imposing the "supremacy of market values on all political and social values."[19]

In Soros's opinion, the only way to prevent the coming of a social catastrophe of global proportions is to create a democratic global system of political decision-making with the power to create and enforce substantial reforms. Moreover, he expressed his hope that the struggle between globalism and its opponents might assume a different trajectory—one that both abandons the globalist rhetoric of reform and bypasses the doomsday scenario of a violent backlash. In short, Soros believes that the prospects for a more humane global society rest on the feasibility of constructing a global "new deal."

A Global "New Deal"

On the issue of global reform, the most prominent apostate of globalism shares common ground with the antiglobalist left. Internationalist-egalitarian voices have long demanded that the global marketplace be subjected to greater democratic accountability as reflected in stronger rules and effective global regulatory institutions. In their view, most existing international political and economic institutions require serious renovation and philosophical redirection. Indeed, many groups argue that some international organizations would have to be dismantled altogether. Internationalist-egalitarians hope that the counter-systemic pressures generated by deteriorating social conditions will force globalists to the bargaining table before the world descends into a social catastrophe beyond repair. In their view, the implementation of a significant reform agenda represents the only realistic change for reversing the steady rise of global inequality without surrendering to the parochial agenda of the nationalist-protectionist camp.

As was emphasized in the discussion of Polanyi's thesis, sustained efforts to realize a self-regulating free-market system are particularly destructive of communal networks based on values of reciprocity and redistribution. Hence, attempts to rebuild such networks of solidarity on a global scale lie at the very heart of the global "new deal" scenario. In my view, the most important element of such a grand bargain must be a sincere commitment on the part of wealthy countries to improve North–South equity with respect to global credit, global trade, and global economic decision-making. The 2000 summit of the World Social

Forum in Brazil showed that there already exists a plethora of specific initiatives to transform the current shape of globalization with regard to global governance, social and economic equality, and human rights. Concrete policy proposals include, but are not limited to, the following items:

- Blanket forgiveness of all Third World debt.
- Levying of a tax on international financial transactions.
- Abolition of offshore financial centers that offer tax havens for wealthy individuals and corporations.
- Implementation of stringent global environmental agreements.
- Implementation of a more equitable global-development agenda.
- Establishment of a new world-development institution financed largely by the global North through such measures as a financial transaction tax but administered largely by the global South.
- Establishment of international labor-protection standards, perhaps as clauses of a profoundly reformed WTO.
- Greater transparency and accountability provided to citizens by national governments and international institutions.
- Making all governance of globalization explicitly gender-sensitive.[20]

In their study *Globalization from Below*, activists Jeremy Brecher, Tim Costello, and Brendan Smith combine several such policy proposals to offer their own comprehensive blueprint for a global "new deal." Their program is centered on seven basic principles. The *first principle* calls for an upward leveling of labor, environmental, social, and human-rights conditions by forcing on corporations minimum global standards for labor and environment. The *second principle* suggests the democratization of social institutions at every level, from local to global. This includes opening the dialogue on the future of the global economy to all citizens of the world. The *third principle* demands that decision-making processes occur as close as possible to those they affect. This means that corporations should be held accountable to local, community-controlled institutions. The *fourth principle* envisions a closing of the gap between the global rich and poor. In addition to endorsing global redistribution measures, the authors want international financial institutions to cancel the remaining debts of the poorest countries. The *fifth and sixth principles* call for a strict enforcement of international environmental agreements and the creation of prosperity in accordance with human and environmental needs. The *final principle* demands a more effective system of protection against global recessions. One of the most widely cited suggestions in this regard is the establishment of the so-called "Tobin Tax" (named after its chief proponent, a Nobel–prize-winning economist) on international financial transactions, with the proceeds devoted to investment in poor countries' development efforts.[21]

The scenario of a global "new deal" that redistributes wealth to the South and subjects global markets to more effective democratic social control is, indeed, an attractive vision of globalization. There remains, however, a towering political problem: Who are the social agents capable of translating this agenda into practice? Despite their remarkable growth rates in recent years, internationalist-egalitarian alliances are still no match for the hegemonic globalist networks. Moreover, old state-centered strategies of social and economic reform have lost much of their appeal in a neoliberal context that has witnessed the curtailment of the power of nation-states to control the economic activities of the private sector. The fundamental challenge for global new dealers is to reconstruct a Keynesian system of controlled capitalism on a global scale.

Responding to this very challenge, Michel Rocard, the former social democratic prime minister of France, envisions the formation of an "alliance of progressive forces" consisting of unions, social-democratic parties, and NGOs. In his view, such an international network would be the agent of social change most capable of challenging dominant neoliberal power structures.[22] But given the willingness of most labor parties and unions to embrace the neoliberal tenets of the "third way," it is not very likely that social-democratic and left-liberal forces in their current form would endorse dramatic reforms. Indeed, under current conditions, it is hard to imagine that the movers and shakers of globalism would even condescend to sit down with their opponents at a "globalization summit" dedicated to fundamentally reshaping the existing system of political and economic power.

Given the combination of power and intransigence exhibited by globalist forces, the grand vision of a more humane global system does not seem to possess a high likelihood of being realized in the near future. Taking into account the three possible trajectories emerging from the ideological struggle between globalism and its challengers, I would expect the continuation of the current pattern. The rhetoric of "globalism with a human face" may keep the neoliberal ship afloat for some time, but it will fail to put an end to the series of antiglobalist mass protests that appeared on the world scene in 1999. The current dominance of globalism as a neoliberal system of widely shared ideas and beliefs about globalization makes it extremely difficult for dissenters to build large popular constituencies around the notion of weakening the power of market forces over society. Daunting as it may be, however, the rise of countervailing ideological visions and political strategies following the "Battle of Seattle" has proven that the construction of a more egalitarian world order is not entirely an impossible task.

Conclusion

In this book, I have argued that it is insufficient to analyze globalization as if it were simply the outcome of objective material processes that are "out there." Globalization also has important normative and ideological dimensions that are part of social and economic processes. Hence, we must understand the dynamics of our age, in part at least, as the result of intricately interacting ideas, values, and beliefs. Endowing globalization with conflicting meanings, globalists and their opponents simplify social reality and legitimate political programs, and shape personal and collective identities. For better or worse, no human being—not even an academic "observer" of the phenomenon—can remain untouched by this ideological battle, for there is no exterior vantage point that offers an objective, value-free assessment of globalization.

While the professional commitment to intellectual openness requires that scholars and educators always facilitate the expression of different perspectives, the spirit of criticism demands that they also accept the duty of ethical judgment. Thus my efforts to offer the reader a critical theory of globalization reflect not only my conviction that ideas matter in politics and economics, but also my desire to contribute to a normative project that contests the neoliberal worldview. In my view, globalism is ethically unsustainable because it routinely privileges self-interested market relations over other-regarding social relations. Market relations may indeed be necessary, but in order to serve human needs, they must be subordinated to the welfare of *all* people on this planet. The wealth of the rich ought not to be maintained through neglect of the poor. A life of political participation, dignity, and relative material security ought to be a real possibility for people on all five continents, and not only for those who enjoy the advantage of privileged birth or those who claim to "build the better mousetrap."

This study, then, ends in a plea for the reconsideration of ethics in global politics and economics. As suggested by the Dalai Lama, Pope John Paul II, Archbishop Desmond Tutu, and many other prominent spiritual leaders, the neoliberal market ideology of our age must be confronted by a global ethic that serves as the normative framework for a democratic global society.[23] The Swiss theologian Hans Küng also has formulated a global ethic that contains four commitments: to a culture of nonviolence and respect of life; to a culture of solidarity and a just economic order; to a culture of tolerance and a life of truthfulness; and to a culture of equal rights, particularly racial and gender equality.[24]

Profound social change is most likely to occur when the rise of new ideas coincides with persistent structural crises. As we have seen in the past century, such times harbor both grave dangers and great opportunities. In many ways, our era of globalization resembles the period from 1870 through 1914. Like our own time, the late nineteenth-century witnessed the flourishing of new technologies that revolutionized virtually everything, from communication to agriculture. Like ours, it was a time of corporate mergers, urban growth, and massive migration. Based on claims that justified boundless individual self-interest rooted in the "natural laws of the marketplace," Social Darwinism emerged as the prevailing narrative in the West. The exploitation of the global South reached new heights as the major imperialist powers engaged in a frantic scramble for new markets, raw materials, and national glory. The reformist movements that arose to counter this earlier form of globalism constituted a late response that altered the prevailing social dynamics only at the margins. Thus reformism failed to prevent the first war of global proportions as well as the ensuing social catastrophes of the following three decades.

Once again, we stand at a critical juncture. Lest we are willing to let global inequality climb to levels that virtually ensure a violent backlash scenario, we must embark on a profound reformist course before it is too late. For educators, one obvious step in this reformist project is to both contest and revise the script of globalism, thereby undercutting the dominance that neoliberal ideas currently enjoy. Indeed, education and the media are key in any progressive strategy that aims at contesting dominant ideas. As the Dalai Lama has noted, imparting a sense of universal responsibility on the young is especially important. Ideals constitute the engine of progress, hence it is imperative to introduce the young generation to an ethical vision for a global society.[25]

Once globalism and its corresponding neoliberal power base begin to lose their grip on the construction of meaning, alternative interpretations of globalization will circulate more freely in public discourse. As a result, more and more people will realize that there is nothing "inevitable" or "irreversible" about the liberalization of markets and the deregulation of the economy. There is nothing wrong with the term "globalization" as a signifier for current transformative social processes. However, I fervently hope that new meanings will link this central concept of our time to a progressive political tradition that seeks to give institutional expression to a more democratic and egalitarian international order.

NOTES

Chapter One

1. For the main arguments of the debate, see Lyman Tower Sargent, *Contemporary Political Ideologies: A Comparative Analysis*, 11th ed. (Fort Worth: Harcourt Brace College Publishers, 1999), 10–12; Mostafa Rejai, ed., *Decline of Ideology?* (Chicago: Aldine-Atherton, 1971); and Chaim I. Waxman, ed., *The End of Ideology Debate* (New York: Funk & Wagnalls, 1968).

2. Daniel Bell, *The End of Ideology: On the Exhaustion of Political Ideas in the Fifties* (Glencoe, IL: Free Press, 1960). See especially 13–18, 369–75.

3. Francis Fukuyama, "The End of History?" *National Interest* 16 (summer 1989):4. See also Francis Fukuyama, *The End of History and the Last Man* (New York: Free Press, 1992).

4. Fukuyama, "The End of History?" 18.

5. Francis Fukuyama, "Economic Globalization and Culture: A Discussion with Dr. Francis Fukuyama," *Merrill Lynch Forum* <http://www.ml.com/woml /forum/global.htm> (2000); and Francis Fukuyama, "Second Thoughts: The Last Man in a Bottle," *National Affairs* 56 (summer 1999):16–44.

6. Fred Dallmayr, *Alternative Visions: Paths in the Global Village* (Lanham, MD: Rowman & Littlefield, 1998), 73.

7. For various definitions of ideology, see, for example, Sargent, *Contemporary Political Ideologies*; Michael Freeden, *Ideologies and Political Theory: A Conceptual Approach* (Oxford: Clarendon Press, 1996); Slavoj Zizek, ed., *Mapping Ideology* (London: Verso, 1994); Terry Eagleton, *Ideology: An Introduction* (London: Verso, 1991); Istvan Meszaros, *The Power of Ideology* (New York: New York University Press, 1989); David McLellan, *Ideology* (Milton Keynes, UK: Open University Press, 1986); Paul Ricoeur, *Lectures on Ideology and Utopia*, ed. George H. Taylor (New York: Columbia University Press,

1986); Goran Therborn, *The Ideology of Power and the Power of Ideology* (London: New Left Books, 1980); Jorge Larrain, *The Concept of Ideology* (London: Hutchinson, 1979); and Karl Mannheim, *Ideology and Utopia: An Introduction to the Sociology of Knowledge* (London: Routledge, 1991 [1936]).

8. Terrell Carver, "Ideology: The Career of a Concept," in *Ideals and Ideologies: A Reader*, 3rd ed., ed. Terrence Ball and Richard Dagger (New York: Longman, 1998), 9.

9. Robert J. Samuelson, "Why We're All Married to the Market," *Newsweek* (27 April 1998):47–50. I am grateful to Brian Michael Goss, who pointed these headlines out to me during his paper presentation at the 1998 Border Subjects 3 Conference at Illinois State University.

10. Ricoeur, *Lectures on Ideology and Utopia*. My summary of Ricoeur's discussion of ideology draws on George Taylor's "Editor's Introduction," in Ricoeur, *Lectures on Ideology and Utopia*, ix–xxxvi.

11. Ibid., 266.

12. William I. Robinson, *Promoting Polyarchy: Globalization, U.S. Intervention, and Hegemony* (Cambridge: Cambridge University Press, 1996), 30. My explanation of Gramsci's notion of hegemony draws heavily on Robinson's excellent explication. A good selection of Gramsci's political writings is contained in Antonio Gramsci, *Selections from Prison Notebooks* (New York: International Publishers, 1971).

13. For a succinct explanation and critique of Ricardo's economic theories, see Theodore Cohn, *Global Political Economy: Theory and Practice* (New York: Longman, 2000), 200–203.

14. For a detailed exposition of Herbert Spencer's social and economic theories, see M. W. Taylor, *Men Versus the State: Herbert Spencer and Late Victorian Individualism* (Oxford: Clarendon Press, 1992); and David Wiltshire, *The Social and Political Thought of Herbert Spencer* (Oxford: Oxford University Press, 1978). For a representative selection of Spencer's writings, see Herbert Spencer, *On Social Evolution*, ed. J. D. Y. Peel (Chicago: University of Chicago Press, 1972).

15. Jan Knippers Black, *Inequity in the Global Village: Recycled Rhetoric and Disposable People* (West Hartford, CT: Kumarian Press, 1999); and Edward Luttwak, *Turbo-Capitalism: Winners and Losers in the Global Economy* (New York: HarperCollins, 1999). For a more detailed discussion of the rise of neoliberal ideology in Europe and the United States, see also Robert Gilpin, *The Challenge of Global Capitalism: The World Economy in the 21st Century* (Princeton, NJ: Princeton University Press, 2000); Peter Gowan, *The Global Gamble: Washington's Faustian Bid for World Dominance* (London: Verso, 1999); Daniel Yergin and Joseph Stanislaw, *The Commanding Heights: The Battle Between Government and the Marketplace That Is Remaking the Modern World* (New York:

Simon & Schuster, 1998); John Gray, *False Dawn: The Delusions of Global Capitalism* (New York: New Press, 1998); and Robert Kuttner, *Everything For Sale: The Virtues and the Limits of the Market* (New York: Knopf, 1997).

16. For a critical discussion of "market fundamentalism," see George Soros, *The Crisis of Global Capitalism: Open Society Endangered* (New York: Public Affairs, 1998).

17. See Claire Turenne Sjolander, "The Rhetoric of Globalisation: What's in a Wor(l)d?" *International Journal* 51, no. 4 (1996):603–16.

18. See Harvey Cox, "The Market as God: Living in the New Dispensation," *Atlantic Monthly* (March 1999):18–23.

19. Mustafa Koc, "Globalization as Discourse," in *From Columbus to Con Agra: The Globalization of Agriculture and Food*, ed. Alessandro Bonanno (Lawrence: University Press of Kansas, 1994), 265.

20. See, for example, James H. Mittelman, *The Globalization Syndrome: Transformation and Resistance* (Princeton, NJ: Princeton University Press, 2000), especially ch. 9, 165–78; Ulrich Beck, *What Is Globalization?* (Cambridge: Polity Press, 2000); Barry K. Gills, ed., *Globalization and the Politics of Resistance* (New York: St. Martin's Press, 2000); Richard Falk, *Predatory Globalization: A Critique* (Cambridge: Polity Press, 1999); Noam Chomsky, *Profit Over People: Neoliberalism and Global Order* (New York: Seven Stories Press, 1999); Pierre Bourdieu, *Acts of Resistance: Against the Tyranny of the Market* (New York: New Press, 1998); and Gray, *False Dawn*.

21. For a general introduction to critical theory, see Jürgen Habermas, *Knowledge and Human Interests* (Boston: Beacon Press, 1973); Stephen Leonard, *Critical Theory in Political Practice* (Princeton, NJ: Princeton University Press, 1990); Stephen Eric Bronner and Douglas Kellner, eds., *Critical Theory and Society: A Reader* (London: Routledge, 1989); Stephen Eric Bronner, *Of Critical Theory and Its Theorists* (Malden, MA: Blackwell, 1994); and Stephen Eric Bronner, *Ideas in Action: Political Tradition in the Twentieth Century* (Lanham, MD: Rowman & Littlefield, 1999).

22. For various perspectives on developing a critical theory of globalization, see Jan Aart Scholte, "Beyond the Buzzword: Towards a Critical Theory of Globalization," in *Globalization: Theory and Practice*, ed. Eleonore Kaufman and Gilian Young (London: Pinter, 1996), 43–58; Douglas Kellner, "Globalization and the Postmodern Turn," in *Globalization in Europe: Theoretical and Empirical Investigations*, ed. Roland Axtmann (Washington, DC: Pinter, 1998), 23–42; and James H. Mittelman, "How Does Globalization Really Work?" in *Globalization: Critical Reflections*, ed. James H. Mittelman (Boulder, CO: Lynne Rienner, 1996), 229–41.

Chapter Two

1. The parable of the "Blind Scholars and the Elephant" originated most likely in the Pali Buddhist Udana, which was apparently compiled in the second century B.C.E. Its many versions spread to other religions as well, most significantly Hinduism and Islam. For example, in his *Theology Revived*, Muhammad al-Ghazzali (1058–1128) refers to the tale in a discussion on the problem of human action in which the inadequacy of natural reason becomes evident. I am grateful to Ramdas Lamb in the Department of Religion at the University of Hawai'i at Mānoa for explaining to me the origins of the parable.

2. Stephen J. Rosow, "Globalisation as Democratic Theory," *Millennium: Journal of International Studies* 29, no. 1 (2000):31.

3. For various definitions of globalization, see, for example, Frank J. Lechner and John Boli, eds., *The Globalization Reader* (Oxford: Blackwell Publishers, 2000); Robert J. Holton, *Globalization and the Nation-State* (New York: St. Martin's Press, 1998); Mittelman, *Globalization*; Malcolm Waters, *Globalization* (London: Routledge, 1995); Roland Robertson, *Globalization: Social Theory and Global Culture* (London: Sage, 1992); Anthony Giddens, *The Third Way: The Renewal of Social Democracy* (Cambridge: Polity Press, 1998); and *The Consequences of Modernity* (Stanford, CA: Stanford University Press, 1990); and David Harvey, *The Condition of Postmodernity* (Malden, MA: Blackwell, 1989).

4. Richard J. Barnet and John Cavanagh, *Global Dreams: Imperial Corporations and the New World Order* (New York: Simon & Schuster, 1994). See also Paul Krugman, *The Accidental Theorist* (New York: Norton, 1998), 73; and Gilpin, *The Challenge of Global Capitalism*, 294.

5. Craig Calhoun, "Nationalism and Ethnicity," *Annual Review of Sociology* 19 (1993):215–16.

6. Susan Strange, *The Retreat of the State: The Diffusion of Power in the World Economy* (Cambridge: Cambridge University Press, 1996), xii–xiii. My discussion of this aspect of the globalization debate has greatly benefited from Ian Clark's excellent exposition in his *Globalization and International Relations Theory*, 34–40.

7. Linda Weiss, *The Myth of the Powerless State: Governing the Economy in a Global Era* (Ithaca, NY: Cornell University Press, 1998), 212.

8. Holton, *Globalization and the Nation-State*, 196.

9. Paul Hirst and Graham Thompson, *Globalization in Question: The International Economy and the Possibilities of Governance*, 2nd ed. (Cambridge: Polity Press, 1999).

10. Ibid., 2. For a similar conclusion, see Michael Veseth, *Selling Globalization: The Myth of the Global Economy* (Boulder, CO: Lynne Rienner, 1998); Paul N. Doremus, William W. Keller, Louis W. Pauly, and Simon Reich, *The Myth of the Global Corporation* (Princeton, NJ: Princeton University Press,

1998); and John Zysman, "The Myth of a 'Global' Economy: Enduring National Foundations and Emerging Regional Realities," *New Political Economy* 1, no. 2 (1996):157–84.

11. See, for example, David Held, Anthony McGrew, David Goldblatt, and Jonathan Perraton, *Global Transformations: Politics, Economics, and Culture* (Stanford, CA: Stanford University Press, 1999).

12. Gilpin, *The Challenge of Global Capitalism*, 294–95. For a similar assessment, see Dani Rodrik, *Has Globalization Gone Too Far?* (Washington, DC: Institute for International Economics, 1997), 7–8; and Gary Burtless, Robert Z. Lawrence, Robert E. Litan, and Robert J. Shapiro, *Globaphobia: Confronting Fears about Open Trade* (Washington, DC: Brookings Institution, 1998), 6–7.

13. Immanuel Wallerstein, *The Capitalist World Economy* (Cambridge: Cambridge University Press, 1979), and *The Politics of the World Economy* (Cambridge: Cambridge University Press, 1984); Andre Gunder Frank, "A Theoretical Introduction to 5,000 Years of World-System History," *Review* 13, no. 2 (1990):155–248, and *ReORIENT: Global Economy in the Asian Age* (Berkeley: University of California Press, 1998). See also Christopher Chase-Dunn, *Global Formation: Structures of the World Economy* (Lanham, MD: Rowman & Littlefield, 1998).

14. Immanuel Wallerstein, "Culture as the Ideological Battleground of the Modern World System," in *Global Culture*, ed. Mike Featherstone (London: Sage, 1990), 38.

15. William Carroll, Radhika Desai, and Warren Magnusson, *Globalization, Social Justice and Social Movements: A Reader* (Victoria, ON: University of Victoria, 1996), 21, 107; and Samir Amin, "The Challenge of Globalization," *Review of International Political Economy* 3, no. 2 (1996):244–45.

16. Ash Amin, "Placing Globalization," *Theory, Culture and Society* 14, no. 2 (1997):123–38.

17. See, for example, Leslie Sklair, "Social Movements and Global Capitalism," in *The Cultures of Globalization*, 291–311.

18. For various accounts of economic globalization, see, for example, *The Globalization Reader*, 145–94; Hugo Radice, "Taking Globalisation Seriously," in *Global Capitalism Versus Democracy: The Socialist Register 1999*, ed. Leo Panitch and Colin Leys (New York: Monthly Review Press, 1999); Hirst and Thompson, *Globalization in Question*; Gowan, *The Global Gamble*; Daniel Singer, *Whose Millennium? Theirs or Ours?* (New York: Monthly Review Press, 1999), 184–213; Saskia Sassen, *Globalization and Its Discontents: Essays on the New Mobility of People and Money* (New York: New Press, 1998); Holton, *Globalization and the Nation-State*, 50–79; Luttwak, *Turbo-Capitalism*; Mittelman, *Globalization* and *The Globalization Syndrome*; and Waters, *Globalization*, 65–95; and Robert Reich, *The Work of Nations* (New York: Vintage, 1992).

19. The most comprehensive treatment of this nature is Robert O. Keohane,

After Hegemony (Princeton, NJ: Princeton University Press, 1984). For a recent update of Keohane's position on globalization, see Robert O. Keohane and Joseph S. Nye, Jr., "Globalization: What's New? What's Not? (And So What)?" *Foreign Policy* 118 (spring 2000):104–19; and Robert Keohane, "Governance in a Partially Globalized World," *American Political Science Review* 95, no. 1 (March 2001):1–13.

20. Gilpin, *The Challenge of Global Capitalism*, 299.

21. Ibid., 19.

22. Perhaps the most accessible example of this genre is Robert K. Schaeffer's very readable study, *Understanding Globalization* (Lanham, MD: Rowman & Littlefield, 1997).

23. Luttwak, *Turbo-Capitalism*, xii, 27.

24. Gilpin, *The Challenge of Global Capitalism*, 65–75.

25. Ibid., 20.

26. Manuel Castells, "Information Technology and Global Capitalism," in *Global Capitalism*, ed. Will Hutton and Anthony Giddens (New York: New Press, 2000), 53.

27. Ibid., 55. See also Gowan, *The Global Gamble*, 3–12.

28. Gilpin, *The Challenge of Global Capitalism*, 20.

29. See David Ashley, *History Without a Subject: The Postmodern Condition* (Boulder, CO: Westview Press, 1997), 109; Gary Gereffi, "The Elusive Last Lap in the Quest for Developed-Country Status," in Mittelman, *Globalization*, 64–69; and Gary Gereffi and Miguel Korzeniewicz, eds., *Commodity Chains and Global Capitalism* (Westport, CT: Greenwood Press, 1993).

30. Gilpin, *The Challenge of Global Capitalism*, 24.

31. See, for example, Robert T. Kurdle, "The Three Types of Globalization: Communication, Market, and Direct," in *Globalization and Global Governance*, ed. Raimo Väyrynen (Lanham, MD: Rowman & Littlefield, 1999), 3–23; C. P. Rao, ed., *Globalization, Privatization and Free Market Economy* (Westport, CT: Quorum Books, 1998); Burtless et al., *Globaphobia*; and Lowell Bryan and Diana Farrell, *Market Unbound: Unleashing Global Capitalism* (New York: Wiley, 1996).

32. Bryan and Farrell, *Market Unbound*, 187.

33. Kenichi Ohmae, *The End of the Nation-State: The Rise of Regional Economies* (New York: Free Press, 1995) and *The Borderless World: Power and Strategy in the Interlinked World Economy* (New York: Harper Business, 1990). For additional examples of the "end of the nation-state thesis," see Lester Thurow, *The Future of Capitalism: How Today's Economic Forces Shape Tomorrow's World* (New York: William Morrow, 1996); John Naisbitt, *Global Paradox* (London: Nicholas Brealey Publishing, 1995); and Nicholas Negroponte, *Being Digital* (London: Hodder & Stoughton, 1995). For a thoughtful rebuttal of this thesis, see Michael Mann, "Has Globalization Ended the Rise of the Nation-

State?" *Review of International Political Economy* 4, no. 3 (autumn 1997): 472–96.

34. Caroline Thomas, "Globalization and the South," in *Globalization and the South*, ed. Caroline Thomas and Peter Wilkin (New York: St. Martin's Press, 1997), 6. See also, Roger Burbach, Orlando Nunez, and Boris Kagarlitsky, *Globalization and Its Discontents: The Rise of Postmodern Socialisms* (London: Pluto Press, 1997). A more popular version of this argument can be found in William Greider, *One World, Ready or Not: The Manic Logic of Global Capitalism* (New York: Simon & Schuster, 1997).

35. See, for example, Ethan B. Kapstein, *Sharing the Wealth: Workers and the World Economy* (New York: Norton, 1999); Gowan, *The Global Gamble*; Luttwak, *Turbo-Capitalism*; Wolfgang Reinicke, *Global Public Policy* (Washington, DC: Brookings Institution, 1998); Doremus et al., *The Myth of the Global Corporation*; Weiss, *The Myth of the Powerless State*; and David C. Korten, *When Corporations Rule the World* (West Hartford, CT: Kumarian Press, 1995).

36. Singer, *Whose Millennium?*, 186–87.

37. Saskia Sassen's work emphasizes the key role played by global cities in the organization and control of globally-oriented economic and social processes. See Saskia Sassen, *The Global City: New York, London, Tokyo* (Princeton, NJ: Princeton University Press, 1991), *Losing Control? Sovereignty in an Age of Globalization* (New York: Columbia University Press, 1996), and *Globalization and Its Discontents*.

38. Jan Aart Scholte, *Globalization: A Critical Introduction* (New York: St. Martin's Press, 2000), 42.

39. For an excellent exposition of this argument, see Edward S. Cohen, "Making Sense of Globalization: Can We Learn Anything from the Confusion?" (paper presented at the 58th Annual Meeting of the Midwest Political Science Association, Chicago, April 27–30, 2000). See also Geoffrey Garrett, *Partisan Politics in the Global Economy* (Cambridge: Cambridge University Press, 1998); Leo Panitch, "Rethinking the Role of the State," in Mittelman, *Globalization*, 83–113; Eric Helleiner, "Post-Globalisation: Is the Financial Liberalisation Trend Likely to Be Reversed?" in *States Against Markets: The Limits of Globalisation*, ed. Robert Boyer and Daniel Drache (London: Routledge, 1996) and Helleiner, *States and the Reemergence of Global Finance* (Ithaca, NY: Cornell University Press, 1994); and Stephen Krasner, "Economic Interdependence and Independent Statehood," in *States in a Changing World: A Contemporary Analysis*, ed. Robert H. Jackson and Alan James (Oxford: Clarendon Press, 1993), 301–21.

40. Gray, *False Dawn*, 23.

41. Ibid., 218.

42. Manual Castells, *The Information Age: Economy, Society, and Culture*, 3 vols. (Oxford: Blackwell, 1996–1998), 3:356.

43. Ibid., 3:368.

44. Ibid., 3:379.

45. See, for example, the various essays collected in Väyrynen, *Globalization and Global Governance*; and David A. Smith, Dorothy J. Solinger, and Steven C. Topic, eds., *States and Sovereignty in the Global Economy* (London: Routledge, 1999).

46. Falk, *Predatory Globalization*.

47. David Held, "Democracy and the New International Order," in *Cosmopolitan Democracy: An Agenda for a New World Order*, ed. Daniele Archibugi and David Held (Cambridge: Polity Press, 1995), 96–120. For a more detailed elaboration of Held's vision, see David Held, *Democracy and the Global Order* (Stanford, CA: Stanford University Press, 1995), and Daniele Archibugi, David Held, and Martin Koehler, eds., *Re-Imagining Political Community: Studies in Cosmopolitan Democracy* (Stanford, CA: Stanford University Press, 1998).

48. Falk, *Predatory Globalization*, 7. See also, Richard Falk, *Human Rights Horizons: The Pursuit of Justice in a Globalizing World* (New York: Routledge, 2000), "The World Order between Inter-State Law and the Law of Humanity: The Role of Civil Society Institutions," in Archibugi and Held, *Cosmopolitan Democracy*, 163–79, and *On Humane Governance: Toward a New Global Politics* (Cambridge: Polity Press, 1995).

49. See Holton, *Globalization and the Nation-State*, 202–3.

50. Tomlinson, *Globalization and Culture*, 1.

51. Ibid., 28.

52. George Ritzer, *The McDonaldization of Society: An Investigation Into the Changing Character of Contemporary Social Life* (Thousand Oaks, CA: Pine Forge Press, 1993).

53. Benjamin R. Barber, *Jihad vs. McWorld* (New York: Ballantine Books, 1996), 17.

54. Ibid., 19. For a neo-Marxist perspective on the rise of a global capitalist monoculture, see Herbert Schiller, "The Global Information Highway: Project for an Ungovernable World," in *Resisting the Virtual Life*, ed. James Brook and Iain A. Boal (San Francisco: City Lights, 1995), 17–33.

55. Serge Latouche, *The Westernization of the World* (Cambridge: Polity Press, 1996), 3.

56. See, for example, Arjun Appadurai, *Modernity at Large: Cultural Dimensions of Globalization* (Minneapolis: University of Minnesota Press, 1996); and Ulf Hannerz, *Cultural Complexity: Studies in the Social Organization of Meaning* (New York: Columbia University Press, 1992), and *Transnational Connections: Cultures, People, Places* (London: Routledge, 1996).

57. Robertson, *Globalization* and "Glocalization: Time–Space and Homogeneity–Heterogeneity," in ed. Mike Featherstone, Scott Lash, and Roland Robertson, *Global Modernities* (London: Sage, 1995), 25–44.

58. Hannerz, *Cultural Complexity*, 96.

59. Beck, *What Is Globalization?*, 102.

60. Appadurai, *Modernity at Large*, 33.

61. Martin Albrow, *The Global Age: State and Society Beyond Modernity* (Cambridge: Polity Press, 1996), 192.

62. For a more detailed account of this debate, see Scholte, *Globalization*, 24–25; Tomlinson, *Globalization and Culture*, 32–70; and Kate Nash, *Contemporary Political Sociology: Globalization, Politics, and Power* (Malden, MA: Blackwell, 2000), 71–88.

63. One of the most comprehensive surveys of the subject can be found in Held et al., *Global Transformations*.

64. Fredric Jameson, "Preface," in ed. Fredric Jameson and Masao Miyoshi, *The Cultures of Globalization* (Durham, NC: Duke University Press, 1998), xi–xii.

65. Ian Clark, *Globalization and International Relations Theory* (Oxford: Oxford University Press, 1999), 39. For a plea for better definitions of globalization, see Scholte, *Globalization*, 41–42.

66. See Claus Offe, *Modernity and the State: East, West* (Cambridge: Polity Press, 1996), 5.

67. Hans-Georg Gadamer, *Truth and Method* (New York: Seabury Press, 1975).

68. Robert W. Cox, "A Perspective on Globalization," in Mittelman, *Globalization*, 21–30; Stephen Gill, "Globalization, Democratization, and the Politics of Indifference," in Mittelman, *Globalization*, 205–28, and Gill, "Globalisation, Market Civilisation, and Disciplinary Neoliberalism," *Millennium: Journal of International Studies* 24, no. 2 (1995):399–423. See also Chomsky, *Profit Over People*; Bourdieu, *Acts of Resistance*; and Falk, *Predatory Globalization*.

69. Alan Scott, "Introduction: Globalization: Social Process or Political Rhetoric?" in ed. Alan Scott, *The Limits of Globalization: Cases and Arguments* (London: Routledge, 1997), 2.

70. For an impressive exposition of this argument, see Veseth, *Selling Globalization*.

Chapter Three

1. All citations are taken from Aaron Bernstein, "Backlash: Behind the Anxiety over Globalization," *BusinessWeek* (April 24, 2000):44. This *BusinessWeek*–Harris poll on globalization was conducted by Harris Interactive between April 7–10, 2000. A total of 1,024 interviews were conducted.

2. Ibid., 38–40.

3. See Zygmunt Bauman, *In Search of Politics* (Stanford, CA: Stanford University Press, 1999), 28–29, 127–28; and Bourdieu, *Acts of Resistance*, 95.

4. Judith Butler, "Gender as Performance," in *A Critical Sense: Interviews with Intellectuals*, ed. Peter Osborne (London: Routledge, 1996), 112.

5. Michel Foucault, *The Archeology of Knowledge* (New York: Pantheon, 1972), 59–68.

6. Sandra Masur cited in Mark Rupert, "Globalization and the Reconstruction of Common Sense in the U.S.," in *Innovation and Transformation in International Studies*, ed. Stephen Gill and James Mittelman (Cambridge: Cambridge University Press, 1997), 138–52. For a detailed description of this "transnational historic bloc of internationally-oriented capitalists," see Mark Rupert, *Ideologies of Globalization: Contending Visions of a New World Order* (London: Routledge, 2000), 16–17, 154.

7. Andrew Chadwick, "Studying Political Ideas: A Public Political Discourse Approach," *Political Studies* 48 (2000):283–301.

8. Claude Lefort, *Les formes de l'histoire* (Paris: Gallimard, 1978). Relevant passages cited in Miguel de Larrinaga, "(Re)Politicizing the Discourse: Globalization Is a S(h)ell Game," *Alternatives* 25 (2000):157. See also Ernesto Laclau and Chantal Mouffe, *Hegemony and Socialist Practice: Towards a Radical Democratic Politics* (London: Verso, 1985), 96.

9. See Chadwick, "Studying Political Ideas," 290–92.

10. Veseth, *Selling Globalization*, 16–18.

11. Friedrich Hayek, *Law, Legislation, and Liberty*, 3 vols. (London: Routledge & Kegan Paul, 1979), 1:55.

12. Isaiah Berlin, "Two Concepts of Liberty," in *Four Essays on Liberty* (London: Oxford University Press, 1969), 121–22.

13. For an apt summary of the market principles of economic liberalism, see Timothy J. Gaffaney, "Citizens of the Market: The Un-Political Theory of the New Right," *Polity* 32(2) (winter 1999):181–84.

14. Milton Friedman, *Capitalism and Freedom* (Chicago: University of Chicago Press, 1962), 9.

15. *BusinessWeek* (December 13, 1999):212.

16. Joan E. Spiro, "The Challenges of Globalization," speech at the World Economic Development Congress in Washington, DC, September 26, 1996 <http://www.state.gov/www/issues/economic/960926.html>.

17. Martin Wolf, "Why This Hatred of the Market?" in Lechner and Boli, *The Globalization Reader*, 9–11; and Peter Martin, "The Moral Case for Globalization," in Lechner and Boli, *The Globalization Reader*, 12–13.

18. Charlene Barshefsky cited in Mark Levinson, "Who's in Charge Here?" *Dissent* (fall 1999):22.

19. Michael Camdessus cited in Levinson, "Who's in Charge Here?"; and Michael Camdessus, "Globalization and Asia: The Challenges for Regional Cooperation and Implications for Hong Kong," address to Hong Kong Mone-

tary Authority, Hong Kong, March 7, 1997 <http://www.imf.org/external/np/speeches/1997/MDS9703.html>.

20. Fred Theobald, "It Is Called Globalization" (undated) <http://www.theesusgroup.com/article%201.html>.

21. Tom Weidemeyer, "Open Trade Without Open Skies: The Contrast Between Globalization, Free Trade, and Restricted Aviation Rights," speech to the FAA Aviation Conference in Washington, DC, March 8, 2000 <http://www.ups.com/news/speech/20000308opentrade.html>.

22. See, for example, William Bole, "Tales of Globalization," *America* 181, no. 18 (December 4, 1999):14–16.

23. Friedman, *The Lexus and the Olive Tree*, xii, 23–24.

24. Ibid., 9.

25. Ibid., 104, 152.

26. Ibid., 105.

27. Ibid., 109–10.

28. Stuart Eizenstat, "The U.S. Perspective on Globalization," April 1999 <http://www.odc.org/commentary/vpapr.html>.

29. John Micklethwait and Adrian Woolridge, *A Future Perfect: The Challenge and Hidden Promise of Globalization* (New York: Crown Publishers, 2000), xxi.

30. For a detailed discussion of these neoliberal policy initiatives, see ibid., 22–54.

31. Luttwak, *Turbo-Capitalism*, 152.

32. Beck, *What Is Globalization?*, 122.

33. See Robert W. McChesney, "Global Media, Neoliberalism, and Imperialism," *Monthly Review* (March 2001) <http://www.monthlyreview.org/301rwm.html>.

34. For a critical assessment of Thatcher's experiment, see Gray, *False Dawn*, 24–34.

35. Bill Clinton, "Remarks by the President on Foreign Policy," San Francisco, Febraury 26, 1999 <http://www.pub.whitehouse.gov/urires/12R?urn:pdi://oma.eop.gove.us/1999/3/1/3.text.1.html>.

36. President Clinton cited in Sonya Ross, "Clinton Talk of Better Living," *Associated Press*, October 15, 1997 <http://more.abcnews.go.com/sections/world/brazil1014/index.html>.

37. Stuart Eizenstat, "Remarks to Democratic Leadership Council," January 19, 1999 <http://www.usinfo.org/wf/990120/epf305.html>.

38. "International Finance Experts Preview Upcoming Global Economic Forum," April 1, 1999 <http://www.econstrat.org/pctranscript.html>.

39. Friedman, *The Lexus and the Olive Tree*, 407.

40. Rahul Bajaj, "Interview with *The Rediff Business Interview*," February 2,

1999 <http://rediff.com/business/1999/feb/02bajaj.html>. See also <http://www.ascihyd.org/asci701.html>.

41. Manuel Villar, Jr., "High-Level Dialogue on the Theme of the Social and Economic Impact of Globalization and Interdependence and their Policy Implications," New York, September 17, 1998 <http://www.un.int/philippines/villar.html>.

42. Masaru Hayami, "Globalization and Regional Cooperation in Asia," Tokyo, March 17, 2000 <http://www.boj.or.jp/en/press/koen049.html>.

43. John R. Malott, "Globalization, Competitiveness, and Asia's Economic Future," Kuala Lumpur, Malysia, March 13, 1998 <http://www.csis.org/pacfor/pac1198.html>.

44. Roman Herzog cited in Martin and Schumann, *The Global Trap*, 6.

45. Alain Lipietz, *Towards a New Economic Order* (Oxford: Oxford University Press, 1993), x.

46. David Smith, "Putting a Human Face on the Global Economy: Seeking Common Ground on Trade," 1999 DLC Annual Conference, Washington, DC, October 14, 1999 <http://www.dlcppi.org/speeches/99conference/99conf_panel1.html>.

47. Cox, "The Market as God," 18–23. See also Thomas Frank, *One Market under God: Extreme Capitalism, Market Populism, and the End of Economic Democracy* (New York: Doubleday, 2000).

48. Beck, *What Is Globalization?*, 122.

49. Lorenzo Zambrano, "Putting the Global Market in Order" <http://www.globalprogress.org/ingles/Mexico/Zamprano.html>.

50. "Economic Globalization and Culture: A Discussion with Dr. Francis Fukuyama" <http://www.ml.com/woml/forum/global2.html>.

51. Friedman, *The Lexus and the Olive Tree*, 474–75. See also Friedman's remark on page 294: "Today, for better or worse, globalization is a means for spreading the fantasy of America around the world. . . . Globalization is Americanization."

52. Gray, *False Dawn*, 131.

53. Steven Kline, "The Play of the Market: On the Internationalization of Children's Culture," *Theory, Culture and Society* 12 (1995):110.

54. See Barber, *Jihad vs. McWorld*, 119–51.

55. Micklethwait and Woolridge, *A Future Perfect*, xxii.

56. Krugman, "We Are Not the World," in *The Accidental Theorist*, 78.

57. Robert Hormats, "PBS Interview with Danny Schechter," February 1998 <http://pbs.org/globalization/hormats1.html>.

58. Friedman, *The Lexus and the Olive Tree*, 112–13.

59. Steward Brand, "Financial Markets," Global Business Network Book Club, December 1998 <http://www.gbn.org/public/services/bookclub/reviews/ex_8812.html>.

60. Michael Hardt and Antonio Negri, *Empire* (Cambridge, MA: Harvard University Press, 2000), 3.

61. Cited in Richard Gott, *In the Shadow of the Liberator: Hugo Chávez and the Transformation of Venezuela* (London: Verso, 2000), 52–53.

62. Will Hutton, "Anthony Giddens and Will Hutton in Conversation," in *Global Capitalism*, ed. Will Hutton and Anthony Giddens (New York: Free Press, 2000), 41.

63. Friedman, *The Lexus and the Olive Tree*, 381.

64. Ibid., 464.

65. Statement of Joseph Gorman before the Subcommittee on Trade of the Committee on Ways and Means, March 18, 1997 <http://fasttrack.org/track/congress/gorman.html>.

66. Remarks by Samuel R. Berger, Columbia University, New York City, May 2, 2000 <http://www.usis.it/file2000_05/alia/a0050415.html>.

67. Economic Communiqué, Lyon G7 Summit, June 28, 1996 <http://library.utoronto.ca/www/g7/96ecopre.html>.

68. Robert Rubin, "Reform of the International Financial Architechture," *Vital Speeches* 65, no. 15 (1999):455.

69. Remarks by Joan Spiro, World Economic Development Congress, Washington, DC, September 26, 1996 <http://www.state.gov/www/issues/economic/960926.html>.

70. Denise Froning, "Why Spurn Free Trade?" *Washington Times* 15 September 2000.

71. Alan Greenspan, "The Globalization of Finance," October 14, 1997 <http://cato.org/pubs/journal/cj17n3-1.html>.

72. Peter Sutherland, "Expand the Debate on Globalization," *Time* (February 2, 1998) <http://cgi.pathfinder.com/time/mag...02/special_report.expand_th25.html>.

73. George David, "The Critics of Globalization are Wrong," Fortune Global Forum, Bangkok, Thailand, March 26, 1997 <http://www.utc.com/ARCHIVE/bangkok.html>.

74. Jay Mazur, "Labor's New Internationalism," *Foreign Affairs* (January/February 2000):80–81.

75. "Tropical Disease Drugs Withdrawn," *BBC News*, October 31, 2000.

76. John J. Meehan, Chairman of the Public Securities Association, "Globalization and Technology at Work in the Bond Markets," speech given in Phoenix, March 1, 1997 <http://www/bondmarkets.com/news/Meehanspeechfinal.shtml>.

77. Newt Gingrich, interview with Danny Schechter at the 1998 World Economic Forum in Davos, Switzerland <http://www.pbs.org/globalization/newt.html>.

78. See Barber, *Jihad vs. McWorld*, 77–87.

79. Friedman, *The Lexus and the Olive Tree*, 364.

80. Micklethwait and Woolridge, *A Future Perfect*, xxvii.

81. Robert Hormats, interview by Danny Schechter, February 1998 <http://www.pbs.org/globalization/hormats1.html>.

82. Ibid.

83. Thomas Friedman, "Under the Volcano," *New York Times*, September 29, 2000.

84. Phil Knight cited in "Political, Business Leaders Call for Enlightened Strategies to Fight Globalization Trap" <http://www.weforum.org/pressreleases.nsf/ghtenedstrategiesttofightglobalizationtrap.html>.

85. Phil Condit before the Subcommittee on Trade of the Committee on Ways and Means, U.S. House of Representatives, March 4, 1999 <http://www.boeing.com/news/speeches/current/condit030499.html>.

86. Caio K. Koch-Weser, "Address to the XI Malente Sympsium," Lübeck, Germany, October 17, 1996 <http://www.worldbank.org/html/extdr/extme/ckwsp005.html>.

87. Doug Henwood, "Stiglitz and the Limits of 'Reform,'" *Nation* (October 2, 2000):20.

88. 1999 UN Human Development Report <http://www.undp.org/hdro/report/html>.

89. Juan Somavia cited in "U.N. to Examine Why Poverty Persists Despite Freer Trade," *Honolulu Advertiser*, July 1, 2000.

90. "Economic Globalization and Culture: A Discussion with Dr. Francis Fukuyama" <http://www.ml.com/woml/forum/global2.html>.

91. Hillary Rodham Clinton, "Growth of Democracy in Eastern Europe," Warsaw, October 5, 1999 <http:/www.whitehouse.gov/WH/EOP/First Lady/html/generalspeeches/1999/19991005.html>.

92. Robinson, *Promoting Polyarchy*, 56–62.

93. Friedman, *The Lexus and the Olive Tree*, 187.

94. R. C. Longworth, "Democracies Are Paying the Price," *Chicago Tribune*, November 19, 1999.

95. Friedman, *The Lexus and the Olive Tree*, 191–92.

96. Mike Moore, "Address to the Development Committee of the European Parliament," February 21, 2000 <http://www.wto.org/wto/speeches/mm25.html>.

97. Charlene Barshefsky cited in Walen Bello, "Reforming the WTO Is the Wrong Agenda," in *Globalize This! The Battle Against the World Trade Organization and Corporate Rule*, ed. Kevin Danaher and Roger Burbach (Monroe, ME: Common Courage Press, 2000), 115.

98. Martin Khor, "Seattle Debacle: Revolt of the Developing Nations," in Danaher and Burbach, *Globalize This!*, 50–51.

99. Benjamin R. Barber, "Globalizing Democracy," *American Prospect Online* 11, no. 20 (September 11, 2000) <http://www.prospect.org/archives/V11-20/barber-b.html>.

Chapter Four

1. Norberto Bobbio, *Left & Right: The Significance of a Political Distinction* (Chicago: University of Chicago Press, 1996), 60–71.

2. Ibid., 90.

3. Anthony Giddens, *Beyond Left and Right: The Future of Radical Politics* (Stanford, CA: Stanford University Press, 1994), 251.

4. See Gilpin, *The Challenge of Global Capitalism*, 297.. Gilpin also identifies two antiglobalist camps, but he uses different terminology to describe them: The populist perspective of the political right, and the communitarian perspective of the political left. As will become clear later in the chapter, I find Gilpin's labels somewhat imprecise.

5. Margaret Canovan, *Populism* (New York: Harcourt Brace Jovanovich, 1981).

6. Chip Berlet and Matthew N. Lyons, *Right-Wing Populism in America: Too Close for Comfort* (New York: Guilford Press, 2000), 5–6. For two additional sources on populism, see Carl Boggs, *The End of Politics: Corporate Power and the Decline of the Public Sphere* (New York: Guilford Press, 2000); and Michael Kazin, *The Populist Persuasion: An American History* (New York: Basic Books, 1995).

7. Reform party, "Principles and Issues" <http://www.reform-party-usa.org>.

8. Patrick J. Buchanan, *The Great Betrayal: How American Sovereignty and Social Justice Are Being Sacrificed to the Gods of the Global Economy* (Boston: Little, Brown, 1998), 97.

9. Ibid., 288.

10. Patrick J. Buchanan, *A Republic, Not An Empire: Reclaiming America's Destiny* (Washington, DC: Regnery Publishing, 1999), xi–xii.

11. Unless indicated otherwise, all citations below are taken from Patrick J. Buchanan, "Address to the Chicago Council on Foreign Relations," November 18, 1998 <http://www.chuckbaldwinlive.com/read.freetrade.html>.

12. Surprisingly, Buchanan does not seem to be bothered by the fact that the central intellectual features of economic nationalism were also designed by Europeans—most importantly, by the early nineteenth-century German thinkers J. G. Fichte and Friedrich List.

13. For example, Buchanan relies on the work of the American economist Alan Tonelson. See Alan Tonelson, *The Race to the Bottom: Why a Worldwide*

Worker Surplus and Uncontrolled Free Trade Are Sinking American Living Standards (Boulder, CO: Westview Press, 2000).

14. Buchanan, *The Great Betrayal*, 104–8.

15. Patrick Buchanan, press release April 24, 2000 <http://www.issues2000. org/Pat_Buchanan_Free_Trade_&_Immigration.html>.

16. Patrick Buchanan, press release July 2, 1999 <http://www.issues2000. org/Pat_Buchanan_Free_Trade_&_Immigration.html>.

17. "Remarks by Patrick Buchanan, Republican Presidential Candidate" to the Conservative Political Action Conference, Omni Shoreham Hotel, Washington, DC, *Federal News Service*, February 20, 1992.

18. Speech by Patrick Buchanan, May 28, 1999 <http://www.gopatgo2000. com/000-immigration.html>.

19. Patrick Buchanan, "The Millennium Conflict: America First or World Government," speech to Boston World Affairs Council, Boston, January 6, 2000 <http://www.buchanan.org/pa-00-0106-worldgovernment.html>.

20. Patrick J. Buchanan, "Address to the Chicago Council on Foreign Relations," November 18, 1998 <http://www.chuckbaldwinlive.com/read.free-trade.html>.

21. Buchanan, *The Great Betrayal*, 101, 105.

22. Buchanan, "Address to the Chicago Council on Foreign Relations."

23. Thomas Friedman, "America's Labor Pains," *New York Times*, May 9, 2000 <http://www.nytimes.com>.

24. See, for example, Mark P. Worrell, "The Veil of Piacular Subjectivity: Buchananism and the New World Order," *Electronic Journal of Sociology* 4, no. 3 (1999) <http://www.sociology.org/content/vol1004.003/buchanan.html>. See also Hans-Georg Betz, *Radical Right-Wing Populism in Western Europe* (New York: St. Martin's Press, 1994), 22–35.

25. Worrell, "The Veil of Piacular Subjectivity."

26. Patrick J. Buchanan, "Speech to the Daughters of the American Revolution," Washington, DC, April 22, 1992, cited in Frederick W. Mayer, *Interpreting NAFTA: The Science and Art of Political Analysis* (New York: Columbia University Press, 1998), 232.

27. For a more detailed description of these groups and their antiglobalist agenda, see Rupert, *Ideologies of Globalization*, chs. 5 and 6.

28. Pat Robertson, *The New World Order* (Dallas: Word Publishing, 1991), 37.

29. Hans-Georg Betz, "Introduction," in *The New Politics of the Right: Neo-Populist Parties and Movements in Established Democracies*, ed. Hans-Georg Betz and Stefan Immerfall (New York: St. Martin's Press, 1998), 5–6.

30. Toby Axelrod, "Current Trends in Right-Wing Extremism in Germany," American Jewish Committee (fall 2000) <http://www.ajc.org/pre/German Right.html>.

31. Geir Moulson, "German Far-Right Crime Soars to the Highest Level Since WW II," *Chicago Tribune*, March 3, 2001.

32. DVU homepage, "Our Aims and Principal Policies" <http://www.dvu-berlin.de/e-index.html>.

33. Ibid.

34. Cited in Betz, *Radical Right-Wing Populism in Western Europe*, 114.

35. Leonard Weinberg, "The American Radical Right in Comparative Perspective," in *The Revival of Right-Wing Extremism in the Nineties*, ed. Peter H. Merkl and Leonard Weinberg (London: Frank Cass, 1997), 251.

36. For a detailed account of these events, see Gott, *In the Shadow of the Liberator*.

37. Pablo Aiquel, "Can Chávez Perform an Economic Miracle?" *Le Monde Diplomatique* (November 2000) <http://monde-diplomatique.fr/en/html>.

38. Gott, *In the Shadow of the Liberator*, 27–28.

39. Ibid., 5.

40. Ibid., 131–32; and Larry Rohter, "The World: A Man With Big Ideas, a Small Country . . . and Oil," *New York Times*, September 24, 2000.

41. Chávez cited in Gott, *In the Shadow of the Liberator*, 190.

42. Chávez cited in Scott Wilson, "Chávez, Castro Sign Oil Accord," *Washington Post Foreign Service*, October 31, 2000.

43. Gott, *In the Shadow of the Liberator*, 190–91, 201.

44. Chávez cited in Daniel Eisenberg, "Oil's New Boss," *Time.com* 156, no. 15 (2000) <www.time.com/time/magazine/printout/0,8816,56401,00.html>.

45. "OPEC Summit Begins with Call for Unity," *Latin American News*, September 27, 2000 <http://www.quepasa.com>.

46. Christopher Marquis, "Bush Could Get Tougher on Venezuela's Leader," *New York Times*, December 28, 2000.

47. Gott, *In the Shadow of the Liberator*, 228.

48. Jorge G. Castaneda, *Utopia Unarmed: The Latin American Left After the Cold War* (New York: Knopf, 1993), 19.

49. "The Chávez Revolution," interview with Hugo Chávez in *Time* 154, no. 5 (August 9, 1999) <http://www.time.com>.

50. Larry Rohter, "Leader Moves to Dominate Civic Groups in Venezuela," *New York Times*, September 10, 2000 <http://www.nytimes.com>.

51. Chávez cited in Gott, *In the Shadow of the Liberator*, 198.

52. Ralph Nader, "Statement of Ralph Nader, Announcing his Candidacy for the Green Party's Nomination for President," delivered February 21, 2000, Washington, DC <www.votenader.org/press/000221/pressannounce.html>.

53. Green Party Platform, as ratified at the National Convention, June 25, 2000 <http://www.gp.org>.

54. Ralph Nader, "Acceptance Statement for the Association of State Green

Parties Nomination for President of the United States," June 25, 2000, Denver <http://votenader.org/press/000625acceptance_speech.html>.

55. *Time.com* online interview with Patrick Buchanan and Ralph Nader, November 28, 1999 <http://www.time.com/community/transcripts/1999/112899buchanan-nader.html>.

56. Ralph Nader, "Global Trade Concentrates Power and Homogenizes the Globe," *Public Interest* (December 7, 1999) <http://www.issues2000.org/Ralph_Nader_Free_Trade_&_Immigration.html>.

57. Ralph Nader, "Introduction," in Lori Wallach and Michelle Sforza, *The WTO: Five Years of Reasons to Resist Corporate Globalization* (New York: Seven Stories Press, 1999), 7.

58. Nader cited in Harold Meyerson, "Nader Speaks," *LA Weekly*, June 30–July 6, 2000 <http://www.laweekly.com/ink/00/32/cover-meyerson2.shtml>.

59. PBS Interview with Ralph Nader, March 1998 <http://www.pbs.org/globalization/nader.html>.

60. Nader, "Acceptance Statement for the Association of State Green Parties Nomination for President of the United States."

61. See 2000 U.N. Human Development Report and 1999 U.N. Human Development Report <http://www.undp.org/hdr2000>; <http://www.undp.org/hdr1999>. See also Thomas W. Pogge, "The Moral Demands of Global Justice," *Dissent* (fall 2000):37–43.

62. Nader, "Introduction," in Wallach and Sforza, *The WTO*, 12.

63. Ralph Nader, "The Concord Principles: An Agenda for a New Initiatory Democracy," February 1, 1992 <http://petra.greens.org/~cls/nader/concord.html>.

64. Nader, "Acceptance Statement for the Association of State Green Parties Nomination for President of the United States."

65. See, for example, Jeremy Brecher, Tim Costello, and Brendan Smith, *Globalization from Below: The Power of Solidarity* (Cambridge, MA: South End Press, 2000); Falk, *Predatory Globalization*; Joshua Karliner, *The Corporate Planet: Ecology and Politics in the Age of Globalization* (San Francisco: Sierra Club Books, 1997).

66. Candido Grzybowski, "Civil Societies Responses to Globalization," Rio de Janeiro, November 8, 1995 <http://www.corpwatch.org/trac/feature/planet/gr_twn.html>.

67. Martin Khor, "How the South Is Getting a Raw Deal at the WTO," in Sarah Anderson, ed., *Views from the South: The Effects of Globalization and the WTO on Third World Countries* (Chicago: Food First Books, 2000), 47. For more information on Third World Network see <http://www.twnside.org>.

68. "History of the IFG" <http://www.ifg.org/about/html>.

69. For more information on Global Exchange see <http://www.globalexchange.org>.

70. Diane Elson, ed., *Male Bias in the Development Process*, 2nd ed. (Manchester, UK: Manchester University Press, 1995); and Isabella Bakker, *The Strategic Silence* (London: Zed Books, 1994).)

71. See, for example, Angela Miles, "Local Activisms, Global Feminisms and the Struggle Against Globalization," *Canadian Woman Studies* 20, no. 3 (fall 2000):6–10; and Rita Mae Kelly, Jane H. Bayes, Mary E. Hawkesworth, and Brigitte Young, eds., *Gender, Globalization, and Democratization* (Lanham, MD: Rowman & Littlefield, 2001).

72. Valentine M. Moghadam, "Transnational Feminist Networks: Collective Action in an Era of Globalization," *International Sociology* 15, no. 1 (March 2000):57–86.

73. Walden Bello, "From Melbourne to Prague: The Struggle for a Deglobalized World," talk delivered at a series of engagements on the occasion of demonstrations against the World Economic Forum (Davos) in Melbourne, Australia, September 6–10, 2000 <http://www.globalexchange.org/economy/alternatives/bello090600.html> For more information of Focus on the Global South see <http://focusweb.org>.

74. Jan Nederveen Pieterse, "Globalization and Emancipation: From Local Empowerment to Global Reform," in Gills, *Globalization and the Politics of Resistance*, 192.

75. R. J. Barry Jones, "Globalization versus Community: Stakeholding, Communitarianism and the Challenge of Globalization," in Gills, *Globalization and the Politics of Resistance*, 65.

76. Alexander Cockburn, Jeffrey St. Clair, and Allan Sekula, *5 Days That Shook the World: Seattle and Beyond* (London: Verso, 2000), 65; and Public Citizens Health Research Group, "Let the 'Non-Governments' Beware: Multinational Organizations Are Out to Co-opt You and Your Tactics," *Health Letter* 2 (February 2001):5–7.

77. Subcomandante Marcos, "First Declaration of La Realidad," August 3, 1996 <http://www.apostate.com/politics/realidad2.html>. For a comprehensive collection of Marcos's early speeches, see Subcomandante Marcos, *Shadows of Tender Fury: The Letters and Communiqués of Subcomandante Marcos and the Zapatista Army of National Liberation*, ed. and introduction by John Ross (New York: Monthly Review Press, 1995).

78. Subcomandante Marcos, "Do Not Forget Ideas Are Also Weapons," excerpted from "La droite intellectuelle et le fascisme liberal," *Le Monde diplomatique*, August 2000 <http://www.theexperiment.org>.

79. Jean-Bertrand Aristide, *Eyes of the Heart: Seeking a Path for the Poor in the Age of Globalization* (Monroe, ME: Common Courage Press, 2000), 49.

80. Steven Greenhouse, "After Seattle, Unions Point to Sustained Fight on Trade," *New York Times*, December 6, 1999.

Chapter Five

1. Jane Slaughter, "The Next Seattle: Naomi Klein Looks into the Future of the Movement," *In These Times* (December 25, 2000).

2. Buchanan cited in Martin Koppel, "Buchanan Courts Labor Officials with His 'America First' Politics," *Militant* 63, no. 42 (November 29, 1999).

3. "Neither Left Nor Right," *Southern Poverty Law Center Intelligence Report* (winter 2000) <http://www.splcenter.org/intelligenceproject/ip-4m3.html>. I want to thank Mark Potok, the editor of the *Southern Poverty Law Center Intelligence Report*, for his personal correspondence of January 25, 2001, clarifying my questions about the presence of the radical right in Seattle.

4. Martin Khor, "Seattle Debacle: Revolt of the Developing Nations," in Danaher and Burbach, *Globalize This!*, 48; and Mary Kaldor, "'Civilising' Globalisation? The Implications of the 'Battle in Seattle,'" *Millennium: Journal of International Studies* 29, no. 1 (2000):105–15.

5. For more detailed accounts of the "Battle of Seattle" from the perspective of the protesters, see Danaher and Burbach, *Globalize This!*; and Cockburn et al., *5 Days That Shook the World*.

6. Danaher and Burbach, *Globalize This!*, 24–25.

7. Cockburn et al., *5 Days That Shook the World*, 39, 101.

8. Danaher and Burbach, *Globalize This!*, 23; and Cockburn et al., *5 Days That Shook the World*, 51.

9. Cockburn et al., *5 Days That Shook the World*, 34.

10. Ibid., 51–52.

11. Ibid., 38. Jeffrey St. Clair asserts that at the very moment President Clinton was publicly expressing some sympathy with the demonstrators, his aides were ordering Seattle Mayor Shell to use all available force to clear the streets (see ibid., 39).

12. Charlene Barshefsky cited in Martin Khor, "Seattle Debacle: Revolt of the Developing Nations," in Danaher and Burbach, *Globalize This!*, 51.

13. Cockburn et al., *5 Days That Shook the World*, 8.

14. See Mazur, "Labor's New Internationalism," 79–93.

15. Cockburn et al., *5 Days That Shook the World*, 70–71.

16. Anthony Williams cited in John Kifner and David E. Sanger, "Financial Leaders Meet as Protests Clog Washington," *New York Times*, April 17, 2000.

17. Desko Vladic cited in Joseph Kahn, "Protesters Assemble, Hoping for a Rerun of Seattle's Show," *New York Times*, September 23, 2000.

18. Stefan Theil, "Taking It to the Streets," *Newsweek* (Atlantic edition), (September 25, 2000):40.

19. Ibid., 40.

20. Joseph Kahn, "Protests Diminish at Conference in Prague on Worldwide Aid," *New York Times*, September 28, 2000.

21. For a description of the demonstrations in Nice, see Suzanne Daley, "Europeans, and Protesters, Meet on the Riviera," *New York Times*, December 8, 2000.

22. "Police Quell Davos Protests," *BBC News*, January 28, 2001 <http:www.bbc.co.uk>; and Onna Coray, "Swiss Police Catch Heat for Anti-Global Melee," *Chicago Tribune*, January 30, 2001.

23. David Greising, "Free Speech Not on Agenda of Global Leaders," *Chicago Tribune*, January 28, 2001.

24. Onna Coray, "Swiss Police Catch Heat for Anti-Global Melee," *Chicago Tribune*, January 30, 2001.

25. Hannah Arendt, *On Violence* (New York: Harcourt Brace Jovanovich, 1970), 56.

26. McChesney, "Global Media, Neoliberalism, and Imperialism," 12.

27. William S. Solomon, "More Form Than Substance: Press Coverage of the WTO Protests in Seattle," *Monthly Review* 52, no. 1 (May 2000) <http://www.monthlyreview.org/500solo.html>.

28. See David Demers, *Global Media: Menace or Messiah?* (Cresskill, NJ: Hampton Press, 1999). See also Edward S. Herman and Robert W. McChesney, *The Global Media: The New Missionaries of Corporate Capitalism* (London: Cassell, 1997).

29. McChesney, "Global Media, Neoliberalism, and Imperialism," 3.

30. Christopher Dixon cited in McChesney, "Global Media, Neoliberalism, and Imperialism," 2.

31. Solomon, "More Form Than Substance."

32. All citations taken from Seth Ackerman, "Prattle in Seattle: Media Coverage Misrepresents Protests," in Danaher and Burbach, *Globalize This!*, 61.

33. Editorial, *Chicago Tribune*, November 30, 1999.

34. See, for example, Cathy Young, "The Fuzzy Goals of Antiglobalization Activists," *Boston Globe*, October 1, 2000; and "Clueless in Seattle," *Economist* (December 14, 1999):17.

35. Malcolm Wallop, "Memo to Business: The Greens Intend to Place Profits on the Endangered List," *Investor's Business Daily*, January 8, 2001.

36. Richard D. McCormick, "Why the Protesters Are Wrong," in "Debating Globalization," *BBC News*, January 26, 2001 <http://www.bbc.co.uk>.

37. Caio Koch-Weser cited in "Meet the New Face of Globalization," *Toronto Star*, September 24, 2000.

38. Carl Ware cited in Anita Munson, "Coca-Cola Executive Defends Globalization Based on His Experience," *South Bend Tribune*, November 16, 2000; Alan Greenspan cited in Rob Garver, "Greenspan to Bank: Champion Free

Trade," *American Banker* (November 15, 2000):4; Aaron Lucas cited in the *Proceedings of the Cato Institute Policy Forum*, October 6, 2000 <http://cato.org/events/transcripts/001006et.pdf>; Warren Staley cited in "Ideas Must Flow about Free Trade," *City Business*, January 21, 2000.

39. Bill Clinton, "Remarks by the President to the Community of the University of Warwick," 2000 <http://www.usembassy.org.uk/potus00/oo1214b.html>.

40. Kofi Annan, address to the World Economic Forum in Davos, Switzerland, January 28, 2001 <http://www.un.org/News/dh/latest/address_2001.html>.

41. Editorial, *BusinessWeek* (November 6, 2000):228.

42. Pete Engardia and Catherine Belton, "Global Capitalism: Can it Be Made to Work Better?" *BusinessWeek* (November 6, 2000):40.

43. Jagdish Bhagwati, *The Wind of the Hundred Days: How Washington Mismanaged Globalization* (Cambridge, MA: MIT Press, 2000), 317–22.

44. Friedman, *The Lexus and the Olive Tree*, 438–68.

45. See, for example, Susan George, "Another World Is Possible," *Dissent* (winter 2001):5–8; Mazur, "Labor's New Internationalism," 79–98; Richard Falk, "Meeting the Political Challenge of Globalization," *Australian Financial Review* (January 7, 2000):17; and Stephen Gill, "Toward a Postmodern Prince? The Battle in Seattle as a Moment in the New Politics of Globalisation," *Millennium: Journal of International Studies* 29, no. 1 (2000):131–40.

46. Luis Hernandez Navarro, "The Revolt of the Globalized," in Danaher and Burbach, *Globalize This!*, 43.

47. See, for example, Jan Aart Scholte, "Cautionary Reflections on Seattle," *Millennium: Journal of International Studies* 29, no. 1 (2000):115–21; and Fred Halliday, "Getting Real about Seattle," *Millennium: Journal of International Studies* 29, no. 1 (2000):123–29.

48. See, for example, Kaldor, "'Civilising' Globalisation?," 113.

49. Bernard Cassen cited in Tony Smith, "Anti-Globalization Summit Opens," *AP International News*, January 25, 2001 <http://www.news.excite.com/news/ap/010125/20/int-world-social-forum.html>.

Chapter Six

1. Nancy Birdsall, "Building a Market-Friendly Middle Class," remarks delivered at the Annual World Bank Conference on Development Economics, April 18, 2000 <http://odc.org/commentary/bird-wb.html>.

2. Martin Khor, "A Year after Seattle, No Progress at WTO," *South–North Development Monitor* no. 4797 (December 5, 2000) <http://twnside.org.sg/title/twr123a.html>.

3. Bill Berkowitz, "Desert Camouflage," *In These Times* (March 19, 2001): 16.

4. For a full text of the manifesto, including critical marginal notes by Jo-anne Barkan, see Tony Blair and Gerhard Schröder, "The Third Way/*Die Neue Mitte*," *Dissent* (spring 2000):51–65.

5. Giddens, *The Third Way*; and "Anthony Giddens and Will Hutton in Conversation," in Hutton and Giddens, *Global Capitalism*, 1–51.

6. "Anthony Giddens and Will Hutton in Conversation," in Hutton and Giddens, *Global Capitalism*, 11–12.

7. Perry Anderson, "Renewals," *New Left Review* 1 (January/February 2000):17.

8. Karl Polanyi, *The Great Transformation: The Political and Economic Origins of Our Time* (Reprint, Boston: Beacon Press, 1957), 29.

9. Ibid., 141.

10. Ibid., 132.

11. For the concise explication of Polanyi's ethical theory, see Gregory Baum, *Karl Polanyi on Ethics and Economics* (Montreal: McGill-Queen's University Press, 1996).

12. Polanyi, *The Great Transformation*, 237.

13. Southern Poverty Law Center, "Neither Left Nor Right: The Spreading Battle Against the Forces of Economic Globalism Is Shaping the Extremism of the New Millennium" <http://splcenter.org>.

14. See Pressebüro Savanne, "Right–Left—A Dangerous Flirt" <http://www.savanne.ch/right-left.html>. See also Berlet and Lyons, *Right-Wing Populism in America*, 342–43.

15. Ryan Lizza, "Silent Partner," *New Republic Online*, January 10, 2000 <http://www.tnr.com/magazines/tnr/011000/lizza011000html>. See also Mark S., "The Progressive Left's Dirty Little Secret: Public Citizen, IFG, and the Far Right," May 14, 2000 <http://www.tao.ca/~resist/thelftsdirtylittle secret.html>.

16. Interview with Patrick Buchanan and Ralph Nader, *Time.com*, November 28, 1999 <http://time.com/time/community/transcripts/1999/112899bu chanan-nader.html>.

17. See "Protest in Ecuador Escalates," SAPRIN Network, February 6, 2001 <http://conaie.nativeweb.org>.

18. See Clifford Kraus, "Argentina Paralyzed by Strike Over President's Austerity Policy," *New York Times*, June 9, 2000 <http:www.nytimes.com/yr/mo/day/late/09cnd-argentina.html>.

19. Soros, *The Crisis of Global Capitalism*, xv–xxix.

20. For a detailed description of such a reform agenda, see Jan Nederveen Pieterse, ed., *Global Futures: Shaping Globalization* (London: Zed Books, 2000), ch. 12; and Cable, *Globalization and Global Governance*, chs. 4–7.

21. Brecher, Costello, and Smith, *Globalization from Below*, 67–80.

22. Michel Rocard, "Does Social Democracy Have a Future?" in Peter Rus-

sell, ed., *The Future of Social Democracy: Views of Leaders from Around the World* (Toronto, ON: University of Toronto Press, 1999), 15–22.

23. See Dalai Lama, *Ethics for the New Millennium* (New York: Riverhead Books, 1999); Pope John Paul II, *Crossing the Threshold of Hope*, ed. Vittorio Messori (New York: Knopf, 1994); and Desmond Tutu, *No Future Without Forgiveness* (New York: Doubleday, 1999).

24. Hans Küng, *A Global Ethic for Global Politics and Economics* (New York: Oxford University Press, 1998), 111.

25. Dalai Lama, *Ethics for the New Millennium*, 197.

SELECTED BIBLIOGRAPHY

Albrow, Martin. *Globalization*. London: Routledge, 1995.

———. *The Global Age: State and Society Beyond Modernity*. Cambridge: Polity Press, 1996.

Amin, Samir. *Capitalism in the Age of Globalization: The Management of Contemporary Society*. London: Zed Books, 1997.

Anderson, Sarah, ed. *Views from the South: The Effects of Globalization and the WTO on Third World Countries*. Chicago: Food First Books, 2000.

Anderson, Sarah, and John Cavanagh, with Thea Lee. *Field Guide to the Global Economy*. New York: New Press, 2000.

Appadurai, Arjun. *Modernity at Large: Cultural Dimensions of Globalization*. Minneapolis: University of Minnesota Press, 1996.

Archibugi, Daniele, David Held, and Martin Koehler, eds. *Re-Imagining Political Community: Studies in Cosmopolitan Democracy*. Stanford, CA: Stanford University Press, 1998.

Arendt, Hannah. *On Violence*. New York: Harcourt Brace Jovanovich, 1970.

Aristide, Jean-Bertrand. *Eyes of the Heart: Seeking a Path for the Poor in the Age of Globalization*. Monroe, ME: Common Courage Press, 2000.

Ashley, David. *History Without a Subject: The Postmodern Condition*. Boulder, CO: Westview Press, 1997.

Axtmann, Roland, ed. *Globalization in Europe: Theoretical and Empirical Investigations*. Washington, DC: Pinter, 1998.

Bakker, Isabella. *The Strategic Silence*. London: Zed Books, 1994.

Bamyeh, Mohammed A. *The Ends of Globalization*. Minneapolis: University of Minnesota Press, 2000.

Barber, Benjamin R. *Jihad vs. McWorld*. New York: Ballantine Books, 1996.

Barker, Chris. *Television, Globalization and Cultural Identities*. Buckingham, PA: Open University Press, 1999.

Barnet, Richard J., and John Cavanagh. *Global Dreams: Imperial Corporations and the New World Order.* New York: Simon & Schuster, 1994.

Bauman, Zygmunt. *Globalization: The Human Consequences*. New York: Columbia University Press, 1998.

———. *In Search of Politics*. Stanford, CA: Stanford University Press, 1999.

Beck, Ulrich. *Risk Society*. London: Sage, 1992.

———. *What Is Globalization?* Cambridge: Polity Press, 2000.

Bell, Daniel. *The End of Ideology: On the Exhaustion of Political Ideas in the Fifties*. Glencoe, IL: Free Press, 1960.

Berlet, Chip, and Matthew N. Lyons. *Right-Wing Populism in America: Too Close for Comfort*. New York: Guilford Press, 2000.

Berlin, Isaiah. *Four Essays on Liberty*. London: Oxford University Press, 1969.

Betz, Hans-Georg. *Radical Right-Wing Populism in Western Europe*. New York: St. Martin's Press, 1994.

Betz, Hans-Georg, and Stefan Immerfall, eds. *The New Politics of the Right: Neo-Populist Parties and Movements in Established Democracies*. New York: St. Martin's Press, 1998.

Bhagwati, Jagdish. *The Wind of the Hundred Days: How Washington Mismanaged Globalization*. Cambridge, MA: MIT Press, 2000.

Black, Jan Knippers. *Inequity in the Global Village: Recycled Rhetoric and Disposable People*. West Hartford, CT: Kumarian Press, 1999.

Bobbio, Norberto. *Left & Right: The Significance of a Political Distinction*. Chicago: University of Chicago Press, 1996.

Boggs, Carl. *The End of Politics: Corporate Power and the Decline of the Public Sphere*. New York: Guilford Press, 2000.

Bourdieu, Pierre. *Acts of Resistance: Against the Tyranny of the Market*. New York: New Press, 1998.

Boyer, Robert, and Daniel Drache, eds. *States Against Markets: The Limits of Globalisation*. London: Routledge, 1996.

Braman, Sandra, and Annabelle Sreberny-Mohammadi, eds. *Globalization, Communication and Transnational Civil Society*. Cresskill, NJ: Hampton Press, 1996.

Brecher, Jeremy, and Tim Costello. *Global Village or Global Pillage? Economic Reconstruction from the Bottom Up,* 2nd ed. Cambridge, MA: South End Press, 1998.

Brecher, Jeremy, Tim Costello, and Brendan Smith. *Globalization from Below: The Power of Solidarity*. Cambridge, MA: South End Press, 2000.

Bronner, Stephen Eric. *Of Critical Theory and Its Theorists*. Malden, MA: Blackwell, 1994.

————. *Ideas in Action: Political Tradition in the Twentieth Century.* Lanham, MD: Rowman & Littlefield, 1999.

Bronner, Stephen Eric, and Douglas Kellner, eds. *Critical Theory and Society: A Reader.* London: Routledge, 1989.

Brook, James, and Iain A. Boal. *Resisting the Virtual Life.* San Francisco: City Lights, 1995.

Bryan, Lowell, and Diana Farrell. *Market Unbound: Unleashing Global Capitalism.* New York: Wiley, 1996.

Buchanan, Patrick J. *The Great Betrayal: How American Sovereignty and Social Justice Are Being Sacrificed to the Gods of the Global Economy.* Boston: Little, Brown, 1998.

————. *A Republic, Not An Empire: Reclaiming America's Destiny.* Washington, DC: Regnery Publishing,1999.

Buelens, Frans. *Globalisation and the Nation-State.* Northampton, MA: Edward Elgar Publishing, 2000.

Burbach, Roger. *Globalization and Postmodern Politics: From Zapatistas to High Tech Robber Barons.* London: Pluto Press, 2001.

Burbach, Roger, Orlando Nunez, and Boris Kagarlitsky. *Globalization and Its Discontents: The Rise of Postmodern Socialism.* London: Pluto Press, 1997.

Burns, Timothy, ed. *After History? Francis Fukuyama and His Critics.* Lanham, MD: Rowman & Littlefield, 1994.

Burtless, Gary, Robert Z. Lawrence, Robert E. Litan, and Robert J. Shapiro. *Globaphobia: Confronting Fears about Open Trade.* Washington, DC: Brookings Institution, 1998.

Cable, Vincent. *Globalization and Global Governance.* London: Royal Institute of International Affairs, 1999.

Callinicos, Alex. *Social Theory: A Historical Introduction.* New York: New York University Press, 1999.

Canovan, Margaret. *Populism.* New York: Harcourt Brace Jovanovich, 1981.

Carnoy, Martin, Manuel Castells, and Stephen S. Cohen., eds. *The Global Economy in the Information Age.* University Park: Pennsylvania State University Press, 1993.

Carroll, William, Radhika Desai, and Warren Magnusson. *Globalization, Social Justice and Social Movements: A Reader.* Victoria, ON: University of Victoria, 1996.

Castaneda, Jorge G. *Utopia Unarmed: The Latin American Left After the Cold War.* New York: Knopf, 1993.

Castells, Manuel. *The Information Age: Economy, Society and Culture,* 3 vols. Oxford: Blackwell, 1996–1998.

Chase-Dunn, Christopher. *Global Formation: Structures of the World Economy.* Lanham, MD: Rowman & Littlefield, 1998.

Chomsky, Noam. *Profit Over People: Neoliberalism and Global Order.* New York: Seven Stories Press, 1999.

Clark, Ian. *Globalization and International Relations Theory.* Oxford: Oxford University Press, 1999.

Cockburn, Alexander, Jeffrey St. Clair, and Allan Sekula. *5 Days That Shook the World: Seattle and Beyond.* London: Verso, 2000.

Cohn, Theodore H. *Global Political Economy: Theory and Practice.* New York: Longman, 2000.

Cox, K. R., ed. *Spaces of Globalization: Reasserting the Power of the Local.* New York: Guilford Press, 1997.

Cox, Robert W. *Production, Power, and World Order: Social Forces in the Making of History.* New York: Columbia University Press, 1987.

Crothers, Lane, and Charles Lockhart, eds. *Culture and Politics: A Reader.* New York: St. Martin's Press, 2000.

Cvetkovich, Ann, and Douglas Kellner. *Articulating the Global and the Local: Globalization and Cultural Studies.* Boulder, CO: Westview Press, 1996.

Dallmayr, Fred. *Alternative Visions: Paths in the Global Village.* Lanham, MD: Rowman & Littlefield, 1998.

Danaher, Kevin, and Roger Burbach, eds. *Globalize This! The Battle Against the World Trade Organization and Corporate Rule.* Monroe, ME: Common Courage Press, 2000.

————. *Democratizing the Global Economy: The Battle Against the World Bank and the IMF.* Monroe, ME: Common Courage Press, 2001.

DeMartino, George F. *Global Economy, Global Justice: Theoretical Objections and Policy Alternatives to Neoliberalism.* London: Routledge, 2000.

Demers, David. *Global Media: Menace or Messiah?* Cresskill, NJ: Hampton Press, 1999.

Derber, Charles. *Corporation Nation.* New York: St. Martin's Press, 1998.

Dirlif, Arif. *Postcolonial Aura: Third World Criticism in the Age of Global Capitalism.* Boulder, CO: Westview Press, 1997.

Doremus, Paul, William W. Keller, Louis W. Pauly, and Simon Reich. *The Myth of the Global Corporation.* Princeton, NJ: Princeton University Press, 1998.

Dunkerley, David, and John Beynon. *The Globalisation Reader.* London: Athlone, 1999.

Eagleton, Terry. *Ideology: An Introduction.* London: Verso, 1991.

Elson, Diane, ed. *Male Bias in the Development Process,* 2nd ed. Manchester, UK: Manchester University Press, 1995.

Eschle, Catherine. *Feminism, Social Movements, and the Globalization of Democracy.* Boulder, CO: Westview Press, 2001.

Falk, Richard A. *On Humane Governance: Toward a New Global Politics.* Cambridge: Polity Press, 1995.

————. *Predatory Globalization: A Critique.* Cambridge: Polity Press, 1999.

―――. *Human Rights Horizons: The Pursuit of Justice in a Globalizing World.* New York: Routledge, 2000.

Featherstone, Mike. *Consumer Culture and Postmodernism.* London: Sage, 1991.

―――. *Undoing Culture: Globalization, Postmodernism and Identity.* London: Sage, 1995.

Featherstone, Mike, ed. *Global Culture.* London: Sage, 1990.

Featherstone, Mike, Scott Lash, and Roland Robertson, eds. *Global Modernities.* London: Sage, 1995.

Ferleger, Lou, and Jay Mandle. *Dimensions of Globalization.* Thousand Oaks, CA: Sage, 2000.

Fishlow, Albert, and Karen Parker, eds. *Growing Apart: The Causes and Consequences of Global Wage Inequality.* New York: Council of Foreign Relations Press, 1999.

Foucault, Michel. *The Archeology of Knowledge.* New York: Pantheon, 1972.

Frank, Andre Gunder. *ReORIENT: Global Economy in the Asian Age.* Berkeley: University of California Press, 1998.

Frank, Thomas. *One Market under God: Extreme Capitalism, Market Populism, and the End of Economic Democracy.* New York: Doubleday, 2000.

Freeden, Michael. *Ideologies and Political Theory: A Conceptual Approach.* Oxford: Clarendon Press, 1996.

French, Hilary. *Vanishing Borders: Protecting the Planet in the Age of Globalization.* New York: Norton, 2000.

Friedman, Milton. *Capitalism and Freedom.* Chicago: University of Chicago Press, 1962.

Friedman, Thomas L. *The Lexus and the Olive Tree.* New York: Farrar, Straus & Giroux, 1999.

Fukuyama, Francis. *The End of History and the Last Man.* New York: Free Press, 1992.

―――. *The Great Disruption: Human Nature and the Reconstitution of Social Order.* New York: Free Press, 1999.

Gadamer, Hans-Georg. *Truth and Method.* New York: Seabury Press, 1975.

Gardels, Nathan, ed. *The Changing Global Order.* London: Blackwell, 1997.

Garrett, Geoffrey. *Partisan Politics in the Global Economy.* Cambridge: Cambridge University Press, 1998.

Gereffi, Gary, and Miguel Korzeniewicz, eds. *Commodity Chains and Global Capitalism.* Westport, CT: Greenwood Press, 1993.

Germain, Randall D. *Globalization and Its Critics: Perspectives from Political Economy.* New York: St. Martin's Press, 2000.

Giddens, Anthony. *The Consequences of Modernity.* Stanford, CA: Stanford University Press, 1990.

―――. *Beyond Left and Right: The Future of Radical Politics.* Stanford, CA: Stanford University Press, 1994.

———. *The Third Way: The Renewal of Social Democracy*. Cambridge: Polity Press, 1998.

———. *Runaway World*. London: Routledge, 2000.

Gill, Stephen, and James Mittelman, eds. *Innovation and Transformation in International Studies*. Cambridge: Cambridge University Press, 1997.

Gills, Barry K., ed. *Globalization and the Politics of Resistance*. New York: St. Martin's Press, 2000.

Gilpin, Robert. *The Challenge of Global Capitalism: The World Economy in the 21st Century*. Princeton, NJ: Princeton University Press, 2000.

Gott, Richard. *In the Shadow of the Liberator: Hugo Chávez and the Transformation of Venezuela*. London: Verso, 2000.

Gowan, Peter. *The Global Gamble: Washington's Faustian Bid for World Dominance*. London: Verso, 1999.

Gramsci, Antonio. *Selections from Prison Notebooks*. New York: International Publishers, 1971.

Gray, John. *False Dawn: The Delusions of Global Capitalism*. New York: New Press, 1998.

Greider, William. *One World, Ready or Not: The Manic Logic of Global Capitalism*. New York: Simon & Schuster, 1997.

Habermas, Jürgen. *Knowledge and Human Interests*. Boston: Beacon Press, 1973.

Hannerz, Ulf. *Cultural Complexity: Studies in the Social Organization of Meaning*. New York: Columbia University Press, 1992.

———. *Transnational Connections: Cultures, People, Places*. London: Routledge, 1996.

Hardt, Michael, and Antonio Negri. *Empire*. Cambridge, MA: Harvard University Press, 2000.

Hart, Jeffrey A., and Aseem Prakash. *Coping with Globalization*. London: Routledge, 2000.

———. *Responding to Globalization*. London: Routledge, 2000.

Harvey, David. *The Condition of Postmodernity*. Oxford: Blackwell, 1989.

Hayek, Friedrich. *Law, Legislation, and Liberty*, 3 vols. London: Routledge & Kegan Paul, 1979.

Held, David. *Democracy and the Global Order*. Stanford, CA: Stanford University Press, 1995.

Held, David, and Anthony G. McGrew. *The Global Transformations Reader: An Introduction to the Globalization Debate*. Cambridge: Polity Press, 2000.

Held, David, Anthony McGrew, David Goldblatt, and Jonathan Perraton. *Global Transformations: Politics, Economics, and Culture*. Stanford, CA: Stanford University Press, 1999.

Helleiner, Eric. *States and the Reemergence of Global Finance*. Ithaca, NY: Cornell University Press, 1994.

Henderson, Hazel. *Beyond Globalization: Shaping a Sustainable Global Economy*. West Hartford, CT: Kumarian Press, 1999.

Herman, Edward S., and Robert W. McChesney. *The Global Media: The New Missionaries of Corporate Capitalism*. London: Cassell, 1997.

Hirschman, Albert O. *The Rhetoric of Reaction*. Cambridge, MA: Harvard University Press, 1991.

Hirst, Paul, and Graham Thompson. *Globalization in Question: The International Economy and the Possibilities of Governance*, 2nd ed. Cambridge: Polity Press, 1999.

Hodges, Michael R., John J. Kirton, and Joseph P. Daniels, eds. *The G8's Role in the New Millennium*. Aldershot, UK: Ashgate, 1999.

Holton, Robert J. *Globalization and the Nation-State*. New York: St. Martin's Press, 1998.

Huntington, Samuel P. *The Clash of Civilization: Remaking of World Order*. New York: Simon & Schuster, 1996.

Hurrell, Andrew, and Ngaire Woods, eds. *Inequality, Globalization, and World Politics*. Oxford: Oxford University Press, 1999.

Hutton, Will, and Anthony Giddens, eds. *Global Capitalism*. New York: Free Press, 2000.

Jackson, Robert H., and Alan James, eds. *States in a Changing World: A Contemporary Analysis*. Oxford: Clarendon Press, 1993.

Jacoby, Russell. *The End of Utopia*. New York: Westview Press, 1999.

Jameson, Fredric, and Masao Miyoshi, eds. *The Cultures of Globalization*. Durham, NC: Duke University Press, 1998.

Kagarlitsky, Boris. *The Twilight of Globalization: Property, State and Capitalism*. London: Pluto Press, 2000.

Kalb, Don, Marco van der Land, Richard Staring, Bart van Steenbergen, and Nico Wilterding, eds. *The Ends of Globalization: Bringing Society Back In*. Lanham, MD: Rowman & Littlefield, 2000.

Kapstein, Ethan B. *Sharing the Wealth: Workers and the World Economy*. New York: Norton, 1999.

Karliner, Joshua. *The Corporate Planet: Ecology and Politics in the Age of Globalization*. San Francisco: Sierra Club Books, 1997.

Kazin, Michael. *The Populist Persuasion: An American History*. New York: Basic Books, 1995.

Kelly, Rita Mae, Jane H. Bayes, Mary E. Hawkesworth, and Brigitte Young, eds. *Gender, Globalization, and Democratization*. Lanham, MD: Rowman & Littlefield, 2001.

Keohane, Robert O. *After Hegemony*. Princeton, NJ: Princeton University Press, 1984.

Klak, Thomas. *Globalization and Neoliberalism: The Caribbean Context*. Lanham, MD: Rowman & Littlefield, 1998.

Kofman, Eleonore, and Gillian Young, eds. *Globalization: Theory and Practice.* London: Pinter, 1996.

Korten, David C. *When Corporations Rule the World.* West Hartford, CT: Kumarian Press, 1995.

———. *The Post-Corporate World.* West Hartford, CT: Kumarian Press, 1999.

Krugman, Paul. *The Accidental Theorist.* New York: Norton, 1998.

Küng, Hans. *A Global Ethic for Global Politics and Economics.* New York: Oxford University Press, 1998.

Kuttner, Robert. *Everything For Sale: The Virtues and the Limits of the Market.* New York: Knopf, 1997.

Laclau, Ernesto, and Chantal Mouffe. *Hegemony and Socialist Practice: Towards a Radical Democratic Politics.* London: Verso, 1985.

LaFeber, Walter. *Michael Jordan and Global Capitalism.* New York: Norton, 1999.

Larrain, Jorge. *The Concept of Ideology.* London: Hutchinson, 1979.

Latouche, Serge. *The Westernization of the World.* Cambridge: Polity Press, 1996.

Lechner, Frank J., and John Boli, eds. *The Globalization Reader.* Oxford: Blackwell, 2000.

Leonard, Stephen. *Critical Theory in Political Practice.* Princeton, NJ: Princeton University Press, 1990.

Lipietz, Alain. *Towards a New Economic Order.* Oxford: Oxford University Press, 1993.

Luttwak, Edward. *Turbo-Capitalism: Winners and Losers in the Global Economy.* New York: HarperCollins, 1999.

Mander, Jerry, and Edward Goldsmith, eds. *The Case Against the Global Economy.* New York: Random House (Sierra Club), 1999.

Mannheim, Karl. *Ideology and Utopia: An Introduction to the Sociology of Knowledge.* 1936. Reprint, London: Routledge, 1991.

Marcuse, Peter, and Ronald van Kempen. *Globalizing Cities: A New Spatial Order?* Malden, MA: Blackwell, 2000.

Martin, Hans-Peter, and Harald Schumann. *The Global Trap: Globalization and the Assault on Democracy and Prosperity.* London: Zed Books, 1997.

Mayer, Frederick W. *Interpreting NAFTA: The Science and Art of Political Analysis.* New York: Columbia University Press, 1998.

McBride, Stephen Kenneth, and John Richard Wiseman. *Globalization and its Discontents.* New York: St. Martin's Press, 2000.

McLellan, David. *Ideology.* Milton Keynes, UK: Open University Press, 1986.

McNeill, J. R. *Something New under the Sun: An Environmental History of the Twentieth-Century World.* New York: Norton, 2000.

Meszaros, Istvan. *The Power of Ideology.* New York: New York University Press, 1989.

Meyer, Birgit, and Peter Geschiere. *Globalization and Identity: Dialectics of Flow and Closure.* Oxford: Blackwell, 1999.

Micklethwait, John, and Adrian Woolridge. *A Future Perfect: The Challenge and Hidden Promise of Globalization.* New York: Crown Publishers, 2000.

Mishra, Ramesh. *Globalization and the Welfare State.* Cheltenham, UK: Elgar, 1999.

Mittelman, James H., ed. *Globalization: Critical Reflections.* Boulder, CO: Lynne Rienner, 1996.

————. *The Globalization Syndrome: Transformation and Resistance.* Princeton, NJ: Princeton University Press, 2000.

Mokhiber, Russell, and Robert Weissman. *Global Predators: The Hunt for Mega-Profits and the Attack on Democracy.* Monroe, ME: Common Courage Press, 1999.

Mooney, Harold A. *The Globalization of Ecological Thought.* Oldendorf, Germany: Ecology Institute, 1998.

Mosler, David, and Robert Catley. *Global America: Imposing Liberalism on a Recalcitrant World.* Westport, CT: Praeger, 2000.

Munck, Ronaldo, and Peter Waterman, eds. *Labour Worldwide in the Era of Globalization: Alternative Union Models in the New World Order.* New York: St. Martin's Press, 1999.

Naisbitt, John. *Global Paradox.* London: Nicholas Brealey Publishing, 1995.

Nash, Kate. *Contemporary Political Sociology: Globalization, Politics, and Power.* Malden, MA: Blackwell, 2000.

Negroponte, Nicholas. *Being Digital.* London: Hodder & Stoughton, 1995.

Offe, Claus. *Modernity and the State: East, West.* Cambridge: Polity Press, 1996.

Ohmae, Kenichi. *The Borderless World: Power and Strategy in the Interlinked World Economy.* New York: Harper Business, 1990.

————. *The End of the Nation-State: The Rise of Regional Economies.* New York: Free Press, 1995.

O'Meara, Patrick, Howard M. Mehlinger, and Matthew Krain, eds. *Globalization and the Challenges of a New Century: A Reader.* Bloomington: Indiana University Press, 2000.

O'Rourke, Kevin H., and Jeffrey G. Williamson. *Globalization and History: The Evolution of a Nineteenth-Century Atlantic Economy.* Cambridge, MA: MIT Press, 1999.

Osborne, Peter, ed. *A Critical Sense: Interviews with Intellectuals.* London: Routledge, 1996.

Panitch, Leo, and Colin Leys, eds. *Global Capitalism versus Democracy: The Socialist Register 1999.* New York: Monthly Review Press, 1999.

Petras, James. *The Left Strikes Back: Class Conflict in the Age of Neoliberalism.* Boulder, CO: Westview Press, 1998.

Pieterse, Jan Nederveen, ed. *Global Futures: Shaping Globalization*. London: Zed Books, 2000.

Polyani, Karl. *The Great Transformation: The Political and Economic Origins of Our Time*. 1944. Reprint, Boston: Beacon Press, 1957.

Prakash, Aseem, and Jeffrey A. Hart. *Globalization and Governance*. London: Routledge, 1999.

Rajaee, Farhang. *Globalization on Trial: The Human Condition and the Information Civilization*. West Hartford, CT: Kumarian Press, 2000.

Rangan, Subramanian, and Robert Z. Lawrence. *A Prism on Globalization: Corporate Responses to the Dollar*. Washington, DC: Brookings Institute Press, 1999.

Rao, C. P., ed. *Globalization, Privatization and Free Market Economy*. Westport, CT: Quorum Books, 1998.

Reich, Robert. *The Work of Nations*. New York: Vintage, 1992.

Reinicke, Wolfgang. *Global Public Policy*. Washington, DC: Brookings Institution, 1998.

Rejai, Mostafa, ed. *Decline of Ideology?* Chicago: Aldine-Atherton, 1971.

Ricoeur, Paul. *Lectures on Ideology and Utopia*, ed. George H. Taylor. New York: Columbia University Press, 1986.

Ritzer, George. *The McDonaldization of Society*. Thousand Oaks, CA: Pine Forge Press, 1993.

———. *The McDonaldization Thesis: Explorations and Extensions*. Thousand Oaks, CA: Pine Forge Press, 1997.

Robbins, Bruce. *Feeling Global*. New York: New York University Press, 1999.

Roberts, J. Timmons, and Amy Hite, eds. *From Modernization to Globalization*. Oxford: Blackwell, 2000.

Robertson, Roland. *Globalization: Social Theory and Global Culture*. London: Sage, 1992.

Robinson, William I. *Promoting Polyarchy: Globalization, U.S. Intervention, and Hegemony*. Cambridge: Cambridge University Press, 1996.

Rodrik, Dani. *Has Globalization Gone Too Far?* Washington, DC: Institute for International Economics, 1997.

Rorty, Richard. *Achieving Our Century*. Cambridge, MA: Harvard University Press, 1998.

Rosenau, James. *Along the Domestic–Foreign Border: Exploring Governance in a Turbulent World*. Cambridge: Cambridge University Press, 1997.

Rupert, Mark. *Ideologies of Globalization: Contending Visions of a New World Order*. London: Routledge, 2000.

Sargent, Lyman Tower. *Contemporary Political Ideologies: A Comparative Analysis*, 11th ed. Fort Worth, TX: Harcourt Brace College Publishers, 1999.

Sassen, Saskia. *The Global City: New York, London, Tokyo.* Princeton, NJ: Princeton University Press, 1991.

———. *Losing Control? Sovereignty in an Age of Globalization.* New York: Columbia University Press, 1996.

———. *Globalization and Its Discontents: Essays on the New Mobility of People and Money.* New York: New Press, 1998.

Schaeffer, Robert K. *Understanding Globalization.* Lanham, MD: Rowman & Littlefield, 1997.

Scholte, Jan Aart. *Globalization: A Critical Introduction.* New York: St. Martin's Press, 2000.

Scott, Alan, ed. *The Limits of Globalization: Cases and Arguments.* London: Routledge, 1997.

Sen, Amartya. *Development as Freedom.* New York: Knopf, 1999.

Sernau, Scott. *Bound: Living in the Globalized World.* West Hartford, CT: Kumarian Press, 2000.

Shapiro, Ian, and Lea Brilmayer. *Global Justice.* New York: New York University Press, 1999.

Shils, E. A., and H. A. Finch, eds. *Max Weber on the Methodology of the Social Sciences.* New York: Free Press, 1949.

Singer, Daniel. *Whose Millennium? Theirs or Ours?* New York: Monthly Review Press, 1999.

Smith, David A., Dorothy J. Solinger, and Steven C. Topic, eds. *States and Sovereignty in the Global Economy.* London: Routledge, 1999.

Soros, George. *The Crisis of Global Capitalism: Open Society Endangered.* New York: Public Affairs, 1998.

Spencer, Herbert. *On Social Evolution,* ed. J. D. Y. Peel. Chicago: University of Chicago Press, 1972.

Steger, Manfred B. *The Quest for Evolutionary Socialism: Eduard Bernstein and Social Democracy.* Cambridge: Cambridge University Press, 1997.

———. *Gandhi's Dilemma: Nonviolent Principles and Nationalist Power.* New York: St. Martin's Press, 2000.

Steger, Manfred B., and Nancy Lind, eds. *Violence and Its Alternatives: An Interdisciplinary Reader.* New York: St. Martin's Press, 1999.

Strange, Susan. *The Retreat of the State: The Diffusion of Power in the World Economy.* Cambridge: Cambridge University Press, 1996.

———. *Mad Money: When Markets Outgrow Governments.* Ann Arbor: University of Michigan Press, 1997.

Tabb, William K. *The Amoral Elephant: Globalization and the Struggle for Social Justice in the Twenty-First Century.* New York: Monthly Review Press, 2001.

Taylor, M. W. *Men Versus the State: Herbert Spencer and Late Victorian Individualism.* Oxford: Clarendon Press, 1992.

Therborn, Goran. *The Ideology of Power and the Power of Ideology*. London: New Left Books, 1980.

Thomas, Caroline, and Peter Wilkin, eds. *Globalization and the South*. New York: St. Martin's Press, 1997.

Thurow, Lester. *The Future of Capitalism: How Today's Economic Forces Shape Tomorrow's World*. New York: William Morrow, 1996.

Tomlinson, John. *Globalization and Culture*. Chicago: University of Chicago Press, 1999.

Tonelson, Alan. *The Race to the Bottom: Why a Worldwide Worker Surplus and Uncontrolled Free Trade Are Sinking American Living Standards*. Boulder, CO: Westview Press, 2000.

Väyrynen, Raimo, ed. *Globalization and Global Governance*. Lanham, MD: Rowman & Littlefield, 1999.

Veseth, Michael. *Selling Globalization: The Myth of the Global Economy*. Boulder, CO: Lynne Rienner, 1998.

Wallach, Lori, and Michelle Sforza. *The WTO: Five Years of Reasons to Resist Corporate Globalization*. New York: Seven Stories Press, 1999.

Wallerstein, Immanuel. *The Capitalist World Economy*. Cambridge: Cambridge University Press, 1979.

———. *The Politics of the World Economy*. Cambridge: Cambridge University Press, 1984.

Waters, Malcolm. *Globalization*. London: Routledge, 1995.

Waxman, Chaim I., ed. *The End of Ideology Debate*. New York: Funk & Wagnalls, 1968.

Weiss, Linda. *The Myth of the Powerless State: Governing the Economy in a Global Era*. Ithaca, NY: Cornell University Press, 1998.

Went, Robert. *Globalization: Neoliberal Challenge, Radical Responses*. London: Pluto Press, 2000.

Wiltshire, David. *The Social and Political Thought of Herbert Spencer*. Oxford: Oxford University Press, 1978.

Woods, Ngaire, ed. *The Political Economy of Globalization*. Basingstoke, UK: Macmillan, 2000.

Yergin, Daniel, and Joseph Stanislaw. *The Commanding Heights: The Battle Between Government and the Marketplace That Is Remaking the Modern World*. New York: Simon & Schuster, 1998.

Zizek, Slavoj, ed. *Mapping Ideology*. London: Verso, 1994.

Zolo, Danilo. *Democracy and Complexity*. University Park: Pennsylvania State University Press, 1992.

INDEX

academic debate over globalization,
    17–41
  parable relationship, 17–18
  principal participants in, 18–19
AFL-CIO, 93
Albrow, Martin, 38
alliance of progressive forces, 147
Alliance for Sustainable Jobs and
    the Environment, 123
Amin, Ash, 23
Anderson, Perry, 139
Annan, Kofi, 132
antiglobalist people's movements,
    internationalization of, 110–16
AOL-Time Warner, 129
Appadurai, Arjun, 37
Arendt, Hannah, 128
Argentina, mass strike in, 144
Aristide, Jean-Bertrand, 115
  poor people's movement, 85
Aristide Foundation for Democracy,
    116
Asian Development Bank, 125
Association for Taxation of Financial
    Transactions for Aid of Citi-
    zens, 134

Atlantic Monthly, 58
Austrian Freedom Party, 84

Bajaj, Rahul, 56
Bakker, Isabella, 112
Barber, Benjamin, 60, 69, 79, 129,
    142
  "McWorld," 35–36
Barshefsky, Charlene, 49, 78, 122
"Battle of Seattle," 118–23
  aftermath, 128–33
Beam, Louis, 119
Beck, Ulrich, 37, 54, 58
Bell, Daniel, 135
  ideology analysis, 1–3
Bello, Walden, 112, 113
Berger, Samuel, 66
Berlet, Chip, 86
Bertelsmann, 129
Betz, Hans-Georg, 95
Bhagwati, Jagdish, 132–33
Birdsall, Nancy, 136
Black Bloc, 120–21
Blair, Tony, 137–38
Blair–Schröder manifesto, 138
Bobbio, Norberto, 81–82, 83

Bolivar, Simon, 101
Bove, Jose, 119
Brazilian Institute for Social and
    Economic Analysis, 110
Brecher, Jeremy, 146
Bretton Woods
    conference, major achievements
        of, 25–26
    institutions, 125
    system, collapse of, 26
British Petroleum, 67
Bryan, Lowell, 29
Buchanan, Patrick J., 84, 86, 105–6,
    119, 130, 143
    economic nationalism, 86–95
Business Roundtable, Task Force on
    Trade and Investment, 72
BusinessWeek, 48
    globalization feature, 43–45
Butler, Judith, 45

Caldera, Rafael, 99
Calhoun, Craig, 20
Camdessus, Michael, 49
Canovan, Margaret, 86
Cargill Inc., 131
Carver, Terrell, 5
Cassen, Bernard, 134
Castells, Manuel, 27
    "network society" study, 31–32
Castro, Fidel, 102
Cato Institute's Trade Center, 131
CEMEX Corporation, 59
Center for International Trade and
    Economics, 67
Ceresole, Norberto, 101
Chadwick, Andrew, 46
Chávez, Hugo, 84, 99–100
    Bolivarian national populism,
        99–104
Chicago Tribune, 76, 130

child labor, 70–71
Chipko movement, 85
Christian Coalition, 95
Christian Science Monitor, 104
Clark, Ian, 40
Clay, Henry, 89
Clinton, Bill, 55, 132, 137
Clinton, Hillary Rodham, 74
Coca-Cola, 131
Collins v. Jordan, 121
comparative-advantage theory, 10
CONAIE. See Confederation of
    Indigenous Nations of
    Ecuador
Condit, Phil, 72
Confederation of Indigenous
    Nations of Ecuador
    (CONAIE), 143
Costello, Tim, 146
Cox, Harvey, 58
Cox, Robert W., 40
critical theory, xi

Daer, Rudolfo, 144
Dalai Lama, 149, 150
Dallmayr, Fred, 4
David, George, 67–68
De Fabel van de Illegaal, 142–43
Deutsche National Zeitung, 96
Deutsche Wochenzeitung, 96
Die Neue Mitte, 138
Direct Action Network, 119
Disney, 129
Dixon, Christopher, 129

Eastman Kodak, 46
Ecologist, 143
economic nationalism, 86–95
    definition of, 88
Economic Security Council, 64
Economist, 52, 130

Ecuador, antiglobalist protest movement in, 143–44
Eizenstat, Stuart, 52, 55
"Electronic Herd," 51, 62, 75–76, 77
Elson, Diane, 112
The End of Ideology (Bell), 1–2
    criticism of, 2–3
Engels, Friedrich, 61
The Esus Group, 49
EU. *See* European Union
European Union (EU), 24, 95
    Summit, 126
EZLN. *See* Zapatista Army of National Liberation

Falk, Richard, 32, 33–34, 52
False Dawn (Gray), 142
Farrell, Diana, 29
FedEx Corporation, 55
Financial Times, 49
Fini, Gianfranco, 84
FOCUS. *See* Focus on the Global South
Focus on the Global South (FOCUS), 85, 112–13
formula, ideological, 53
Foucault, Michel, 45
Frank, Andre Gunder, 23
free market
    theories, 10–11, 26
    United States as model for, 59–60
French National Front, 84
Frey, Gerhard, 84, 96
    German right-wing extremism, 95–99
Friedman, Milton, 11, 26, 48, 54
Friedman, Thomas, 13, 52, 55–56, 59, 61–62, 64, 70, 71, 77, 130, 133
    on "Electronic Herd," 75–76
    on globalization, 50–51

Froning, Denise, 67
Fukuyama, Francis, 3–4, 59, 74, 135, 138
future prospects, 135–39
    global "new deal," 145–48
    violent backlash, 139–45

G7 Summit, 66–67
G8 Economic Summit, 118
Gadamer, Hans-Georg, 41
GATT. *See* General Agreement on Tariffs and Trade
Geertz, Clifford, 8
General Agreement on Tariffs and Trade (GATT), 25, 88
General Motors, 28
German People's Union, 84, 96–98
German right-wing extremism, 95–99
GEX. *See* Global Exchange
Giddens, Anthony, 83, 84, 138–39
Gill, Stephen, 40
Gilpin, Robert, 22–23
    on transnational corporations, 28
Gingrich, Newt, 69
"Global Age," 39
"global commodity chains," 28
Global Exchange (GEX), 85, 111–12, 119
Global Trade Watch, 104–5
globalism, 13, 41
    authors view of, 148–49
    as dominant political ideology, 6–7
    globalization differences, 13–14
    ideological dynamics of, 14
    ideology and, 1–9
    neoliberalism and, 9–12
globalists, neoliberal, 12
globalization, ix–xi
    academic debate over, 17–41

benefits everyone, 66–73
as cultural process, 34–38
definition of, 19
democracy relationship, 73–79
as economic process, 24–28
1870 through 1914 period of, 149
formula, 53
Friedman on, 50–51
future prospects concerning,
    135–50
globalism differences, 13–14
ideology and, 38–41
important aspects of, 27–28
is inevitable and irreversible,
    54–61, 92
market liberalization and integra-
    tion, 47–54
marketing, 43–47
markets and technology in charge
    of, 61–66
as political process, 28–34
skeptics, 19–24
Globalization from Below (Brecher,
    Costello, and Smith), 146–47
"Golden Straitjacket," 50, 51, 54
Goldman Sachs International, 61, 67
Goldsmith, Edward, 143
Gore, Al, 105
Gorman, Joseph, 65–66
Gott, Richard, 100
Gramsci, Antonio, 8–9, 66, 79, 128
Gray, John, 31, 59, 142
The Great Transformation (Polanyi),
    140
Greenspan, Alan, 67, 131
Grzybowski, Candido, 110

Haider, Jorg, 84
Hale, Matt, 119
Hannerz, Ulf, 37
Hardt, Michael, 62–63
Hayek, Friedrich, 11, 26, 47

hegemony, 8–9
Held, David, 32–33, 34
Helms, Jesse, 88
Heritage Foundation, 67
Herzog, Roman, 57
Hirst, Paul, 21
Hirst-Thompson thesis, 21–22
Hoffa, James, 93
Holton, Robert, 20–21
homo economicus theory, 9–10
Hormats, Robert, 61, 70–71
Human Development Report, 108
Human Rights Watch, 137
Hussein, Saddam, 103
Hutton, Will, 64

ideology
    debate, end of, 1–5
    definition of, 5
    elements and functions of, 5–9
    globalization and, 38–41
    political, 5–7
IFG. *See* International Forum on
    Globalization
IMF. *See* International Monetary
    Fund
immigrants, invasion of legal and
    illegal, 91
Intercontinental Gathering for
    Humanity and Against Neo-
    liberalism, 114
International Association of Femi-
    nist Economists, 112
International Bank for Reconstruc-
    tion and Development, 25
International Forum on Globaliza-
    tion (IFG), 85, 111, 119
International Monetary Fund (IMF),
    25, 49, 63, 72, 85, 90
    World Bank meetings, 124–26,
    135, 137
Investor's Business Daily, 130

Italian National Alliance, 84

"J18," 118
Jackson, Andrew, 92
Jameson, Fredric, 39
Jennings, Peter, 130
"Jihad," 36
Jihad vs. McWorld (Barber), 142
John Birch Society, 95
Joseph, Keith, 11

Kanbur, Ravi, 72–73
Keynes, John Maynard, 11
Khor, Martin, 111
Klein, Naomi, 118
Kline, Steven, 60
Knight, Phil, 71
Koch-Weser, Caio K., 72, 131
Krugman, Paul, 22, 61
Kung, Hans, 149

La Jornada, 133
Latouche, Serge, 36
Le Monde Diplomatique, 134
Le Pen, Jean-Marie, 84
Lectures on Ideology and Utopia
     (Ricoeur), 7
Lefort, Claude, 46
Left & Right (Bobbio), 81
left populism, 104–9
The Lexus and the Olive Tree (Fried-
     man), 50
   excerpts from, 61–62, 64
Liberty Lobby, 95
Life magazine, 104
Lipietz, Alain, 57
Locke, John, 54
Los Angeles Times, 129
Luttwak, Edward, 53

McChesney, Robert, 128
McCormick, Richard, 131

"McDonaldization," 35
"McWorld," 35–36
Malott, John, 57
Marcos, Subcomandante, 114, 115
market forces, irreversible, 54–61
marketization, 43–47
markets
   free, 10–11, 26, 59–60
   liberalization and integration of,
      47–54
   self-regulating, 47
   social, 11
Marshall Plan, 49
Martin, Peter, 49
Masur, Sandra, 46
Mazur, Jay, 68
media corporations, 129
Meehan, John, 69
mercantilism, 9
Mill, John Stuart, 54
Milliken, Roger, 143
Moghadam, Valentine, 112
Moore, Mike, 77–78
Moynihan, Daniel Patrick, 104
multiculturalism, 91
Mussolini, Benito, 103

Nader, Ralph, 85, 110, 143
   left populism, 104–9
NAFTA. *See* North American Free
   Trade Association
Nation, 104
National Alliance, 119
nationalism, 20
nationalist-protectionist right,
   86–104
Navarro, Luis Hernandez, 133
negative liberty, 48
Negri, Antonio, 62–63
neoliberalism, 9–12
   central tenets of, 8
"network society" study, 31–32

New Economic Information Service, 76

New Left Review, 139

New Republic, 143

"New World Order," 84

New York Times, 13, 77, 129, 130

News Corporation, 129

Newsweek, 6, 8

Nike Corporation, 28, 71

Nixon, Richard, 26

North American Free Trade Association (NAFTA), 24, 87–88, 114

Ohmae, Kenichi, 29

OPEC. *See* Organization of Petroleum Exporting Countries

Organization of Petroleum Exporting Countries (OPEC), 91, 102

Overseas Development Council, 67

parable, blind scholars and elephant, 17–18

Perez, Carlos Andres, 99

Peron, Juan Domingo, 103

Perot, H. Ross, 87–88

Philadelphia Inquirer, 130

Pieterse, Jan Nederveen, 113

Polanyi, Karl, analysis, 140–41, 145

politics

    antiglobalist people's movements, 110–16

    Bolivarian national populism, 99–104

    German right-wing extremism, 95–99

    globalization and, 28–34

    ideology connection, 5–7

    internationalist-egalitarian left, 104–16

    left populism, 104–9

    left/right distinction, 81–85

nationalist-protectionist right, 86–104

polyarchy, concept of, 74

Pope John Paul II, 149

populism, 86

    left, 104–9

    national, 99–104

Posse Comitatus Act of 1887, 121

Project Bolivar 2000, 101

Public Citizen, 102, 143

Rainforest Action Network, 119

Ramsey, Charles, 124, 125

Reagan, Ronald, 11

Reform party, 87

Ricardo, David, 9

    comparative-advantage theory, 10

Ricoeur, Paul, 7–8, 57, 59

Ritzer, George, 35

Robertson, Pat, 95

Robertson, Roland, 36–37

Robinson, William I., 8–9, 74, 75

Rocard, Michel, 147

Rosow, Stephen J., 19

Roth, Kenneth, 137

Rousseau, Jean-Jacques, 51

Rua, Fernando de la, 144

Rubin, Robert, 67

Ruckus Society, 119, 123

Scholte, Jan Aart, 30

Schröder, Gerhard, 137–38

Scott, Alan, 41

"Second-Coming Capitalism," 11

self-regulating markets, 47

Shell, Paul, 121

Singer, Daniel, 30

single global market, 29

Smith, Adam, 9–10

Smith, Brendan, 146

Smith, David, 58

Smith, Frederick W., 55

social market, 11
Social Statics (Spencer), 10
Solomon, William, 129
Somavia, Juan, 73
Sony, 129
Soros, George, 144–45
Spencer, Herbert, 9, 60
   free-market competition theory,
      10–11
Spiro, Joan, 48–49, 52, 67
Staley, Warren, 131
Stiglitz, Joseph, 72, 73
Strange, Susan, 20
Summers, Larry, 72
Summit of the Americas, antiglobal-
      ist activities at, 135
Sumner, William Graham, 60
Sutherland, Peter, 67
Sweeney, John, 93

Teamsters, 93
technologies, new, 122–23
Thatcher, Margaret, 11, 55
Theobald, Fred, 49
"The Third Way," 138
Third World Network (TWN), 111
Thomas, Caroline, 30
Thompson, Graham, 21
Time magazine, 105
TNCs. *See* transnational corpora-
      tions
Tobin Tax, 147
Tomlinson, John, 34–35
transnational corporations (TNCs),
      27–28, 70
TRW Inc., 65
"Turbo-Capitalism," 11
Tutu, Desmond, 149
TWN. *See* Third World Network

U.N. Development Report, 73
U.N. General Assembly, 73

U.N. International Labor Organiza-
      tion, 73
U.S. Business Roundtable, 46
U.S. Federal Reserve Board, 67
U.S. News, 130
U.S. Public Securities Association,
      69
U.S. Subcommittee on Trade of the
      House Committee on Ways
      and Means, 72
U.S. Union of Needletrades, Indus-
      trial, and Textile Employees,
      68
United Technologies, 67
"United We Stand," 87
Unsafe at Any Speed (Nader), 104
UPS Airlines, 49–50

Velasco, Juan, 103
Veseth, Michael, 47
Viacom, 129
Villar, Manuel, 56
Vivendi, 129

Wallerstein, Immanuel, 23
Wallop, Malcolm, 130
Ware, Carl, 131
Washington Consensus, ten areas of,
      63–64
Weber, Max, 7
WEF. *See* World Economic Forum
Weidemeyer, Tom, 49–50
Weiss, Linda, 20
Williams, Anthony A., 125
Williamson, John, 63
Wolf, Martin, 49
Wolfensohn, James, 114
World Bank, 25, 63, 72, 85, 90,
      114
   International Monetary Fund
      meetings, 124–26, 135, 137
World Church of the Creator, 119

World Economic Forum (WEF), 71
   antiglobalist activities at, 123–24
   Asia-Pacific Summit of, 125
   Davos meeting, 127
World Social Forum (WSF), 134,
   145–46
World Trade Organization (WTO),
   25, 63, 77, 79, 85, 88, 106, 137
   Seattle meeting, 78
   Third Ministerial Conference, 118

World Wide Web, 29
world-system theorists, 23, 24
WSF. *See* World Social Forum
WTO. *See* World Trade
   Organization

Zambrano, Lorenzo, 59
Zapatista Army of National
   Liberation (EZLN), 114
Zapatista rebellion, 85

About the Author

Manfred B. Steger is associate professor of politics and government at Illinois State University, and affiliate faculty member of the Globalization Research Center at the University of Hawai'i at Mānoa. His academic fields of expertise include ideologies and theories of globalization, comparative political and social theory, theories of nonviolence, and international politics. His most recent publications include *The Quest for Evolutionary Socialism: Eduard Bernstein and Social Democracy* (1997), *Engels After Marx* (1999), *Violence and Its Alternatives: An Interdisciplinary Reader* (1999), and *Gandhi's Dilemma: Nonviolent Principles and Nationalist Power* (2000).